...UTIFUL FOR EVER

Helen Rappaport read Russian Special Studies at Leeds University and was an actress in TV and films before moving into publishing. She worked as a free - lance editor for academic publishers before becoming a full-time writer in 1998, specializing in Victorian social history and the Russian Revolution. She is the author of *No Place for Ladies: The Untold Story of Women in the Crimean War*, *Ekaterinburg: The Last Days of the Romanovs*, *Conspirator: Lenin in Exile* and *Magnificent Obsession: Victoria, Albert and the Death that Changed the Monarchy*. Helen Rappaport lives in Oxford.

www.helenrappaport.com

79 589 530 7

HELEN RAPPAPORT

Beautiful For Ever

Madame Rachel of Bond Street –
Cosmetician, Con-Artist and Blackmailer

VINTAGE BOOKS
London

FOR PETE AND CHRIS

Published by Vintage 2012

2 4 6 8 10 9 7 5 3 1

Copyright © Helen Rappaport 2010

Helen Rappaport has asserted her right under the Copyright, Designs
and Patents Act 1988 to be identified as the author of this work

First published in Great Britain in 2010 by
Long Barn Books

Vintage
Random House, 20 Vauxhall Bridge Road,
London SW1V 2SA

www.vintage-books.co.uk

Addresses for companies within The Random House Group Limited
can be found at: www.randomhouse.co.uk/offices.htm

The Random House Group Limited Reg. No. 954009

A CIP catalogue record for this book
is available from the British Library

ISBN 9780099570134

The Random House Group Limited supports The Forest Stewardship
Council (FSC®), the leading international forest certification
organisation. Our books carrying the FSC label are printed on FSC®
certified paper. FSC is the only forest certification scheme endorsed
by the leading environmental organisations, including Greenpeace.
Our paper procurement policy can be found at:
www.randomhouse.co.uk/environment

Printed and bound by CPI Group (UK) Ltd, Croydon, CR0 4YY

Contents

Preface & Acknowledgements

I CAME ACROSS the story of Madame Rachel quite by
chance several years ago when searching for potential
Victorian subjects. Something about her story as I then
found it, briefly told in a 1920s collection of famous
Victorian trials, captured my imagination. The time was not
right to publish her story then, so I nursed it along, adding
to it whenever I had time, in the hope that eventually it
would be commercially viable. For this reason, *Beautiful For
Ever* has been a very special book for me as a writer. It
has been an exciting journey of discovery winkling out this
story so long lost to history, and I am proud to have been
able to do so. Madame Rachel's story is told here almost
entirely from the newspapers and journals of her day –
which means we can hear her, and many others involved in
that story – speak with their own, real voices.

That much of the story I have done alone. In order,
however, to discover the truth of Madame Rachel's family
background, I was hugely fortunate to discover others
who have trod the same genealogical path. Historical
research is often about chance and how one connection

leads to another. In pursuit of Madame Rachel I tried to find material about her children, in particular her opera singer daughter Hélène. A speculative research trip to the Royal Academy of Music put me in touch with the Royal College of Music and the ultimate serendipity – an entirely unexpected link to a family historian Patricia Oliver. Thanks to her extraordinary diligence and that of Dan Russell in Australia and Gordon Ashbury in England I have been able to ascertain the elusive Madame Rachel's true identity – something none of her Victorian contemporaries ever knew for sure – and I won't spoil it here by going into specifics. Patricia Oliver also put me in touch with Arna Samuels in North London, who, as a mature student at the Open University, had written about Madame Rachel for a thesis on women fraudsters and had worried at the story like a dog at a bone, discovering valuable detail. I am indebted to Arna for passing on her research material to me.

Various other people helped along the way: my stalwart colleague Phil Tomaselli dug out what survives of Rachel's prison records at the Public Record Office, Kew; John Ward offered valuable information on the Carl Rosa Opera Company and opera in the nineteenth century; Corinne Garstang's excellent website filled me in on the history of Woking Invalid Convict Prison; Lesley Schoenfield at Harvard Law Library provided me with scans of the very rare accounts of Rachel's first trial in August 1868; Steve Mendoza at the University of

California Library helped me to track down a photograph in Paris; Douglas Austin offered information on chemicals used in cosmetics; Bridget Palmer at the Library of the Royal Academy of Music provided access to their admissions registers and minute books and Paul Collen at the Centre for Performance History at the Royal College of Music put me in touch with Patricia Oliver; Paul Frecker generously shared his dissertation on the Victorian cosmetics trade with me.

My wonderful Paris researcher Emilie Bremond-Poulle spent many hours searching for evidence of Rachel and her family in Paris and finally pulled out the plum of crucial evidence in the Archives de la Préfecture. In my search for information on the career of Alma Verdini I drew a fairly large blank and would welcome any information readers might have; I would particularly like to trace Paul François Quinsac's 1881 painting of 'Mlle Verdini', as well as any information on Léontine Rachel's cosmetics salon in rue de la Paix, Paris, and Madame Rachel's house in Saint Cloud. The portrait of Cecilia Maria Pearse by Joseph Jopling was apparently bought by the publisher John Lane, but I have been unable to trace it. Any comments or information readers would like to share with me would be most welcome via the contact page on my website: *www.helenrappaport.com*

I would like to express my grateful thanks to the following for granting permission to reproduce illustrations in this book: the Guildhall Library for New Bond Street; Matthew Lloyd for the sheet music 'Mrs Plucker Sparrowtail'; the

Bodleian Library, University of Oxford for the 1868 anti-Semitic cartoon; the Victoria & Albert Museum for the photograph of George Lewis; the Historical & Special Collections at Harvard Law School Library for 'The History & Trial of Mdm. Rachel'; the British Library for cartoons from the *Illustrated Police News*; Mr Edmund Brudenell for the portrait of the Countess of Cardigan; PictureHistory.com and the Bibliothèque Nationale Française for the *cartes de visite* of Hélène Crosmond and Alma Verdini respectively.

I remain indebted to Susan Hill who believed in this book from the moment she read the proposal and commissioned the hardback edition. I am grateful to Vintage for bringing it out in this paperback edition and to my editor there, Frances Jessop, and my publicist Indira Birnie. Finally, my continuing thanks go as always to my agent Charlie Viney for understanding my passion about this story and my determination to write it. My brothers Pete and Chris, to whom this book is dedicated, have given me endless, unqualified support for and encouragement in all my work and in the maintenance of my website.

HELEN RAPPAPORT

Oxford, March 2012

LIST OF ILLUSTRATIONS

between pages 146 and 147

1. *Carte de visite* of Madame Rachel, 1868
   (Author's collection)

2. New Bond Street 1860, lithograph by Robert Dudley
   (Guildhall Library, London)

3. Lord Ranelagh cartoon from *Vanity Fair*, 1868
   (Author's collection)

4. Mrs Mary Tucker Borradaile (Author's collection)

5. Sheet music for Arthur Lloyd's 1868 song 'Mrs Mary
   Plucker Sparrowtail' (Matthew Lloyd)

6. Madame Rachel's trial at the Old Bailey 1868, *Penny
   Illustrated Paper* (Author's collection)

7. Anti-Semitic cartoon from 'Life, Trial and Sentence
   of Madame Rachel', 1868 ((Bodleian Library,
   University of Oxford)

8. Sir George Lewis, photograph by Frederick Hollyer
   (Victoria & Albert Museum)

9. Front cover of 'History & Trial of Mdm. Rachel',
   1868 (Historical & Special Collections, Harvard Law
   School Library)

10. 'Madame Rachel under the Hammer', *Illustrated Police
    News* 1869 (British Library)

Epigraph

God hath given you one face and you make
yourselves another.

Shakespeare, *Hamlet* , Act 3: sc. 1.

The Lady in the Cab

THE GAS LAMPS had already been lit along Northumberland Avenue that spring evening in April 1888, but the thoroughfare was still thick with the crush of horse-drawn cabs and omnibuses. Shortly before 8 p.m. an attractive woman of about thirty-five emerged from amidst the marble pillars and thick velvet drapes of the lobby of the Grand Hotel. Slim and pretty, with bright grey eyes and neatly coiffured flaxen curls, she ventured across the congested avenue in the gathering twilight to the cab rank opposite, where she engaged a four-wheel growler to take her to Knightsbridge.

The cab driver asked her where exactly she wanted to be dropped off, to which his fare replied dismissively, 'Oh never mind, I will tell you that when we get there.' Heading north, past the busy railway terminus at Charing Cross and across Trafalgar Square, the cab turned west on the vortex of busy streets that converge at Piccadilly Circus – where the crowds were already out for an evening's entertainment in the clubs and supper rooms of the nearby Haymarket –

and rattled off along the cobbles of Piccadilly. It was just passing Clarges Street opposite Green Park, on the long stretch up to Marble Arch, when the sound of a gunshot rang out from inside. A passer-by heard the shot and a loud scream. Seeing smoke issuing from the cab's broken window he shouted to the driver to stop and rushed forward to pull open the door. Inside a woman lay slumped in a crouching position with her head between her knees. She had shot herself in the head with a five-chambered revolver, which lay on the floor beside her.

Someone rushed to fetch a constable who immediately jumped into the cab, ordering the driver to go as fast as he could to St George's Hospital at Marble Arch, just north of the far end of Piccadilly. But the woman had already lapsed into unconsciousness by the time they arrived. She died of her wounds at 3.25 a.m. the following morning. The resident house surgeon later confirmed that she had died from a single entry wound to the right side of her temple that had 'lacerated the brain'.

The woman's handbag contained thirty shillings in loose change, but there was nothing else to identify her apart from her wedding ring, although it was obvious that she was 'of good social position'. Before blowing out her brains, she had, most thoughtfully, paused to remove the two tortoiseshell combs from her hair and her black straw hat trimmed with velvet and grey birds' wings, clearly not wishing to spoil them.

Later that morning, Friday 28th, the woman's body was identified by her landlady who had seen the news in the early morning paper. The dead woman's brother, David Levison, was contacted and hurried up from Lewisham in south London. When they were children, his sister had been known as Hannah in the family, but in the late 1870s, after training as an opera singer, she had adopted the stage name of Hélène Crosmond. Now widowed, she had been living in a couple of small rooms near the British Museum in Bloomsbury, from where she eked out a living giving singing lessons and the occasional concert performance. Levison had not seen his sister for six or seven weeks, at which time she had seemed cheerful enough, talking about her pupils and her hopes for an operatic tour. But since the death of her husband in 1881, as he ruefully observed to the inquest jury, she 'had had more than the ordinary share of the buffetings of this life' and had become hopelessly addicted to opiates to help her with neuralgia and persistent sleepless nights. However, even though she had been in some 'pecuniary difficulties', as he put it, David Levison knew of no particular recent trouble to account for his sister taking her own life.

At the inquest, Mr John Troubeck, deputy coroner for Westminster, questioned Henry Wood, a shop assistant from Watson Brothers, a gunmakers on Pall Mall. Wood confirmed that he had sold the twenty-five shilling 'bull-dog' revolver and twelve cartridges to the lady on the previous Wednesday evening. She had told him that she was buying the gun as a gift 'for her brother' but that it had to be cheap and – rather oddly – she had added that she had to be sure that the gun 'would kill'. Wood had duly obliged by loading the weapon for her and showing her how to use it. It was not unusual, he said, for ladies to come in and purchase revolvers and he had had no qualms about doing so.

The verdict of the inquest was the inevitable one of 'suicide whilst of unsound mind'. But that was not the whole of the story. Shortly afterwards the press was alerted to the tragic suicide's true identity. The unfortunate Hélène Crosmond was in fact 'a daughter of Madame Rachel'. Everyone in Victorian Britain knew the name: Madame Rachel, aka Sarah Rachel Levison or Leverson, had been at the centre of two scandalous court cases – in 1868 and 1878 – that had rocked Victorian society and had set the titled and wealthy ladies of London a-tremble.

The stigma of her parentage had dogged Hélène all her adult life, even in the years after her mother's death in 1880. In an attempt to shake off this taint of notoriety, she had done her utmost to lead an uncontroversial and exemplary life. But even her 'moral rectitude and a close observance of the conventionalities of society', as the papers so rightly pointed out, had not spared her from continuing allusions to her mother that had caused her acute pain and embarrassment.

The press was therefore much moved by the 'fearful death' of poor Hélène Crosmond. She had made a 'brave fight' holding up her head in a long and weary struggle against the hand of fate, said *The Times*. The *Birmingham Daily Post* agreed: Madame Crosmond had had 'every personal gift to ensure success' as an opera singer but had been 'confronted at every turn by the disgrace incurred by her unhappy mother'. Her suicide apparently had 'long been anticipated by her friends'.

Hélène's financial difficulties had, it turned out, been made worse by the recent cancellation of a much-coveted contract when she had demanded a prima donna role. She had thought of going to the law to seek restitution, but the courtroom was the last thing Hélène Crosmond could bear facing. There had been too much – far too much – of lawyers and courtrooms and criminal procedures already in her family, thanks to her mother's notorious career.

In the brief shelf life of the daily press and the voracious demand for sensational stories to fill newspaper columns, the 'sad fate of a prima donna' was sufficient to shock the British public for a day or so as it gloated over every detail of the unfortunate woman's suicide. But after that Hélène Crosmond was quickly forgotten.

No one, however, was likely to forget her mother, Madame Rachel of 47a New Bond Street, the celebrated 'enameller of ladies' faces', patronized by Her Majesty the Queen and the aristocracy, and notable throughout the land as sole possessor of the secret art of making women Beautiful For Ever.

CHAPTER ONE

Sally Russell of Drury Lane

IF YOU TRY TO find Clare Market today, just down from Holborn tube station in London, virtually nothing remains from the Victorian era. One lone survivor stands out: the quaint, half-timbered shop on the corner of Portugal Street that was supposedly the inspiration for the 1841 Charles Dickens novel, *The Old Curiosity Shop*, now dwarfed by the sprawling new development of the London School of Economics. The whole of this once-teeming part of the parish of St Clement Danes disappeared long ago in the massive programme of slum clearance that from 1900 to 1905 swept away the filthy old rookeries of Clare Market, displacing its 3,000 inhabitants to create the grand sweep of London's Aldwych.

In the seventeenth century the habitations around Clare Market – named after the 2nd Earl of Clare who once had a grand residence nearby – had sprung up on an area of open land called Clement's Inn Fields. The north side of this open space remained an area of elegance and middle-class respectability when lawyers' chambers were established in a grand terrace of houses surrounding a central private garden. Now known as Lincoln's Inn Fields, this little-used haven of trees and grass, whose gates were most firmly locked against the poor, was only a stone's throw from the garbage-ridden alleys and dank and squalid houses of Clare Market that lay just beyond to the south.

Clare Market had been notorious as a haven for the criminal under-classes since the late eighteenth century, when the legendary robber Jack Sheppard had hidden out in nearby Wych Street whilst on the run from the law. This tumbledown area rapidly became the dismal haunt of the downtrodden, of 'human piggeries' and brothels that sprang up alongside the cowsheds and slaughter houses that formed the market's thriving butchers' shambles. Its gin shops were much like those of nearby St Giles immortalized in the engravings of Hogarth; its alehouses crowded out with bedraggled tarts and their sodden-faced pimps who vied for custom among hulking butchers' boys from the nearby market, and actors from Drury Lane. The market had long been a thriving part of the London sex trade, with prostitutes patrolling theatres such as Killigrews or Davenant's at either end of the market, or the Royal Olympic theatre on Wych Street, as well as the far grander Royal Opera House a couple of blocks west on Bow Street. There was a time when all of 'fast London' would assemble in the pubs and drinking dens that crowded round Clare Market to make a night of it. Here, criminals caroused on the beer-slopped floors, whilst groups of pickpockets and cracksmen congregated in the backrooms of the fifteen pubs that served this small area – such as The Fountain on Clare Street and the Hope Tavern in Blackamoor Street – to gamble and share out their day's ill-gotten gains.

Back in the 1850s, with its narrow streets and filthy back alleys daily running with blood from the slaughterhouses and effluent from the overflowing sewers, and flanked by two old and now overcrowded graveyards, Clare Market was a notoriously unhealthy spot. The hungry eyes of desperation stared out at you from the cracked windowpanes of every dirty, gabled house that overhung its stinking, undrained alleys. One observer wrote that he had 'seen miseries of poverty and sickness in the Roman Ghetto and in the plague quarter of Cairo' but that there were places in the neighbourhood of Clare Market 'that would beat them hollow' as nightmares of poverty and disease. Its denizens had to tolerate the never-ending racket of the hundreds of sheep and cattle that were herded in to be slaughtered weekly, as well as the stench of manure, blood and the nearby tripe-boilers that perpetually filled the air. With virtually no police presence, it was bristling with footpads and a dangerous neighbourhood to strangers, who entered the area at night at their peril.

On Wednesday and Saturday market days Clare Market

would be humming with life as the greengrocers, meat and fish purveyors of the shambles were joined by higglers and country butchers from out of town, crowding in with their barrows. It would also be teeming with dirty women haggling over scraps of stale meat and half rotten vegetables in their desperate daily battle to feed their families. Those with enough money could go for a plate of beef-à-la mode at Johnson's Beef House in Clare Court. But most of the inhabitants of Clare Market bought a basin of hot eels or pea soup from street vendors or headed for places like Sarah Russell's hot baked potato and fried fish shop at no. 4 Clare Market, next door to The Fountain pub. Both these foods had become popular staples of the working classes from the 1830s (though the ubiquitous chip was yet to be added to the menu – from the 1860s) and Sarah was one of many Jews living in the area who worked in the Victorian equivalent of the fast-food trade. Theirs was a lucrative one, with hot potatoes at a halfpenny a time a staple of the prostitutes who worked the market. These were baked over a fire in large brass cans and sold during the potato season of August to April or until the stored potatoes started going bad. The plaice and sole dabs that Sarah fried in salad oil were, in particular, sold to be eaten cold by her fellow observant Jews on the Sabbath from Friday evening to Saturday and had a yellowish colour from the turmeric used, Jewish style, to flavour the batter.

Sarah Russell had come to St Clement Danes in

the 1840s from Whitechapel in the East End. She had previously lived in Goulston Street, in the heart of what would later become Jack the Ripper territory, at a time when half the total English population of around 35,000 Jews lived in London. In 1844 she had married a widower and commercial traveller named Joseph Moses at Goulston Street, in a Jewish ceremony conducted by a rabbi from the Great Synagogue based not far away at Duke's Place. But Moses had deserted her in around 1846 to seek his fortune gold prospecting in Australia, leaving her with two daughters, Rachel (born in January 1841 in a courtyard off Drury Lane) and Leah (born nearby in September 1846). By now however, Sarah had taken up with a man named Phillip Levy or Levison, who was a travelling salesman in steel pens for a wholesaler in Houndsditch and who appears to have fathered the rest of her seven children.

Sarah had been working her way up in business ever since she had started out buying and selling old bottles and hare and rabbit skins from a barrow in Wapping, as well as telling penny fortunes round the East End pubs. The profession of huckster or street vendor might be a lowly one, next to that of the rag-and-bone man, but the wily Sarah took a step up the ladder when she moved into St Clement Danes and opened the shop in Clare Market. However, she had no intention of ending her days frying fish for the poor. Living in this area of cheap lodging houses, she was constantly on the move from one temporary home to the next. Hard working and ambitious, Sarah lived by the Jewish ethic of creating a better life for her children. Even if she had to go without, they would all be well educated and, unlike her, be able to read and write.

By the 1850s Sarah was dabbling in numerous business enterprises. As well as frying fish she operated as a 'wardrobe dealer' – not, as one might today imagine, a dealer in second-hand furniture, but in second-hand clothes. It was a step up from the rag picker and the ragman who haunted Petticoat Lane where she had grown up and a more acceptable term than the familiar and racially loaded 'Old Clo', a profession that was a near monopoly among the Jews. Selling what she bought as cheaply as possible for cash, Sarah often dealt with maidservants who sold their mistresses' cast off clothes and also with kept women, often extending credit at a crippling 15 or 20 percent as was the practice. This kind of dealing was, effectively, a form of money lending. Her trade in second hand dresses often took her to Drury Lane where the dancers and actresses were good customers. London theatres then were the focus of a great deal of casual prostitution, with many second-rate actresses being little more than courtesans addicted to too much satin and face paint, who made a little extra on the side in the local brothels. It was a tradition long familiar from the works of Samuel Richardson as well as Hogarth's pictorial evocation of the corruption of innocence in the *Harlot's Progress* and it was common knowledge that procuresses from the local brothels solicited recruits around Drury Lane. In later years it would be alleged that Sarah or 'Sally Russell' as she was known locally, turned her hand to this dubious trade. An eminent barrister had observed her backstage on one occasion when Sarah (though he didn't know who she was at the time) had made an 'insulting proposal' to one of the young actresses she was haggling with over the price of a dress, who had responded by throwing a pot of porter in her face. She was, as later evidence suggests, well-known to the local police and the magistrates at this time.

By 1852 Sarah had two more children – David born in about 1848 and Hannah born in November 1850 – and going by the surname of Levison, when she first ran into trouble with the law. Living in the Drury Lane area and probably working as a sometime procuress, she had begun helping out a friend and neighbour, David Belasco, who had dealt in second-hand clothes at Petticoat Lane before moving into the more lucrative sex trade. Belasco was now running a brothel at 31 Hart Street, an alley off Long Acre opposite Moore's fringe factory and Blackwood's ink manufactory. The nephew of a famous East End Jewish prize fighter Aby Belasco, he had, like him, developed a reputation as a 'fighting man' and had been in trouble in the past for brawling. In April 1852 Belasco had assaulted a drunken patron, Robert Clarke – who had wanted to use the facilities of the brothel without paying for his room – throwing him down the stairs and pitching him out on to the street. Clarke had subsequently died of head injuries.

Sarah was one of two of Belasco's friends who provided him with an alibi at his trial. Still running the fried fish business in Clare Market, she now lived only five minutes walk away in a two-roomed cottage at 10 Russell Place off Bow St – in sight of the Royal Opera House. In court, giving evidence as Sarah Levison, she claimed to have gone over to Hart Street late that night in April to solicit the address of a nursing home for Jewish children in Gravesend – her daughter Rachel was very sick – from Belasco's wife, Mary who was an old friend. She had remained for an hour or so chatting and having a cup of coffee in the downstairs parlour where Belasco had been smoking a pipe, when there had been the sound of an argument upstairs, after which Clarke had mysteriously taken a tumble down them. According to Sarah, in a transparent attempt to invest her brothel-keeper friend with moral integrity, Belasco had been indignant at the altercation, accusing the two tarts who had been with the man of bringing a drunk into the house: 'If you don't all go out, I will send for a policeman' he had said, most reasonably. Sarah was adamant that she had not seen Belasco kick or hit the man and that after he fell the two women had dragged him out of the door. Mr Baron Platt however had not believed her, or the man named Turner who likewise offered a false alibi. He committed them both to Newgate for perjury but it soon became apparent that it would be difficult to establish the charge and three weeks later they were released. Belasco was sentenced to twelve months hard labour for manslaughter but was back in the brothel trade as soon as he was out of jail.

In early June 1854, Sarah's common-law husband, Phillip was himself in court (his name given as 'Levyson'), at the Queen's Bench, Westminster, seeking damages for an alleged defamation of character. One of his regular clients, Mr Broadhurst, a medical practitioner of Brook Street to whom he supplied steel pens, had accused him of theft during a business call to his house. Levison claimed to have suffered greatly by the humiliation of being taken through the streets in handcuffs by three policemen. In court it transpired that he had been misidentified as a man called Baron Jacomini, who had indeed been going round doctors' surgeries in the guise of a commercial traveller, stealing instrument cases. The jury found in Phillip's favour and he was awarded damages. The case in itself was insignificant but its details reveal something of the character of Phillip Levison, who remains an elusive and shiftless figure in this story. Sarah had given birth to another son by him, Aaron, at Vere Street near Clare Market in 1853, and he was now occasionally cohabiting with her at a house in Sheffield Street nearby, along with some of her relatives and, so he claimed, supporting the family to the tune of thirty shillings a week. In 1841 he had stated he was born in 1814 in Spitalfields, but during this 1854 case he described himself as 'Mr Levyson of New York'. He had trained as a butcher, he said, but had never pursued that trade, working as a commercial traveller in steel pens for sixteen years and claiming among his illustrious patrons the Duke of Wellington, Lord Fitzroy Somerset and General Brown. Such elusiveness about his true background and compulsive self-aggrandizement with regard to his clientele was a trait he shared with his common-law wife Sarah.

Those who had witnessed Phillip's visit to the Broadhursts described him as decidedly shabby, with down at heel boots and having a 'foreign accent'; perhaps he was a Yiddish speaker like Sarah. Whether he had fathered her second daughter Leah is unclear – she had been born around the time Joseph Moses had deserted Sarah and gone to Australia. Phillip consistently denied he had ever allowed Sarah to use his surname, yet she did so increasingly, and it is clear later that he was not averse to living off her earnings. At other times he seemed estranged from her, for ever on the move from lodgings to lodgings and constantly denying the true state of their relationship. More enigmatically – and perhaps significantly – in court in June 1854 Phillip revealed that the house Sarah had lived in at Russell Place was a brothel and further ventured that she had at one time lived in another brothel at Gerard Street Soho.

In April 1856 Sarah gave birth to another child, Elizabeth, at lodgings in Drury Lane. Times were hard for the family; Phillip's dealership in steel pens based in Cranbourn Alley near Leicester Square had gone bankrupt in September

1855 and there were now six children to provide for. In 1856 one of them fell victim to the desperate poverty that forced so many of London's underclasses into crime. Out playing in Drury Lane one day, three-year-old Aaron had been cornered by a criminal named Johanna Mack, whose particular bent was the uniquely Victorian profession of child-stripping. Having enticed him away from his home, she had made him drunk on beer and then had stripped him of all his clothing bar his drawers, before doing likewise to another local boy Alfred Mark. Both children had been found some time later wandering bewildered and sick from the beer they had been forced to drink. They had been too young to give evidence at Mack's trial, when she was sentenced to a year's hard labour. Three years later another of the Levison children, this time David, was assaulted by a soldier who swung him round by the legs and broke his arm after David had got into a childish quarrel in the street with the man's younger brother. Phillip Levison had had no qualms in pressing for a prosecution which saw the soldier sentenced to three months in prison.

Life in this part of London was unrelentingly brutish, at a time when there was virtually no public welfare. A few philanthropic institutions were gradually established in the St Clement Danes area to counter the great tide of poverty and neglect – a soup kitchen, a working men's club, a ragged school and an orphan's refuge, but in general it was the debtor's court in Portugal Street that loomed large over everyone's lives. In 1839, however, a much-needed hospital had been established in a disused workhouse near the debtor's court, as a teaching hospital for medical students studying under Professor Robert Bentley Todd at nearby King's College. The hospital was further developed – alarmingly, considering the state of public health in Victorian Britain – on the site of the Old Green Ground – a disused burial ground, without the corpses beneath being first removed. Built to accommodate some 200 or so patients, King's College Hospital soon was inundated with the sick and poor from nearby Clare Market, whose back alleys were breeding grounds for cholera, measles and scarlet fever. In around 1856 Sarah herself was stricken with rheumatic fever and taken to the hospital for treatment, during which time her thick black hair – the one redeeming feature she had and of which she had been inordinately proud – had fallen out. She was distraught; on leaving the hospital she asked the doctor who had prescribed her a hair tonic whilst there to give her the recipe for this 'compound for recovering her hair', and which, so she later claimed, 'speedily reproduced luxuriant and beautiful wavy ringlets, seldom to be equalled'.

Under pressure to support her young family and always on the lookout for lucrative new ventures, Sarah realized that she might be on to a very good thing with this hair tonic and she set about studying cosmetic recipes with the help of her eldest daughter Rachel. She recalled an article read to her from the *Illustrated London News* of January 1846 about the transformative effects of a sacred 'magnetic rock' deep in the Sahara which distilled a precious water 'possessed of extraordinary properties' that increased the vital energies, restored the colour of grey hair and, so it was claimed, gave 'the appearance of youth to persons of considerable antiquity'. Why not manufacture her own 'magnetic hair restorer' and other lotions along the same lines? The hair tonic given to her at King's College Hospital appears to have achieved magical results when she tried it out on others. Word soon spread about Sarah's miracle hair restorative, which, so she was now claiming, was 'compounded from the rarest and most precious of Arabian balms, according to the recipe of a celebrated Eastern physician'. Rumours of her other 'feminine beautifyings' quickly spread beyond Drury Lane to higher quarters and brought carriages and cabs to her humble 'shop' in Clare Court. Before long, Sarah had removed to premises opposite the Royal Opera House in nearby Bow Street.

Before expanding her business further Sarah needed to find a suitable professional persona that would encapsulate her new trade; something foreign-sounding and exotic always seemed to work best with cosmetics. Paris was the world centre of the trade and what could be more fashionable than to make use of the name of one of France's most celebrated tragediennes – Mademoiselle Rachel? The actress was, as it happened, a woman after

Sarah's own heart. She had been born into poverty as Élisa Félix in 1821, one of six children of itinerant Jewish pedlars and old clothes dealers from Alsace. She had started out singing and reciting poetry barefoot in the cafes of Lyon and Paris, before being hired at the age of only seventeen by the Comédie Française, thereafter working her way up to the very top of the French acting profession. As 'Mademoiselle Rachel' she had made a sensational London debut in 1841 during which she had single-handedly propped up the ailing fortunes of Her Majesty's Theatre with her mesmerizing performances from Racine, Voltaire and Corneille. More than that though, she had rescued the financial fortunes of her own family by managing to foist her brother Raphael and her four sisters Sarah, Rebecca, Lia and Dinah on the acting profession too. But Mlle Rachel's career had been a short and tragic one; by July 1857 she was dying. She had been forced to retire from the Comédie Française to Cannes in the south of France – her voice destroyed by the tuberculosis to which she had succumbed after a disastrous tour in America.

Familiar with the acclaim given to Mlle Rachel by London audiences including the Queen herself, the astute Sarah knew that a little manipulation of the truth would be good for business. A supposed distant connection to a fellow Jewess would play on the cachet of the French actress's exotic reputation and ostentatious manner. Mlle Rachel obliged Sarah by dying in January 1858 leaving the newly incarnated English Madame Rachel with a cover that could not easily be challenged and inspiring her greed by also leaving an astronomical legacy of over a million pounds in today's money (throughout her career Mlle Rachel had been notoriously avaricious). The contents of the tragedienne's house at the Place Royale in Paris were auctioned off on 17 April that year. Sarah may well have made a trip over to buy some artefacts to lend credence to her new venture, for within a year she was claiming to be a 'near kinswoman to the late lamented tragedian', and that she herself had manufactured all the costly preparations 'for, and used by that distinguished actress', which was of course a patent lie. By a strange coincidence, Mlle Rachel's sister Sarah, whose own acting career failed after her sister's death, also decided to go into the perfumery business, producing a lotion known as Baume Ottoman, which equally exploited her dead sister, by depicting her as the Ottoman princess in Racine's *Bajazet* on the labels.

Sarah Levison was soon cannily manipulating the spurious connections and confusions with Mademoiselle Rachel to her own financial ends. She made her professional debut in the December 1858 edition of Kelly's London directory as 'Madame Rachel, Hair Restorer', of 5 Conduit St, Regent Street but this address was short-lived and for a while she was still also operating from Bow Street. Knowing her way round the theatres of Drury Lane and Covent Garden as she did, it was only natural that she should seek out custom from actresses who were notorious for being 'fast' and using cosmetics and thus more likely to buy her products. Among her growing list of clients she claimed to have had the celebrated actress Madame Vestris, noted for her flawless white skin into old age, but Vestris had died in 1856 – somewhat predating the Madame Rachel business enterprise. No matter; to Sarah Levison's way of thinking name-dropping never did any harm. It was in fact one of her rivals, Hewlett of Burlington Arcade, who would later peddle his own supposedly exclusive recipe for the 'Vestris Enamel'.

As she began to extend her trade to cosmetics as well as hair treatments, Sarah also pursued business opportunities in the other major social centres, such as Brighton, still a watering hole of the wealthy and the aristocracy although past its Regency heyday. She traded here off-season, from October to March, when the London round of balls, parties and royal drawing rooms were over for the summer. Meanwhile Sarah's children – and she herself from time to time when not away on business – were all now living at 480 New Oxford Street (just north of their old home on Drury Lane), though it is clear that the relationship with Phillip Levison was by now faltering and the couple were becoming increasingly estranged.

It was in November 1857 that Sarah Levison first revealed how opportunistic and tough she could be when it came to exploiting the financial weakness of others. She and Phillip brought a court action for 'goods and money lent' against Mary Ann Christian and Amelie Honoré who ran a dressmaking and millinery business in a case that *Lloyd's Weekly Newspaper* thought instructive of the particular difficulties experienced by the poor, oppressed dressmaker. Sarah, in her capacity as a wardrobe dealer, had apparently called at Christian's shop in order to purchase some soiled dresses. Hearing that the two ladies were in financial difficulty she had advised them to apply to the insolvency court and had volunteered the services of her husband Phillip as a fictitious detaining creditor. She told them to give false names for the debtors on the business (to keep the real debtors from the knowledge of her creditors), suggesting they were in distant places such as Australia, India and New York where they could not be pursued. She also took away some of Christian's property, including furniture, to protect it supposedly from being seized by the court. Meanwhile Sarah, as part of the scam, made a 'friendly arrest' of Miss Christian, who found herself hauled off to Whitecross Street Debtors' Prison for her unpaid debts.

At the hearing in November, Sarah appeared in court but Phillip, who was also called, could not be found. Sarah claimed she knew nothing of his whereabouts – they had separated recently as a result of the circumstances of this case, so she claimed. She swore that she had repeatedly lent Christian and her partner money and to have bought the property which Christian claimed only to have left in her care. It was a pattern of deception and fraud soon to be repeated. The judge was not inclined to believe Sarah but was more preoccupied with the mishandling of the case by Christian's lawyer Mr Olive and did not pursue the matter. It did not however pass the close scrutiny of *Lloyds Weekly*, which suggested the case was underlined by a fraud of a 'very uncommon character'. 'Should not all this be investigated most strictly', it questioned, sensing gross misconduct on the part of 'Mrs Levison'.

Luckily for Sarah, her dubious business practices were not investigated further but they were indeed taken note of by Mary Ann Christian's lawyer, Mr George Lewis of the highly respected legal firm of Lewis & Lewis. Meanwhile, business for the cosmetics side of Sarah's trade was booming. But if she was really going to capitalize on it she needed to move to more salubrious surroundings. It was time to head to the West End and the richer pickings of Mayfair. It was time too to leave behind Sally Russell the fish frier of Clare Market for good and all and take on the mantle of the illustrious Madame Rachel, a woman who moved in a far more rarified world, now patronized by the Crowned Heads of Europe and specially appointed by the Sultana of the Court of Turkey.

CHAPTER TWO

Madame Rachel's Costly Arabian Preparations

IN MID-VICTORIAN LONDON the trade in cosmetics, hair dyes and other beautifiers was an increasingly lucrative growth industry. Despite the moral and social objections to the use of cosmetics as being indicative of promiscuity as well as injurious to the health, Victorian women were becoming increasingly concerned about preserving their looks and enhancing what they had. It mattered not a jot how much the male sex pontificated to them about the pernicious effects of artifice; nor did women want to be lectured on the health-giving properties of regimen, cleanliness and the drinking of copious amounts of spring water as the only acceptable palliative to the loss of looks. Men had since time immemorial worshipped the beauty of the female sex and women in response had sought refuge in the talismanic properties of cosmetics to transform them and make them eternally desirable.

The mysterious arts of the cosmetician date back to the Bible and the wicked Queen Jezebel who painted her face and first gave the use of cosmetics its dangerous and seductive association. In ancient Rome, aside from the legendary use of asses milk for beautifying baths, women used face creams made with pea-flour, barley meal, crushed stag's antlers and narcissus bulbs. Sometimes other unpleasant-sounding organic matter was added such as pulverised snails or placenta, marrow, bile and calves' urine. By the sixteenth century make up was much relied-on to cover the scarring left by venereal disease and smallpox. Works such as *The Secrets of the Reverend Master Alexis of Piemount* published in 1560 offered nostrums to ward off plague as well as recipes for lip balm and for making a natural, marble white skin. One of Alexis's most outlandish concoctions was a 'marvellous' beauty water produced thus: 'Take a young raven from the nest, feed it on hard eggs for forty days, kill it, and distil it with myrtle-leaves, talc and almond oil.' There is no record of the extent of its efficacy.

In the pursuit of beauty, women persisted in taking considerable risks with highly toxic cosmetics in order to retain a fashionably pale complexion. In the sixteenth century, whilst powdered chalk was the staple ingredient, white lead and mercury were often added; mixed with egg white and vinegar the mixture was spread across the face in a mask which would dry to give the appearance of smooth plaster, but which would crack and flake at the slightest facial expression. Urine mixed with rose water was also considered good for the complexion. At this time the profession of the cosmetician was akin to that of the fortune teller and the peddler of quack medicines – an art verging on sorcery that at times could be highly dubious in its associations. By 1770, such was public concern that predatory women were ensnaring husbands under false pretences by the use of cosmetics and other forms of artifice that the British government passed a law, under which any women – be they 'virgins, maids, or widows' – found 'imposing on, seducing or betraying into matrimony … by virtue of scents, paints, cosmetic washes, artificial teeth, false hair, … iron stays or bolstered hips, shall incur the penalty of the law now in force against witchcraft and like misdemeanours, and that the marriage upon conviction, shall stand null and void.'

No wonder cosmeticians were viewed as dangerous. At the court of King Charles II, Mrs Turner touted her 'Oyle of Talck' (talc being a mineral composed of hydrated magnesium that was ground to a powder) as a popular face whitener, and also offered aphrodisiacs on the side. She indulged in the kind of outlandish claims that would characterize Madame Rachel's later sales hype, encouraging young women to gather the dew on May-Day morning and store it in glass phials as the only thing they should ever put on their faces. Interestingly, Mrs Turner also did a little procuring and abortion on the side, which suggests that the professions of cosmetics and vice often went hand in hand.

Many early cosmetics recipes were based on extravagant combinations of expensive herbs and flowers as well as myrrh and even incense, bulked out with animal fats or oil. One such manual, *The Toilet of Flora* published by a trained physician and naturalist, Pierre-Joseph Buc'hoz in 1773, offered an extensive range of recipes for aromatic baths, depilatories, cures for baldness, face washes, hair colours, as well as liquid dentifrices and a mysterious and transformative 'Celestial Water' for rubbing on the face. The recipes in this book required the kind of financial resources enjoyed only by the very rich in order to obtain the exotic products to be variously boiled and mashed together, distilled in brandy and perfumed with aromatic oils. Toothpowders also were produced and were normally made from ground cuttle fish bone, chalk, orris root, red coral and even marble dust.

By the nineteenth century actresses such as Madame Rachel's supposed client Madame Vestris were resorting to more practical methods. Vestris, it was said, slept every night with her face plastered with a paste made of egg whites, alum and sweet almonds spread on a muslin mask. Other actresses wrapped their hands and their faces nightly in thin slices of raw meat for its supposed restorative properties, rather than pay for proprietary masks and forehead pieces of leather impregnated with creams and oils to keep the skin soft and prevent wrinkles. Those with less money at their disposal resorted to going to bed with brown paper soaked in cider vinegar stuck to their foreheads.

The use of cosmetics was of course not solely a female preserve; in the old days men had waxed their hair and moustaches with bear's grease, and beef marrow had been a favourite remedy against baldness. These now had been superseded by hair pomatums made of white wax, spermaceti, lard or suet mixed with essence of bergamot or rose water and oil of almonds For disguising grey hair (a pursuit even then indulged in by both sexes) a rather unpleasant mess of slaked limed, litharge and chalk was combined with white lead in warm water and turned into a paste to be applied to the hair; other hair dyes made use of gall nuts and willow charcoal, lead ore, ebony chips, nitrate of silver, sulphate of copper and nitric acid. There was no end to Victorian ingenuity in driving off those hated grey hairs but what it did to the hair in the process is hard to imagine – some of the products used might well have caused baldness and certainly would have been harmful if they had got into the eyes during application.

By the time Madame Rachel, with the help of her clever eldest daughter, was scouting for recipes for her burgeoning new business, there was a whole range of books on beauty and the toilet that they could draw on. Nevertheless, even by the 1850s, the choice of cosmetics was very limited and the colours were crude, with makeup limited to rouges, red salve for the lips and kohl for the eyes. All were considered extremely vulgar and imitative of the demi-monde but by the mid-century the use of rouge at least was increasingly prevalent among younger women. Numerous books offered homemade recipes for cosmetics, but always with the caution that female beauty 'needs no cosmetics, and that which is not in itself beautiful can never become so by the use of them'. Indulgence in cosmetics, it was generally agreed, was an act of deception which broke the spell of a woman's natural charms; artificial femininity was seen not just as abnormal, but subversive and indicative of something deeper – a falsity of feelings. However, for those insistent on doing it themselves in the privacy of the home there were two basics: 'white cosmetic' (face powder) comprised of various types of fine chalk and sometimes starch which replaced the lethal white lead used in previous centuries, and 'red cosmetic', concocted by stewing a wood with a dark stain such as red sandalwood or pernambuco (brazilwood), with white wine vinegar and pounded alum. After being cooled and strained the mixture would dry out into a pinkish power that could be use as rouge.

Face creams then available were relatively harmless, based usually on white wax and almond oil, though the most prevalent ingredient was spermaceti – a wax extracted from the head cavity of the sperm whale which was then turned into oily white crystals. One of the most popular items gaining hold by the 1860s were the cosmetic face washes for removing every kind of freckle, blemish and eruption on the face; though the more they promised the impossible, the more they succumbed to adulteration. They were often based on highly pernicious chemicals such as white arsenic, bichloride of mercury, hydrochloric acid, corrosive sublimate and even prussic acid – diluted in distilled water and mixed with rose, lavender or orange water to disguise the chemical smell. Many household cupboards contained arsenic, then easily obtainable as a rat poison, which was used for precisely such innocuous home-made beauty remedies leading, it has been claimed, to a preference for poising by arsenic resorted to by several domestic murderesses during the century.

Even the best proprietary balms, washes and blooms for the face used corrosive sublimate to varying degrees of dilution. Metallic compounds, such as 'ceruse' which supposedly gave a brilliancy to faded complexions were dangerously toxic. Paris had led the way in devising new recipes: 'pearl powder', an innocuous sounding product made from crushed seed pearls became popular, though not without risk. Some unscrupulous practitioners in Paris added carbonate of lead and subchloride of bismuth, sufficient to induce slow poisoning in some Parisian actresses who had used it. Even innocent violet powder made with plaster of Paris and talc was sometimes adulterated with quick lime and caustic soda. White lead, out of use since the 1780s, resurfaced in disguise in numerous cosmetic preparations in the nineteenth century, but the fact that this and mercury compounds need only be absorbed through the skin (rather than ingested) to get into the bloodstream and cause terrible damage was only just beginning to dawn on many practitioners. Ladies who used preparations containing bismuth also ran the risk of an unfortunate side-effect: in the presence of sulphur fumes such as coal gas the skin painted with this product turned a deathly shade of grey.

One of the first and most popular commercial brands of English cosmetics and hair dyes was that of Alexander Rowland, a former barber, who brought out his Macassar oil for the hair in the 1790s. His son extended the range between the 1820s and 1850s, adding an 'Olympian Dew' and a 'Bloom of Circassia', as well as an 'Odonto' tooth paste and Rowland's Kalydor face wash, the last of which the advertising hype claimed was 'a never failing specific for cutaneous deformities including freckles, pimples, spots, redness and every other imperfection incident to the skin'. It was one of Rowland's biggest selling products, heavily promoted in the press, where he claimed the patronage of the 'Courts of Europe, the Aristocracy and the Upper Classes'. When Madame Rachel appeared on the scene, Rowland still very much led the field. Also on the ascendant with commercially produced cosmetics were Atkinsons the perfumers, in Bond Street from 1829, and the House of Rimmel. The Frenchman, Eugene Rimmel, had set up a perfumery here in 1834 from where he promoted a highly successful Eau de Cologne and Extract of Spring Flowers, as well as Serkis des Sultanes for protecting the skin and Amandine for softening the face and hands. Rimmel soon had outlets across London and was exporting to Europe and the USA. Unlike many of his dubious rivals including Madame Rachel, he was awarded a bona fide Royal Warrant by Queen Victoria and had been a judge in the perfumery class at the Great Exhibition of 1851. Indeed, the moment a fresh and lovely young queen – Victoria – had come to the throne in 1837, after more than a century of ugly Hanoverian kings, the classified ads had had a field day with such extensive claims of her patronage made that in September 1837 *Figaro in London* had remarked that the queen 'must have had decayed teeth, grey hair, and a head nearly bald, scurf, superfluous hair, a tanned skin, rough and sallow complexion, pimples, spots, redness and cutaneous eruptions' in order to require so many products whose daily use was imputed to her.' With Rowland and Rimmel both producing books extolling the virtues of their own beauty recipes, Madame Rachel had plenty to draw on in putting together her own brochure in 1863. She would soon out-puff Rowland, as she cherry-picked ideas from both her rivals, as well as a whole range of other cosmeticians already crowding out the small ads columns of the newspapers.

***

In November 1858, however, Madame Rachel's first cosmetics venture in Mayfair had ended up in court – a place that would become increasingly familiar to the family. The previous May, in an endeavour to live independently and contribute to the upkeep of the rest of the family who were still living at 480 New Oxford Street, the self-confident Rachel junior, at the age of only sixteen, had taken a two-year lease for £163.16s of first floor rooms at the premises of Jean Georges Atloff, a French bootmaker, at 69 New Bond Street. Here, under her mother's supervision, she was to extend the Madame Rachel franchise, whilst Rachel *mère* was still running the business in Bow Street and pursuing the Brighton end of things. Rachel junior took possession of the rooms at no. 69, along with a servant girl and her five-year old brother Aaron, who was to play the decorative role of page boy. She had paid twelve shillings to have her plate fixed on the door outside, when, four or five days later she had a cab waiting at the door to take her and her trunk of cosmetics to an appointment. According to her barrister, she prepared 'elderly ladies for balls' and on this particular occasion had been called to attend a countess for a party that evening – most of her clients at the time preferring to pay the five guineas for a call out to their own homes. Shortly before leaving Rachel junior had had a disagreement with her landlord Atloff who had claimed her references were not satisfactory. In view of this he now required security for the rent; either that or it should be paid at a weekly rate of three guineas rather than quarterly. Rachel refused and an altercation had ensued, as a result of which Atloff, so Rachel claimed, had locked her in the house, preventing her from fulfilling her engagement. The following morning in attempting to forcibly eject her, he had grabbed her by the arm and dragged her from room to room, tearing her dress; he had also tried to confiscate the trunks containing her valuable cosmetics.

In court, after stating her name to be Miss Rachel Leverson 'a Jewess born in London', Rachel junior made no mention of her mother but proceeded to describe how she went under the business name of Madame Rachel, but that in her circular 'she called herself a Frenchwoman' and also claimed to be of 'Broadway, New York', where, she said, 'her uncle resided'. Under cross-examination she was forced to admit to having defaulted the previous year on payment for the printing of her leaflet and had pleaded 'infancy', being only sixteen at the time. Business had been bad that year, she explained, 'on account of the Indian war' (the Indian Rebellion of 1857) but she intended, when she reached the age of eighteen the following January, to settle up with all her creditors. A doctor was called to confirm bruising to her arm and chest; Miss Leverson had also, in his opinion, suffered a degree of 'nervous excitement' since the incident. Indeed, Rachel claimed she had been unwell since Atloff's attack and her subsequent loss of earnings during the 'middle of a brilliant season' had been considerable. She did not, however, appear to be so traumatized that she was unable to withstand a barbed cross-examination from defending counsel, Mr Temple:

– I see your circular states that you deal in articles "for the restoration and beautifying of the human hair, complexion, and teeth [laughter] … and successful treatment is so fully appreciated by the crowned heads of Europe. Do you mean by that bald heads [laughter], or crowned heads, Kings, Queens, Emperors and such like?

– I mean her Majesty. [laughter]

– What, her present Majesty?

– Yes, Mr Temple.

– Do you go to her majesty to be "done up for a ball"? [laughter]

– No, but I have her Majesty's patronage.

– Then she is the crowned head who so fully appreciates your abilities?

– Yes, Mr. Temple.

– I see you also refer to the aristocracy and the nobility whom you have successfully treated [laughter] … You say you will restore human hair, and I see you have a depilatory powder which is for taking away the hair … Then you have powders to bring hair, and powders to drive it away again?

– Yes. [laughter].

Despite Mr Temple's ridicule, Rachel junior seemed only too proud to elaborate on how she could bring hair on the head with her hair restoratives and take it away on the face by use of her special depilatories; how she dealt in 'blanchinette', a 'sort of preparation by which ladies' faces are made to look white', and rosinette, to make their cheeks look red. She also sold 'Arabian bloom', a snip at 10s. 6d. a box. She made no bones at all about how lucrative her cosmetics business could be; during the season her weekly takings were around £15 (£1,000 a week today) and her weekly stock was worth £30–£40.

The case might well have passed unnoticed had Rachel junior not been so brazen in court in stating the kind of money she earned. A young woman so openly and unrepentantly set on a life in trade at a time when this was still greatly frowned upon inevitably attracted press attention, with articles under headlines such as 'Blooming a Countess' describing the case as a moral tale 'illustrative of fashionable life'. For they underlined not just Rachel junior's opportunism but the degeneracy of the aristocracy who indulged in such things. The greatest amount of column space was accorded the case by the *Morning Post*, whose readers made up the bulk of Madame Rachel's clientele. Whilst the case clearly had some amusement value it also presented Rachel junior as dangerously bold – foreign, elusive and ultimately untrustworthy – reflecting current social anxieties about Jewish 'otherness'. Prior to the case, the defendant Atloff had paid £5 into court, deeming it sufficient compensation, but the jury decided that Rachel's injuries merited £20 in damages. Meanwhile, mother and daughter would have to ride out the response of satirical journals such as *Punch* which had begun to pick up on the story, whilst also exploiting the confusion in the public mind with the late lamented Mademoiselle Rachel, whose memoirs even now were being heavily advertised in London. In its 20 November issue *Punch* carried a parody entitled 'The Cause of the Cosmetics' – the necessary moral lesson to be gleaned from the case of 'Leverson v Atloff' being to leave well alone:

> Trust me, nature ne'er made beauty on this earth as round it
>   whirls,
> Comelier than an English matron's; lovelier than an English
>   girl's.
> Twere enough to make with anguish *Venus de Medici* cry,
> If a woman's beauty stood upon the hazard of a die.

Satirical swipes such as this did not deter Madame Rachel. The most lucrative time of year for her cosmetics trade was fast approaching: the London Season. It was timed to coincide with the Parliamentary Sessions from February to mid-July when MPs – many from the landed classes – left their country estates to sit in the Houses of Parliament. The minute the shooting and fox hunting-season was over the aristocracy would decamp to their London town houses in droves to pursue an elegant procession of drawing rooms (the most sought after being those held by the queen), 'breakfasts' (a misnomer for what were in fact day-long garden parties), balls, house calls, carriage drives in Hyde Park, shopping, visits to the opera and so on. The primary pursuit, on the surface, was to see and be seen in fashionable society, but everyone knew that the true objective of the season was for ambitious mothers from the upper classes to see their daughters well-married, once they had had 'come out' at a formal presentation to the queen. The hopes of older spinsters and widows too were revived with the onset of the season. Seamstresses and dressmakers worked flat out throughout this period to beautify them – and so too did the cosmeticians. In the self-righteous and prudish atmosphere of mid-Victorian Britain, however, the trade in cosmetics still had an 'under the counter' character. Ladies insisted on discretion about their purchases and their beauty treatments, which must be made furtively, in the privacy of their own homes or the salon and never openly in a shop. In response to this, at the beginning of the new season, in March 1859, Madame Rachel launched a new advertising campaign in the *Morning Post*:

BEAUTIFUL WOMEN. – MADAME RACHEL begs to inform her lady patronesses, the nobility and aristocracy generally, that she

has opened her ANNUAL SUBSCRIPTION list for the supply
of her Costly Arabian Preparations for the restoration and
preservation of female loveliness, which have obtained for her
the patronage of royalty – these being manufactured entirely by
MADAME RACHEL, who has no agents, and cannot be obtained
from any other source. Terms as usual, 20 guineas per annum,
which includes every requisite for a most *recherché* toilet, and two
attendances by MADAME RACHEL, viz. one drawing room and
one state ball.

Alarmed by the brazenness of the Madame Rachel publicity
campaign, *Punch* again launched an attack in its March
26 issue with a piece entitled 'Stucco for the Softer Sex',
in which it imagined how Rachel's patronesses might be
'fashioned out of that plastic material, and animated with a
faint life by a disciple of FRANKENSTEIN.' Madame Rachel's
new-fangled 'enamelling' process, which was being touted
in the small ads, promised, in *Punch*'s view, to create a new
breed of artificial women, the nearest thing to which was
perhaps 'a white sepulcher'.

The use of the term 'enamelling of ladies' faces',
although by no means original to Madame Rachel, certainly
gained currency at this time thanks to her extensive
advertising campaign, and was forever after associated with
her name and notoriety. The objective was the age-old one
of producing a smooth and transparently white quality to
the face, as lovely and delicate as a piece of Sèvres porcelain,
for that special ball or dinner or presentation at court and

one whose effects could last for up to a year. The process used by Rachel and her kind was akin to what might today be achieved through the process of 'skin peeling'. In ancient Nineveh women had rubbed their skin with pumice stones to remove the soft fine hair and create a smooth surface; in Egypt and Syria, brides would enamel themselves all over using a liquid depilatory which would leave the skin bright; in the seventeenth century women would cover their faces with oil of vitriol to remove the top layer of skin. But in the hands of Madame Rachel enamelling was elevated to a secret art, which she claimed was conducive to health and beauty, grace and youth, and one that was exclusively hers.

The method was simple – a careful removal of rough hairs or fuzz on the face and bust by the use of various lotions and/or tweezers; followed by the application of copious amounts of alkaline toilet washes, then a filling-in of wrinkles and depressions in the skin with a thick paste (usually made of arsenic or white lead and other ingredients), followed by applications of rouge and powder to finish off. Rich American women were reported to be flocking to London and Paris for the procedure and Madame rode high on the advertising hype, openly asserting her exclusivity in the papers and stating that 'all other persons presuming to style themselves enamellers commit a gross fraud on the public at large'. However, in her celebrity manual, *The Arts of Beauty,* published in 1858, the actress Lola Montes (who in 1868 will make an indirect appearance in our story), had been scathing in her criticism: 'Nothing so effectually writes *memento mori!* on the cheek of beauty as this ridiculous and culpable practice.'

***

The negative publicity that followed Rachel junior's damages case naturally enough acted as an inverted form of publicity for the Madame Rachel franchise. Despite the setback at 69 New Bond Street, during July–August 1859 mother and daughter launched a major campaign in the *Morning Chronicle* and the *Lady's Newspaper* from their home at 480 New Oxford Street, 'opposite Mudie's library' (a popular circulating library) where, they announced, they could be consulted daily from ten to six in order to prepare ladies for the London season. Their new advertising hype preyed on women's innermost anxieties at this most important time of the year: 'How frequently we find that a slight blemish on the face, otherwise divinely beautiful, has occasioned a sad and solitary life of celibacy, unloved, unblessed, and ultimately unwept and unremembered' commiserated Madame Rachel in the advertising columns. But rescue was at hand: 'by prompt and judicious appliances the defect can be removed, and a beauteous loveliness succeeds, so conducive to the happiness and connubial felicity of the fair and graceful being.' Madame Rachel was now becoming ever more brazen in her claims for her products. These 'Costly Arabian Preparations' were being imported to London from far flung Arabia, Syria, Central India, China and Japan 'regardless of expense'; and her exclusive 'Jordan Water' – direct from the legendary river itself – was available expressly for 'State occasions'. All preparations were offered to customers in the very strictest confidence with the stern warning that 'articles purchased elsewhere are spurious'.

The quest for new, more upmarket premises meanwhile continued. In December 1859 a small ad had appeared in *The Times* announcing that 'The late Mrs Parker's preparations for the hair, bark lotion, Quin Julep and Pomade, Vervain and Bandoline Pomade' were continuing to be prepared by her eldest son and successor, Erwin Parker at the depot 47a New Bond Street.' Mrs Parker's business however, appears to have folded some time the following year and Madame Rachel took out a lease on the premises. By early May 1861 she and Rachel junior were once again advertising – in the theatrical profession's trade paper the *Era* – from these New Bond Street premises, offering their exclusive 'Gems of the Season, Alabaster Powder and Magnetic Rock Dew Water'. Rachel junior was now resident at the premises – her presence noted on the 1861 census taken in April that year as a 'perfumer and enamelist' though her father, now working as a stationer, and her remaining siblings were all still living at 480 New Oxford Street. Madame Rachel and her second daughter Leah were nowhere to be found on the census that year and were almost certainly in Paris exploring business ventures there. The beautiful, fifteen-year old Leah, who had now adopted the more exotic name of Leontie, was, it seemed, being groomed to join the business.

While Madame Rachel was out of town, leaving Phillip Levison to care for their children, including a one-year old son, Abraham, who had been born the previous June, Rachel junior, who had been left to mind the shop proceeded to overreach herself and soon ended up in Whitecross Street debtor's prison. She had ordered expensive dresses to a debt of £188 and in the autumn of 1861, at the tender age of twenty, she twice found herself in the bankruptcy court. On 17 September she had petitioned for bankruptcy, on a debt to Messrs Grant & Gask silk mercers of Oxford Street. As the Madame Rachel business appeared to be in Rachel junior's name at this time, she was held responsible but immediately claimed minority, Phillip Levison coming to court to confirm her date of birth as 4 January 1841. Rachel's creditors asked for the case to be adjourned till she came of age in January 1862 when their claim would be valid, but the judge adjourned only till 12 November in order to confer with the Chief Commissioner over the issue of Rachel's minority and culpability; in the meantime she was allowed out of prison on bail.

When Rachel junior returned to court in November 1861 she was obliged to reveal that although she lived

some of the time at New Bond Street, she also stayed
sometimes 'at her mamma's country house at Blackheath'
– a surprising revelation indicating a level of concealed
prosperity enjoyed by the Madame Rachel franchise. She
also travelled to Brighton with her mother on business.
Madame Rachel herself still held 'saloons' for clients at
the premises at 480 Oxford Street. Meanwhile Rachel
junior admitted that she carried another debt contracted
on the business between December 1858 and May 1859
for £149 10s. 5d., to Messrs Burgoyne the Chemists, for
'scents and essential oils used in her preparations'. Some
of the goods supplied, she claimed, were 'spoiled' and of
no use – though, as it was later observed, she had failed
to send any of them back. She made a point of declaring
that she also procured the costly preparations she used in
her enamelling process from abroad. This expense, plus
the obligation to extend credit to many of her patronesses,
whose names were kept in her account books, had brought
her to insolvency. But when pressed for the benefit of
her creditors to reveal what sums were owed to her which
might cover her debts, she refused to say. In any case,
Rachel claimed, because she had been in so much trouble,
she had entrusted these books 'to a friend who had gone
to Australia'. They might, she added as an afterthought,
'have been destroyed.' To produce them and name names
would be to 'ruin her profession' and she bluntly refused
to do so. If her ladies knew that she kept a note of their

names and addresses they would withdraw their patronage from her. The confidentiality of the cosmetician's parlour was, it seemed, equal to that of the doctor's surgery and the lawyer's office.

In court, prosecutor, Mr Macrae, managed to extract the admission from her that she charged on average five to twenty guineas for enamelling a lady's face. 'Oh yes,' responded Rachel with considerable pride, adding that she often charged 'more than twenty guineas' (something like £1,500 today). But she made it clear that the prosecution had no understanding of her *profession*: it was one where the practitioner such as herself whilst charging high prices was also 'compelled to give hundreds of pounds of credit' and she had to help support a large family. No wonder her lady customers wanted the amounts of money they spent kept secret: in the days before the Married Woman's Property Act they were effectively spending their husbands' money and not their own.

With instructions to go away and locate her account books, Rachel junior was once more released on bail, till 17 January the following year. Back in court she still professed to be unable to lay hands on the books but in any event, she now miraculously was owed no money by her lady patronesses. Had these ladies all paid up in order to prevent their names from being aired in court? She must have had a very lucrative trade, suggested Mr Macrae, going on the orders she had placed with Messrs Burgoyne.

When pressed on this Rachel reeled off a list: castor oil, olive oil, attar of roses, bismuth, orris root, lavender oil, white and yellow wax, oils of bergamot and lemon among numerous assorted essences and oils. Mr Macrae could not help observing, to the sound of considerable laughter in court, that she must have received enough otto of roses 'to have sweetened the Thames, as well as perfume sufficient for three parishes, and enough bismuth to destroy the faces of half a million of young ladies.' Her spending was clearly extravagant, as too her exploitation of credit: having failed to pay for the advertisements she had placed across numerous newspapers, Rachel junior had added a further five creditors to her list.

Rachel junior's side of the Madame Rachel franchise had been out of business for more than twelve months pending the bankruptcy hearings. As she was now of age she could be pursued as a bankrupt and was sent back to Whitecross Street Debtor's Prison whilst the magistrates deliberated the legal technicalities of her case. A decision was eventually made that Rachel could after all be allowed to plead infancy retrospectively and she was released from jail. Her creditors appear not to have pursued the matter further. Soon after the resolution of this case, Madame Rachel was once again advertising her 'Beauties of the East', available only at 47 New Bond Street in the *Era*. It would appear that Madame Rachel herself had now reappeared to take control of the business and consolidate its London operation. But she would not avoid controversy for very long. The perpetual trips back and forth to the law courts made by her and her daughter played into her business plan – to keep the name and the brand forever in the public eye. They most certainly reflected an inveterately brazen attitude to the inflated claims made by mother and daughter in promoting the business and the profession of 'enameller of ladies' faces'; the two women also presented an astonishingly fearless attitude towards anyone who denigrated it and a readiness always to sue.

Not long after Madame Rachel's resumption of business, mother and daughter began gearing up for another London season. It was launched with an advertisement in the *Morning Chronicle* reminding women that the Emperor Napoleon of France had judged women's sole business in life to be to dress exquisitely and look lovely. In order to achieve this, 'enamelling', the advertisement claimed, had become 'quite general amongst the ladies of the *elite* who frequent fashionable and crowded assemblies, it being the only method ladies have of displaying their matchless beauty'. And the *only* possessor in the world of that great art, was of course – Madame Rachel. The unwritten subtext was guaranteed to induce anxiety in the vain and gullible: go to Rachel and you will be transformed into a socially acceptable beauty; stay away and you will languish, unnoticed, in the shadows.

In 1862 Madame Rachel's name was back in court and

the papers in a strange case, the truth of which was never made plain. On 3 May, Wentworth Fitzwilliam, Viscount Milton was arraigned at Marlborough Street Magistrates Court by a pawnbroker, Sophia Stephens, for obtaining under false pretences a pair of diamond earrings worth £100, which had been pawned with her by Madame Rachel.

Heir to the 6th Earl Fitzwilliam, Milton had been forced to live most of his life in seclusion, in an attempt by the family to conceal the stigma of his severe epilepsy. No expense had been spared in obtaining the best medical opinion of the day or paying for him to be treated abroad in expensive asylums, but the end result was that Viscount Milton had become irretrievably addicted to a lethal cocktail of drugs and sedatives to control his condition. In the aftermath of a broken engagement, forced on him by his family, Milton went wild in the gaming houses and brothels of the West End. At this time a lady friend of his told him she had lost a pair of diamond earrings 'at a game of cards' with Madame Rachel and Milton had gone to the New Bond Street salon to get them back for her. Having asked to see the diamonds, he was taken by Rachel junior to Sophia Stephens' pawnshop in Brewer Street where they had been pawned for £65. Milton asked them to be brought to Madame Rachel's salon at six that evening and he would redeem them. When the earrings were delivered and placed on a table the Viscount had put them in his pocket and refused to give them up, later claiming that he had wished to place them in the hands of the police until their true ownership had been ascertained.

No mention was made of how the diamonds really had come into Madame Rachel's possession, but the logical assumption was not that they had been won at cards but that they had been left by a lady client as security against a series of beauty treatments for which she had not been able to pay. Colin Penney, assistant to the pawnbroker Sophia Stephens admitted in court he had often been to the New Bond Street salon on business but refused to reveal its nature. In court Milton's barrister, the clever Serjeant Ballantine ('Serjeant' being a legal title short for Serjeant-at-Law) did his best to deflect culpability from his client onto Madame Rachel by insinuating that the earrings had originally been obtained 'by a gross fraud' but without elaborating as to how. Passing references were made to the Belasco perjury case and Rachel junior's bankruptcy, sufficient to rouse antipathy towards Madame Rachel and rekindle the press appetite for stories about her. The judge was not impressed by the defence's blatant attempt to make unfounded accusations of fraud against Rachel, who was not present in court, and remanded the case for a week.

During that time Madame Rachel was quick to defend herself and her business against the calumnies hurled against it. On 3 May, signing herself 'S. R. Levison', Rachel wrote – or rather the clever Rachel junior composed it for her, as her mother could not write – to the editor of *The Times*, complaining of the way in which she and her daughter had been 'most invidiously mentioned' in connection with the Milton case, and that the defence counsel in exculpating his client had made 'speculative, false and unfounded' allegations against her. She would, she asserted, be more than willing to make a statement in court refuting them and would show that the callow Viscount Milton had in fact been 'the dupe of a designing woman, on whose behalf he has, to say the least of it, been most incautiously and imprudently zealous'. With this, Rachel therefore requested that the public would suspend their judgment until the case returned to court.

In the event Madame Rachel did not appear at the second hearing on 10 May when Milton's defence, the upcoming young lawyer, George Lewis, proceeded to argue that this was not a case for sending to trial. His client had acted foolishly but had plenty of money in the bank to pay for the diamonds had he so wished. He had clearly been in an unstable mental condition at the time he had committed this 'indiscretion'. The judge Mr Knox thought the case a very confused one, but, concluding that the act was that of 'a foolish person', he discharged Viscount Milton with a gentle reprimand. The Viscount's irate father immediately ordered his son out of sight and out of the country for bringing shame on the family. The papers for the most part gave little attention to what was seen as the harmless misdemeanour of a member of the aristocracy. It fell to the editor of *Reynolds's News* to draw his readers' attention to the 'benign' treatment Milton had received from the judge. Had he been a working man he would not have got off so lightly. Even the barrister for the prosecution had behaved more like a 'courtier' than a counsellor and had not been able to entertain the idea that the member of an illustrious family was guilty. Names had been suppressed and witnesses kept back in order, effectively, to spare the Milton family honour. The whole affair, remarked *Reynolds's News*, was a 'miserable mockery of justice', showing that 'what is considered criminal in a poor, is pronounced indiscreet in a rich man.' Milton, meanwhile disappeared off to Canada where, aged only 24 and despite his epilepsy, he made a historic journey across the Rocky Mountains, discovering the final stage in the land route linking the Atlantic to the Pacific. For a brief while on his return he was feted in London society, but the epilepsy cut short his life at the age of only 37. No lessons were learned, however, with regard to the biased and indulgent treatment by the courts of the indiscretion of an aristocrat. It would be repeated, with far more slavish deference, when Madame Rachel fell foul of the law again in 1868.

In the meantime, the Milton case added to the slow drip-drip of accumulating gossip and rumour about Madame Rachel and the underlying activities of her business. It had revealed that Rachel junior had pawned diamonds before with Sophia Stephens of Brewer Street. Whose diamonds were they? And where were they coming from? How could Madame Rachel afford to retain such expensive premises in New Bond Street, a house in Blackheath and advertise heavily in the press merely on the proceeds of her enamelling arts? A month later, before the gossip surrounding the Milton case had died down, London society would get a taster of more sinister goings on at New Bond Street.

CHAPTER THREE

The Inner Life
of Fashionable People

WHEN MADAME RACHEL set herself up in premises on New Bond Street she had sent out a clear signal about her exclusivity to the cream of London's fashionable society. The name of Bond Street (technically Old Bond Street and its extension New Bond Street built north of Clifford Street between 1700 and 1721) had for a century or more held a special cachet among the moneyed classes. First developed in the late 1680s, Bond Street was a rather narrow street of small shops of little architectural note, but it lay in the heart of Mayfair, extending from its southern boundary on Piccadilly to Oxford Street at its northern end. It had none of the great flourish of the Parisian shopping boulevards yet nevertheless by the eighteenth century had become London's premier street for luxury goods. At this time it was the preserve of men about town such as the 'Bond Street Loungers' of the early 1700s, the writers Lawrence

Sterne and James Boswell and an assortment of earls, dukes, MPs and dandies, culminating in Beau Brummell, whose favourite tailor, Weston's, had premises at no. 34 Old Bond Street. Emma, Lady Hamilton visited when Nelson was lodging here in the late 1790s and Georgiana, Duchess of Devonshire, helped to popularize Bond Street around the same time. But in general it remained the preserve of men, noted for its gentlemen's tailors, hatters, shoe makers, hair dressers and wig makers, as well as its better class of 'sporting' hotels such as the Clarendon, Long's and Limmer's, which were patronized by Byron and Shelley in their day. Such became the demand for access to the shops on Bond Street that its narrow thoroughfare regularly became gridlocked with carriages, bringing the whole street to a standstill, particularly during the London season, and making it necessary to access the shops there via Conduit Street.

Because of its long association with the male sex, during the first half of the nineteenth century Bond Street was not a place any respectable lady cared to be seen in during the afternoon and if she ventured there in the mornings she would always be chaperoned. By the 1840s however trade in Bond Street began to extend beyond men-only outlets to expensive looking furriers and jewellers, milliners, lacemakers, and linendrapers as well as glass, porcelain and china shops, art galleries and auction houses. Ladies now came to Bond Street for its excellent circulating libraries, such as John Mitchell's, its high-class perfumers including Eugene Rimmel, and Savory & Moore the chemists, who had founded a shop in New Bond Street in 1797 and had long enjoyed the royal warrant above the door.

In 1817 Samuel Pratt, an upholsterer and cabinet maker had established a business at no. 47 New Bond Street, which with his son he had extended in the 1840s to the importing and exhibiting of antique furniture. The business had survived bankruptcy in 1852 and again in 1855 and after the departure of Mrs Parker's perfumery from the ground floor, the premises were leased to Madame Rachel. She first advertised her 'Gems of the Season' from no. 47 in May 1861; by July 1862 the address had been amended to no. 47a and was listed in Kelly's Post Office Directory as that of 'Madame Rachel, Hair Restorer'. The amendment to the house number was no doubt made to differentiate from the Samuel Pratt business occupying the upper floors. A year later the directory listing had been upgraded to 'Perfumer and Enameller'.

Rachel was not the first of her kind to practice in Bond Street – in the late seventeenth century a 'beauty doctor' had practiced at Mr Trout's near the Piccadilly end, claiming in a handbill that she 'worked Night and Day for the good of mankind' producing her miraculous 'Balsamick Essence', along with several other 'incomparable cosmeticks'. These had rendered her clients 'pleasing to their husbands ... that they might not be offended at their deformities and turn to others'. The sales hype preying on women's age-old fear of losing their looks and with it their husbands was thus no different a couple of centuries before Madame Rachel, as too was the claim that 'a great many persons of the first rank' were among the practitioner's select clientele. But what did Madame Rachel have to offer in competition with cosmeticians and perfumers of longer standing in Bond Street such as Francis Truefitt (Perfumer and Court Head [sic] Dresser to Her Majesty) at no. 1, or Rigge, Brockbank & Rigge (Perfumers to the Royal Family) at no. 35, or for that matter Piesse & Lupin's 'Laboratory of Flowers' at no. 2? Competition was intense and she would need to come up with something more inventive than the obviously spurious claim of being 'Purveyor of Arabian Perfumery to the Queen'; similar claims were being made up and down the length of Bond Street by many other businesses.

The front window of Madame's salon at no. 47a, on the corner of New Bond Street and Maddox Street, provided a tantalizing display of what was promised within: exotically shaped bottles, pomade pots, multi-coloured soaps and gaudy packets of powders 'daintily tied with slim silk ribands'. A small screen inside the doorway protected the interior of the long, narrow premises from prying eyes. Beyond it was the shop itself and at the back, a glass door leading into a small parlour, where Madame Rachel offered private consultations until seven in the evening in the winter and even later in the summer. It might have been small but the salon was fitted out in a lavish and deliberately exotic style – suggesting all the mystery and allure of the Orient from where Madame's costly products were brought at such supposedly colossal expense. With its incense burners, latticed screens, rugs and wall tapestries, this 'Temple of Renovation' as Rachel liked to describe it, suggested all the luxury – and sexual mystery – of the harem, the effect finished off by the soothing sound of a tinkling fountain. Arriving at this haven of calm, which society ladies did heavily-veiled in order to protect their anonymity, was like entering a place of worship where the sacred ingredients of its High Priestess Madame Rachel's art were displayed in bottles and jars of all shapes and sizes. Here was a place that promised to work magic on a woman's faded looks. And there to assist lady clients was the imposing figure of Madame Rachel herself, dressed in grand, flowing black robes, with 'crystals and gimcracks clattering at her girdle'. Madame might be large and square-jawed with a heavy, mannish face and a voice to match, but her two charming, exotically Jewish-looking daughters, as well as her son Aaron dressed as a page boy, together imparted a sense of exclusivity to the salon which others in Bond Street could not match. Although Rachel herself was illiterate, she had ensured that all four of her daughters were well educated, wore jewels and the best dresses and took singing and dancing lessons like any other young ladies of Mayfair. Her accomplished eldest daughter Rachel had now been joined at the shop by her second daughter Leontie – a bewitching girl with a caste in her eye who was described by one who saw her as being of almost 'diabolic' beauty. Indeed, Madame claimed to one incredulous client that such were the transformative powers of her products and her own supernormal skills as a cosmetician, that she and her daughters were in fact much older than they appeared; she and Leontie, so she had once claimed to one client, had sat and watched the guillotining of Marie Antoinette during the French Revolution.

***

The exclusivity of Madame Rachel's new address did not however bring with it the hoped-for discreet profile demanded by her lady patronesses, for in June 1862 she once more attracted public attention when she took one of her clients to court for an unpaid debt. Or rather Madame Rachel's 'husband' Phillip Levison went to the Westminster Court of the Exchequer on her behalf in order to recover 928 guineas for services rendered and goods supplied to a Mrs Carnegie, from the lady's husband the Hon. Swinfen Thomas Carnegie, a captain in the Royal Navy and son of the Earl of Northesk. In 1862, as the law then stood, although a woman could posses her own property while she was single, once married, her separate legal identity ceased to exist. Although her father could arrange for separate 'pin money' in the form of a private allowance, all rights to her possessions and any earnings, as well as all liability for her debts, immediately transferred to her husband.

Mrs Louisa Carnegie, who was thirty years younger than her husband, lived at the very upmarket address of Belgrave Square. Her mother was Matilda, Countess Rapp (daughter of one of Napoleon's commanders) and the couple were very well connected in aristocratic circles. In December 1861, having seen Madame Rachel's advertisements in the *Court Journal*, she had sent her maid to New Bond Street with a message requesting Madame visit her at her home. She was worried about the scarring on her breast left after an operation for an abscess in Paris. The procedure had also left her complexion 'very much faded'; she was still young but already fearful of losing her looks. It was now the height of the Christmas holiday season and she had a series of balls and parties to attend, but despite Mrs Carnegie's entreaties Rachel refused to pay a home visit, declaring rather grandly that she 'never attended strange ladies at their residences'. Mrs Carnegie therefore came to Bond Street and, once hooked, returned several times, calling at all hours, on one occasion at midnight and staying till 2 a.m., so Madame claimed. She was desperate for some kind of miracle cure for the scarring on her breast and told Rachel that she was willing to pay anything – 'a thousand pounds' – if she could 'enamel' her and conceal it so that she could at last wear décolleteé gowns in society instead of high-necked ones.

Called to the witness box, Madame Rachel swore the oath on the Old Testament as Rachel Leverson (describing her husband Phillip as a 'perfumer') and declared that she had refused to enamel Mrs Carnegie's breast as she had considered it would be 'injurious to her health', but that she had agreed to enamel her face, neck and arms. At the time, she had made clear to her client her scale of charges, which included 160 guineas 'and upwards' for her special enamelling process. Mrs Carnegie had told Rachel she had her own money and would pay any amount in order to cover the scar and dispel gossip that had been circulated about her that she had 'had one of her breasts cut'. She knew that Madame attended no one but the *élite* of society, which to her seemed guarantee enough of results. Rachel then described how she had exercised her secret art of enamelling on Mrs Carnegie more than four times during the course of eight or ten visits, as well as supplying her with various cosmetics and perfumes.

The Judge, Mr Baron Wilde, asked her to go into more detail about her art. 'I can enamel a lady for one evening – or for ever,' Rachel announced grandly, to peals of laughter in court. Mrs Carnegie had never uttered a word of complaint and seemed satisfied with the products supplied; indeed she had developed something of an addiction to the beauty treatments. 'She could not do without them', averred Rachel. With Madame having worked her magic on her, Mrs Carnegie subsequently attended a fancy dress hunt ball in Monmouthshire in an expensive white tulle dress sewn with feathers to represent 'snow', at which she had been 'much admired'. All this time, Madame Rachel had provided her services and products on extended credit, as was the accepted practice. When she pressed for payment Mrs Carnegie had become flustered and kept stalling her; she offered Rachel some of her jewels including a diamond tiara, and even the rings off her fingers but Rachel had persisted in asking to be paid. Mrs Carnegie promised on her 'honour' as a lady that she would do so. Rachel had no qualms about holding her to that promise; in her estimation she had given value for money. She expected, after generously extending credit to her for three months, to be paid.

Mr John Karslake for the defence now pressed Rachel on what exactly her clients got for their money. Firstly, she said, 'every vestige of dirt is removed from the system by liquid herbs.' The pores are kept open – unlike other cosmetic treatments where they were 'stopped up' – and the whole surface of the skin was 'washed over with liquid flowers'– not, she was anxious to emphasize – with paint. 'I do not paint'. She was most emphatic about that and she was not happy in having to reveal the tricks of her trade in court; her lady clients 'generally required secrecy'. Her process was 'not really enamelling', Rachel continued, her ladies called it so 'because under it, the skin becomes so beautiful, soft and white', that it resembles 'painting on ivory'. Such beautiful transparent skin was highly sought after and so delighted with the results had Mrs Carnegie been that she had declared that she would like Madame Rachel to make her 'beautiful for ever'. When pressed on this point by the defence, Rachel reiterated that her process did indeed have a permanent effect. She had also managed to conceal Mrs Carnegie's wound 'by a process only known to myself'. She now had a lovely figure and her sallow complexion had been transformed. Madame Rachel had indeed made Mrs Carnegie 'beautiful for ever', she was certain of that.

However, after Mrs Carnegie had repeatedly failed to pay Rachel's account for £938 5s. 0d., Rachel had been obliged to send it to her husband Mr Carnegie. Having known nothing of his wife's visits to New Bond Street or condoned the expenditure, he too refused to pay. During the case the defence refused out of delicacy to indulge the 'prurient curiosity of the crowd' and put Mrs Carnegie in the witness box (though she was waiting in a carriage in nearby Palace Yard in case she was called), but it did call her husband, who confirmed that his wife had her own private income of £700-800 a year. In addition, he had always supplied her with 'sufficient necessaries and medical attendance'; she had her own carriage and normally he paid the bills without question. Contrary to the claims of both his wife and Madame Rachel, he thought the scar looked worse now than it had at the beginning of the year.

At the end of the hearing Mr Baron Wilde advised the special jury (of hand-picked, professional men) that the only decision they had to arrive at was whether or not Mr Carnegie had authorized his wife's expenditure at Madame Rachel's salon. Without even leaving the box, and after conferring in a whisper for barely a minute, they returned a verdict for the defendant, exonerating Carnegie of any responsibility for his wife's debt. As with Viscount Milton, it would seem there were unwritten laws relating to social standing in such cases: one for the moneyed classes, and another for the lesser ranks. Rachel had had every legitimate right to pursue payment and should not have lost the case. The decision clearly was a judgment on her as a woman of business and a Jew, and she was left with a £300 bill for costs. One lone voice of sympathy was raised on her behalf in the *Morning Advertiser*, under the rubric 'The labourer was worthy of his hire': if ladies 'put faith in enamelling and derive benefit from it, they are bound, as ladies, to pay for it'.

With Madame Rachel already a familiar name in the press, and the subject of women's increasing addiction to cosmetics a growing topic for discussion, the case was widely reported in the national newspapers. Coverage exposed male anxieties about the rapidly growing vogue for cosmetics as being an assault not just on femininity but on public morality – an assault which ultimately threatened the vary heart of the Victorian patriarchy. The Carnegie case was a grotesque example of the absurd excesses that silly, vain women would go to in their thirst for admiration, wrote the *Glasgow Herald* on 24 June and it had made people begin to cast 'a suspicious eye' on beauty. Presciently, given today's debates over cosmetic surgery, it asked whether this new, manufactured beauty was to be the order of the day. If so, then it was time for Nature to think of 'shutting up shop and emigrating' now that it had to compete with women such as Madame Rachel. Nature was 'growing antiquated', the article continued, she could 'no longer meet the demands of the fair sex for perfection'. But men had a right when they married to expect their brides to be the genuine article and not an enamelled fake: 'We feel alarmed when a beauty looks as if she were going to be betrayed into a smile lest her cheek should suddenly become fractured. We shall watch with tremendous apprehension when some beauty applies her pocket handkerchief to her nose, lest four or five guineas worth of its exquisite proportions should come away with it.'

In its editorial on 21 June the *Birmingham Post* was one of several papers to question the credulity of the upper classes: 'the trial gives a glimpse of the inner life of fashionable people ... which one could imagine genuine enough in the time of the old French monarchy,' it declared, but it was 'altogether out of keeping in the enlightened days of

Queen Victoria'. Enamelling was a 'delusion' and a 'snare', a 'libel on British beauty'. The *Belfast News-Letter* expressed the feeling of most male journalists that Mrs Carnegie should 'leave her face to nature, and sacrifice less to the altar of fashion'. If she did so, she would soon 'regain, without the aid of Madame Rachel, or any other empyric of the sort, the rose of health'. The *Caledonian Mercury* saw the whole female obsession with fashion as denigrating to their sex: 'where and at what expense is the education got that consists in fitting a woman solely for waltzing, and filling church pews with rustling gauze?', it asked, in an article that also lambasted the 'heartless etiquette' that required women's bodies to be distorted by rigid crinolines as part of the whole 'frigid pantomime' of self display. Women looked their most beautiful only when modestly dressed. In the opinion of male newspapermen, they needed only one thing: soap and water; 'all else is gilding'.

Mr Carnegie might have held on to his money and emerged from the case occupying the moral high ground, but despite the financial loss, Madame Rachel was able to capitalize on the case. She was now a household name; her self-confident description of her cosmetic processes had not for one moment buckled when attempts were made to deride them in court. Indeed some of the lawyers present had admitted that a lot of what she had said was perfectly plausible (such as her advocacy of cleanliness of the skin).

As for Mrs Carnegie – her 'costly bid for beauty' had

certainly cost her dear in terms of the humiliation, which was acted out in music hall pastiches that autumn. But it did not seem to have an adverse effect on her husband's career, who retired as an admiral in 1876. The marriage did not, however, survive: Louisa Carnegie subsequently had a torrid affair in Paris with a French diplomat, the Baron de Billing, and Carnegie divorced her in 1872.

The Carnegie case had surprisingly significant repercussions in Victorian society in the months that followed, not just in raising discussion about women's use of cosmetics. It also became the touchstone of mounting discussion about women's greater visibility in the public and business sphere, of their spending power as consumers and their insistence of having the right to do what they wanted with their own money. All these issues played directly into the drafting of the first Married Women's Property Act of 1870 which began the move towards granting women independent control of their finances. Meanwhile, such shifts in conventional female behaviour away from satisfaction with the untainted beauty achieved with soap and water were all perceived as a dangerous sign, symptomatic of more general calls for the emancipation of women. Madame Rachel was a powerful woman who was not frightened of defending her business practices in court or seeking reparation when she felt it was due. The Carnegie case did nothing to deter her bold expansion of the business: throughout the summer of 1862 the press was full of her advertisements, assuring clients of confidentiality and of her attendance exclusively at her New Bond Street Salon. In September she announced that 'Madame Rachel's Royal Arabian Perfume Baths were now open daily, from 10 a.m. to 10 p.m.' Such was the clamour for her skills that at the end of the year Rachel was obliged to place an advertisement in the press scotching rumours among her distressed clientele that she was about to up sticks and go to India. It had been brought to her attention 'through the kindness of Messrs. Thacker & Co, India Agents of 87 Newgate Street', that an Indian newspaper had given out that she was going there to set up in business. Such a report, Rachel was quick to see was 'seriously calculated to injure her in her profession' and she therefore 'begged leave to inform her lady patronesses, the Aristocracy and Nobility that *it is not and never was her intention to visit India.*'

Far from it, Madame Rachel was now preparing to launch a major new marketing campaign in England.

CHAPTER FOUR

Beautiful For Ever

THE CARNEGIE CASE might have appeared, on the surface, a setback for Madame Rachel, but in fact it had an unexpectedly positive outcome. It provided her with that key ingredient in any successful business venture – a marketing catchphrase. On 31 January 1863, an advertisement in the *Era* announced publication of 'Beautiful For Ever', a treatise which promised to be Madame Rachel's exposition on 'Female Grace and Beauty'. Soon even *The Times* was running regular advertisements promoting it.

Rachel was a canny businesswoman who understood her clientele; she knew that whatever the cost and whatever the criticism, there were plenty of rich women in London and beyond, ready to spend their money in the desperate quest, like that of Louisa Carnegie, to remain 'beautiful for ever'. A few months after the case, she set about a concerted campaign of damage limitation by bringing out a short treatise on her methods with the help of her two eldest daughters. At two shillings and sixpence (around £8 today) the twenty-four pages of wisdom imparted within its shiny pink covers promised to reveal the secret of being 'Beautiful For Ever'. Who would not begrudge the money for the secret of Eternal Youth? This pamphlet was no mere quack's patter, but a clever exercise in consumer psychology playing on female insecurities about ageing and the loss of looks and, with its pseudoscience, reassuring Rachel's clientele about the purity of her products.

It opened with a flattering eulogy to the traditional beauty and grace of woman – 'lovely as the bright sunshine at morning's dawn'; 'beautiful as the dew-drops on the flowers'. This was followed by a homily on women through time, as Rachel extolled the virtues of Cleopatra, to Queen Victoria and her daughters, to Alexandra Princess of Wales and even to Britain's new-found heroine – Florence Nightingale – in all cases underlining the moral ascendancy of women over the male sex. Indeed the whole tone of the pamphlet and its title was probably a deliberate play on the title *Faithful Forever* of Coventry Patmore's long poetic tribute to the ideal woman, published in 1860, that was later included in his paean to Victorian domesticity, *The Angel in the House* – a work which graced every respectable Victorian front parlour. In the tones of a religious tract, 'Beautiful For Ever' presented woman as soft, safe and unthreatening in her beauty, eternally self-denying as 'man's guiding-star' and 'gentle counsel', who leads him on to 'deeds of greatness and renown'. The queen herself in her virgin loveliness when she first came to the throne had been an example of Beautiful Woman – as wife, mother and now as grieving widow. The pamphlet went on to praise the nurses of the recent Crimean War of 1854–6, the heroic rowing-boat rescue of drowning men by lighthouse keeper's daughter Grace Darling in 1838 and the courage of the unsung women who had perished at the Siege of Lucknow in the Indian Rebellion of 1857.

Having established woman's unbounded grace, self-sacrifice and modesty Madame Rachel gently proceeded, once again in allusions to Patmore, to insinuate that equal to woman's many domestic obligations was that of maintaining her personal appearance in order that she might be 'the greatest ornament in the house'. The tone then became more mysterious as Rachel described the marvellous properties of the rejuvenating Magnetic Rock Dew of the Sahara, brought to Morocco 'on swift dromedaries, for the use of the court'. This miraculous water, to which Madame Rachel had sole rights and imported to London at 'an enormous outlay', was the holy grail of her list of exclusive products and a testament to her 'world-renowned name' ... 'unrivalled in the beautiful art of which she is the sole possessor'.

The narrative then took a surprisingly personal turn as Rachel alluded to the recent Carnegie court case. Mrs Carnegie's failure to pay for Madame Rachel's expertise had been an act of monstrous ingratitude which had, however, since been 'amply compensated for by the generosity of others', Rachel remarked sententiously. She went on to compare her beauty processes with the medical pioneering of Dr Jenner in smallpox vaccination, flatly rebutting any suggestion that her products were injurious, but rather conducive to health. A lady 'could not be too careful in the arrangement of her toilette, for the future happiness of her life may depend on her first appearance in society', she warned, in a veiled allusion to the constant female preoccupation with marriageability. With this in mind, women should trust to the skills of one person only – Madame Rachel – who had recently been 'specially appointed by the Empress Eugenie and the Court of France as sole importer of Arabian perfumes and toilet requisites'. To go elsewhere was to invite the risk of being sold dangerous cosmetics; Rachel's advertising hype was based on fear – the fear that using cosmetics produced by unscrupulous practitioners could be playing with fire.

Meanwhile Rachel reassured her potential clients that thousands of the 'most delicate and exalted ladies have availed themselves of her successful treatment'. The first step in her beautification procedure was to eradicate all the symptoms of 'bilious attacks and sluggishness of the liver', which she considered to be most destructive to beauty. Rachel was in effect advocating what we might today call a 'detox', in itself an admirable suggestion. The next was to bathe frequently – again admirable – though not in any old bath: ladies must take Madame's 'Arabian medical bath' full of choice and beautiful herbs and spices. Its wonderful restorative effects were, of course, only known to those who indulged in the use of it.

Rachel's masterpiece of commercial promotion, having failed to give away any of her trade secrets but dangling the carrot of further revelation, concluded by announcing similar discussion of the preservation of female loveliness 'with recipes for the same' in future pamphlets; meanwhile 'Beautiful For Ever' could only be obtained at Madame's exclusive Bond Street salon, where her list of preparations and their prices were also available on request.

A considerable shock awaited any woman who ventured to 47a New Bond Street to purchase one of the sixty preparations on Madame Rachel's list. These ranged from washes for the complexion, through face powders, dentifrices and mouth washes, hair preparations, face creams, soaps and perfumes. But none of them came cheap – beginning with 10s. 6d. an ounce for aromatic gum, to Jordan Water at 10 to 20 guineas a bottle. The catalogue abounded in exotic potions such as Rachel's now much-hyped Magnetic Rock Dew Water for Removing Wrinkles and her extensively advertised Circassian Golden Hair Wash. Madame's Royal Arabian Face Cream and Honey of Mount Hymettus soap worked wonders too; as did her 'Arab Bloom' and 'Favourite of the Harem's Pearl White' face powders – not to mention a whole range of fumigated oils, gums, scents and essences of perfumes and herbs from the most exotic and far flung places.

A private one-to-one beauty consultation with Madame cost a minimum of £250; 'Bridal Toilet Cabinets' – their precise nature undisclosed in the price list – cost from 25 to 200 guineas. The premier treatment on offer was 'The Royal Arabian Toilet of Beauty as arranged by Madame Rachel for the Sultana of Turkey', which would set patronesses back an astronomical 100 to 1,000 guineas – this at a time when the average working-class family had to get by on about £1 12s. a week and when housemaids were paid about £11 to £14 a year. The emphasis on such exotic origins for Rachel's products led *Chambers's Journal* to wonder why so much that was good for the appearance came from Circassia, Arabia, Albania and Armenia. Why should there not be 'a Putney Bloom, a Turnham Green Preservative Balm, or even a Camden Town preparation for the Chin?,' their writer asked. 'Why, in the name of native produce and British industry should I not grow Medicated Balm in a box outside my window, like Mignonette?'

Not content with the publication of 'Beautiful For Ever', further press announcements by Rachel in February 1863 cranked up demand, by encouraging lady patronesses to book early in order to ensure her 'special attendance' in time for the first drawing room of the London season. Her advertisements were everywhere: *The Times*, the *Era*,

John Bull, the *Ladies' Newspaper*, court and society journals, as well as in a whole range of regional newspapers, and carried constant exhortations that any cosmetics bearing her name on sale anywhere other than at no. 47a were 'dangerous and spurious' and likely to contain 'most deadly leads and other injurious matter' that had 'blighted many a young and lovely face'. Indeed Rachel went so far as to state unequivocally that 'all other persons presuming to style themselves enamellers commit a gross fraud upon the public'. The recent Carnegie trial, she proclaimed, had proved beyond a doubt that she, Rachel was 'the only enameller in the world'.

Rachel's tactic of proclaiming the wonders of her cosmetics ever louder in the face of a barrage of criticism seemed to work. The hyperbole of her outlandish claims did wonders for custom, even though her saturation advertising was looked on with disdain by her rivals of longer standing. Such was demand that Madame Rachel was now also forwarding her cosmetics three times a week to a subsidiary in Brighton and everybody who considered themselves anybody in society was beating a path to her door. She pumped more money into the business and its interior decor; the Royal Coat of Arms went up above the front door, as too did the famous logo 'Beautiful For Ever'. Women were not the only ones to head for no 47a New Bond Street; in his reminiscences of the 1860s Captain Donald Shaw noted that young men about town also visited Rachel (as they had in the past done barbers) to get her to paint out the black eyes they got at Reeds' sparring rooms in Whitehall.

There was however a sinister undercurrent to the growth of the Bond Street business. The Carnegie case had inevitably brought a degree of notoriety to Rachel and her daughters and they now became the objects of physical and verbal intimidation. The previous year (March 1863) Rachel junior had been threatened by a cab driver when she had come up to town by rail from the family house at Blackheath. Sharing a cab with a male friend who had paid the full fare to Bond Street in advance but had got out at Blackfriars, there had been an altercation when Rachel junior had arrived at New Bond Street. The cabbie who appeared to be drunk, stuck his foot in the door to prevent her entering and stood there demanding he be paid a second time, just as some of Madame's lady clients were attempting to enter and leave the premises. A crowd gathered as Madame Rachel came to the door to ask what was going on, only for the cabbie to jeer at her: 'I've brought one of your painted dolls'. He claimed she had not paid her fare and added threateningly: 'I'll paint her eyes better than you can paint her cheeks.' When taken to court charged with misbehaviour, the cabbie denied any misconduct or that he had demanded payment twice but was fined twenty shillings and costs. In an extraordinary turnaround, Madame Rachel promptly declared that she did not wish any fine to be inflicted on him and paid it for him herself.

One wonders whether this was an act of genuine altruism or a deliberate contrivance to win public sympathy and minimize further adverse publicity. The cabbie incident was by no means the first time that lady clients had found themselves having to run the gauntlet when visiting Rachel's salon. A journalist from the *Pall Mall Gazette* noted that on recently passing the junction of Maddox and New Bond Streets he had seen a carriage outside surrounded by a crowd, just as its owner emerged from the premises. She had been greeted by shouts of 'Beautiful for ever!', followed by quips such as 'Take care of the putty, mum', as she struggled to get into her carriage. And now Madame Rachel was also becoming the object of a series of threatening, anonymous letters. Reporting the story on 28 February 1864, *Reynolds's Newspaper* noted that a large reward had been offered for information leading to the arrest of the 'miscreants' responsible. The article did not quote the content of the letters except to say that they had not only threatened Madame Rachel's life but also accused her of 'most infamous crimes'. She had been so terrified by them that she claimed she 'hardly dared stir from her home'.

In the spring of 1865 it was the turn of an unscrupulous journalist to threaten Rachel with a newspaper exposé. Frederick Beaver was not an accredited reporter, but a second-rate 'penny-a-liner' who operated at the Westminster County Court reporting on lurid cases of murder, suicide, house fires and the like. His profession – so called because his kind were paid three-halfpence a line for news of the sensationalist, tabloid variety – had prompted him to attempt to extort money from Madame Rachel. Beaver had composed an article entitled 'The Notorious Madame Rachel Again', relating to a case called on 7 April 1865 at Westminster, but which had been settled out of court as Madame Rachel had been 'too ill to attend'. That same day Beaver paid a potboy from a nearby pub to deliver the article to Rachel's salon with a note saying he would send it for publication if he did not receive five pounds as a pay-off before midnight. Rachel junior had subsequently met Beaver in a pub in Great Marlborough Street to negotiate; he had demanded money, saying he must have some, in order 'to go and see the boat race' as he had backed Cambridge to win (in the race held on Saturday 8 April Oxford won by three lengths).

When Madame Rachel herself met with Beaver later that evening at New Bond Street he again threatened to send his report to the *Morning Star* if she did not produce the £5 he demanded. Rachel played him along, plying him with glasses of brandy, and agreed to pay ten shillings (in marked half crowns as later was revealed) in return for a signed receipt confirming he would trouble her no more; he should come back the following day for the rest. It transpired that Beaver was no stranger to Madame Rachel; he had called at Bond Street before at her request, to keep her apprised of any adverse reporting about her on his Westminster patch, on which occasion, so he now claimed she had given him a present 'and loaded me with perfumes'. This time, however, he had miscalculated in trying to beat a woman such as Rachel at her own game, for Madame was never reticent in enlisting the strong arm of the law, even though on occasion it went against her. She reported Beaver to the police and he was arrested and indicted for extortion at the Marlborough Street Court on 9 April, at which both Rachel junior and Leontie gave evidence on their mother's behalf, she still being unwell. Beaver was committed for trial but there is no subsequent note of his sentence in the press, indicating that the case was probably dropped. The story he had attempted to blackmail Rachel over may well have been one petitioned for by Rachel against a peer of the realm whose wife, like Mrs Carnegie, had failed to pay her bills. The *Belfast News-Letter* had sailed close to the wind in giving enough clues for everyone in London society to know that it referred to Lord Cardigan (the Crimean War hero) and his scandalous second wife Adeline; enough probably to prompt an out of court settlement and the suppression of the story.

The public barely had time to draw breath before, six months later, Madame Rachel's name was in the papers yet again when she found herself subjected to a little of her own medicine. A woman of 'ladylike appearance' turned up in early December at Marylebone Court – the officials of which by now must have been sick of the sound of Rachel's name – applying for a summons against Rachel for defrauding her of £33 and a ring worth £20. She claimed to have come all the way from the USA to consult with Rachel having read so many recommendations in the papers about her. But all she had received from her in return for her money had been a 'bottle of something like whitewash, which had no effect'. She had demanded her money and ring back, but Rachel had refused. The judge, Mr Tyrwhitt, expressed surprise that the woman had handed over so much money. 'I paid what was demanded of me', was the claimant's terse response. 'I thought that Americans were too sharp for such things' responded the judge incredulously.

Whoever this supposed claimant was, and no one was quite clear at the time, she failed to turn up for the subsequent hearing. Mr Tyrwhitt was about to move to issue a summons when Rachel's lawyer begged leave to put the matter 'in a more correct light', in order to prevent it being misrepresented in the papers. The claim was, he said, both 'grossly fraudulent and scandalous' the complainant was not the lady she claimed to be but an impostor who had been set up by one of Madame Rachel's unscrupulous business rivals deliberately to ruin her. Her name was in fact Aurora Knight, but she called herself 'Lady Jones' and claimed to be the wife of the American consul. She was recently recovered from small pox and had gone to New Bond Street to ask Rachel to 'obliterate' the smallpox scars left on her face. They had agreed on a fee of £100 but the applicant had paid 'only five Napoleons' (gold twenty-franc pieces) on account. Madame had nevertheless attended her for 'eight days and nights' and had recommended a course of baths. However, mindful of the risk of infection, she would not admit her client to her own private Arabian baths, but recommended her to a place at Argyll Street. The complainant, supposedly so willing to spend £100 on her treatment had however gone to the public baths on Endell Street and paid tuppence to take baths there instead. Rachel had had trouble locating her client in order to send in her bill, but eventually traced her to a dubious establishment known as the Café de Lyons in a street off the Strand. Here she was known under various names and had been seen in the company of the man who was so anxious to injure Madame Rachel's reputation.

Soon after receiving Rachel's bill 'Lady Jones' had turned up on her doorstep in a drunken and agitated state and in the company of another 'intoxicated female' and Rachel had been obliged to call the police. Having heard this account the judge only too readily dismissed the summons, but the papers got hold of the story anyway. The true identity of 'Lady Jones' and the person who had put her up to her fraudulent claim remain a mystery but the case was symptomatic of a growing desire to discredit Rachel and bring down her lucrative business empire, as well as to intimidate and unnerve her already highly secretive clientele.

For the time being however, nothing could undermine her continuing successes. In January 1866 she purchased the lease on a house round the corner from her salon, at 50 Maddox Street to use as a private residence near to the business, in addition presumably to the house at Blackheath, from which her eldest daughter still commuted back and forth. Her now considerable income did not however encourage Rachel to pay any of her own many advertising bills on time. One frustrated creditor, on going to the Sheriff's Court to seek payment of £3. 8s. for an advertisement he had inserted for Rachel in an almanac had been asked by the judge whether he really had pressed for his money. 'Oh yes, he replied, 'but she never pays unless she is summoned'. Another creditor got equally short shrift when Rachel used precisely the same ploy as Mrs Carnegie, shifting responsibility for her series of unpaid advertisements in the North Wales newspaper, the *Cambrian Daily Leader*, to the tune of £29. 1s., on to her now estranged husband, Phillip Levison, under the law of couverture. As fast as she was taking people to court for unpaid debts (and the Beaver case suggests there were certainly others that were settled privately) Rachel's many creditors were also in constant pursuit of her.

The secrecy surrounding Rachel's practices at her New Bond Street salon and what exactly was on offer – perhaps beyond perfumes and cosmetics – to the ladies who patronized it was also by now firing the literary imaginations of contemporary writers. She and her beauty products had already been alluded to by name in one of the first mass-market sensation novels, Mary Elizabeth Braddon's *Lady Audley's Secret* – a lurid melodrama of sexual passion, bigamy, murder and fraud – which appeared in 1862 and became a runaway success. But it was Wilkie Collins who boldly created a character clearly based on Rachel in his *Armadale*, which was serialized throughout 1865 in the *Cornhill Magazine*.

Collins had good reason to exploit the Rachel story; with his legal training and contacts in the profession at Lincoln's Inn (he was called to the bar in 1851 but never practised), as well as having friends in the theatre, he had heard numerous unsavoury rumours about Rachel that had long been in circulation. The Carnegie case had been too good not to make use of. Like his contemporary and arch rival, Charles Dickens, Collins was quick to pick up on topical news stories and exploit the all-consuming public appetite for mystery and crime. In *Armadale* he made no attempt to disguise the character of Maria Oldershaw aka 'Mother Jezebel', foster mother and business partner of the novel's antiheroine, the crazed laudanum addict, bigamist and poisoner, Lydia Gwilt, who uses her beauty and sexuality to ensnare men. In this epic melodrama of mixed identities, greed and depravity, Gwilt herself is modelled on the alleged poisoner Madeleine Smith who was sensationally acquitted at her Edinburgh trial in 1857. She is assisted in her crimes by Oldershaw, a professional cosmetician and rejuvenator who runs her mysterious 'Ladies' Toilette Repository' behind heavy velvet drapes at a house in Pimlico; the parallels were obvious to contemporary readers even with the token changes in name and location. Like Rachel, Oldershaw had had years of experience in 'making up battered old faces and worn-out old figures to look like new' by a mysterious process which 'ground people young again'. And like Rachel's Bond Street salon, which now also used the private house on Maddox Street for discreet visits from clients, Mother Oldershaw shares her name plate and business entrance with a quack doctor-cum-abortionist named Dr Downward. In treating women for 'hysteria' and other female complaints, the doctor, like Rachel assumed a sinister French-sounding pseudonym of Dr Le Doux.

In *Armadale* the implication that Rachel was also an abortionist and procuress was clearly made by Collins. Female abortionists often used the title 'Madame', most famously a certain 'Madame Restell' operating in New York at the same time to enormous profit. No evidence has however come to light proving conclusively that abortion was one of Rachel's sidelines but it was certainly a common practice at the time for dubious practitioners to advertise euphemisms for abortifacients among the cosmetics advertisements in the columns of popular ladies' weeklies. It would of course have been perfectly logical for lady clients in this kind of distress to solicit Madame Rachel's help and advice in the privacy of her Bond Street Salon. Collins made clear in an Appendix to the 1866 three-volume edition, that in writing *Armadale* he had carefully researched those aspects of the story touching on the law, medicine and chemistry and had submitted them to the 'scrutiny of professional colleagues'. Nevertheless, he had sailed very close to the wind with the book's libellous allusions to Madame Rachel and his prediction, through the character of Oldershaw, of Rachel's later conviction, even though he deliberately set the story ten years earlier, in 1851, as a smokescreen.

Despite *Armadale*'s damning and ugly allusions to Madame Rachel she made no move to sue, knowing full well that to do so would only be to draw further attention to herself and irreparably damage her business. And right now, at the turn of 1867, she was riding high. She had had an invitation to set up a franchise in New York, had taken an expensive pit tier box at Covent Garden opera for the season at a cost of £400, dined out in the most fashionable restaurants and had a carriage and pair in which she regularly was seen out driving in Hyde Park. Later court evidence shows that Rachel also had acquired a supposedly 'splendid residence' at Saint Cloud in Paris, where she was educating her younger children. Her eldest son David was now studying medicine in Paris's prestigious medical school.

Madame Rachel had good reason to now set her business sights on Paris, for in 1867 the Exposition Universelle was to be staged at the Champs de Mars. The first such had been held in Paris in 1855, inspired by London's Great Exhibition of 1851. But the 1867 one was far more ambitious; running from April to October it would bring huge numbers of wealthy and well-connected visitors to the city, many of whom would be favourably disposed to the services of a good cosmetician. Early that year she sent Rachel junior out to Paris to begin setting up a premises leased at no. 25 rue de Choiseul in the *2ème arondissement*, a fashionable area of shopping arcades on the Right Bank of the River Seine not far from the Tuileries gardens. On 30 May the *Daily News* announced to its English readers that 'Madame Rachel, the celebrated enameller of the ladies of the royal courts of Europe, has arrived in Paris for the season'; within two weeks it was informing them that, according to an announcement in *Galignani's New Paris Guide* tickets were available for her 'Séances [consultations] on Youth and Beauty' at the rue de Choiseul'.

Madame Rachel's salon was the first of its kind in Paris and soon the reputation of '*Rachel l'émailleuse*' was causing quite a stir, as well as arousing a similar kind of notoriety as it had in London, where Rachel junior had returned to take care of things. But then, in August, disaster struck when, out driving on the rue Lafayette, Madame Rachel's carriage was hit by a horse-drawn omnibus. She was badly hurt, breaking several ribs and injuring her right hand. In typical litigious fashion, this did not deter Rachel from immediately suing the Parisian omnibus company for damages and winning compensation before returning to England.

Nothing was going to impede Madame Rachel's bold new business plan. She sent her second daughter Leontie, who was not yet twenty-one out to Paris to replace her. As clever as her sister Rachel, the self-confident Leontie soon adopted a suitably Parisian style of name – Léontine Rachel – as she proceeded to build an enviable French cachet for the family business in the heart of fashionable Paris.

CHAPTER FIVE

Lewis & Lewis

JUST OFF THE noisy interchange of Holborn Circus, on the major route out from the West End to the commercial heart of the City, lies Ely Place, a quiet street of elegant eighteenth-century houses that even today seem suspended in time, at a remove from all the din and distraction of urban life. This private backwater had once given pride of place to the London palace of the Bishop of Ely and here, in 1868, beyond the large iron gates that protected either end of it, stood the premises of Messrs Lewis & Lewis. The name, boldly displayed in large brass letters above the double front doors to number 10 Ely Place admitted clients into the heavy oak interior and reassuring solidity of one of Victorian London's most respected firms of solicitors and to the office of its most sought-after partner, George Henry Lewis.

Lewis's father, James Graham Lewis, a Sephardi Jew, had set up as a solicitor at Ely Place in 1829, where he had been joined by his brother George in 1834. The firm had become noted for its special skills in criminal law, with most of its business conducted in the nearby courts of Bow Street and Marlborough Street. George had specialized in bankruptcies and was solicitor to the Dramatic Authors' Society, though he became a 'celebrity' lawyer favoured by clients in the theatrical profession such as Madame Vestris and Charles Kean. James meanwhile became highly regarded for his compassion and benevolence in often taking on the cases of lowly street criminals.

James's son George Henry had joined the firm in 1851. As a Jew he had been prevented from attending public school or studying law at Oxford or Cambridge, instead attending University College before being articled to his father. George Lewis junior's gift for advocacy soon became well known in the profession, but he chose not to go on and train as a barrister, by 1858 being happy to settle for a partnership. Once installed in his comfortable office at Ely Place with its Turkey carpets and portraits of famous judges along the walls, George had rapidly risen to a position of trust among the moneyed and titled classes. His avuncular manner and gentle, confiding voice underpinned a transparent integrity and rock-solid confidentiality. In the course of preparing a number of criminal cases, including several high profile banking prosecutions during the 1860s, Lewis developed his exceptional gifts for private enquiry, 'playing the game often in defiance of the rules, and relying on his audacity to carry him through'. He rapidly built up a shortlist of preferred leading counsels – Serjeants Ballantine, Sleigh and Parry, the celebrity court performers of their day – and their juniors, Montagu Williams and Douglas Straight. Lewis's reputation for providing well researched and prepared briefs, where every aspect of a witness's testimony had been thoroughly checked beforehand, was second to none. More importantly, by the 1860s he had also brought together his own complex network of spies and informers among London's low life – from prostitutes, to brothel keepers, to reformed criminals whom the firm had previously defended in court.

In his professional capacity George Lewis had already more than once come across Sarah Rachel Levison, aka Madame Rachel, thanks to his own appearances in court and his 'spider's web of narks', who fed him all the gossip. During his long career Lewis became privy to many scandalous secrets in Victorian society; indeed it was said that he 'held the honor of half the British peerage in his keeping'. Rumours had long since filtered through to him, from his uncle's theatrical clients and his own spies, about the darker side of Madame Rachel's business in New Bond Street, the allegations of blackmail and the services that were rumoured to be on offer there.

One morning in March 1868, Lewis, now aged thirty-five, a slim, dapper man with Dundreary whiskers framing his long, delicate face, was settling down to another day's work behind his carved Sheraton desk, when two new clients were ushered in to his presence. Mr Arthur Esdaile was a wealthy, middle aged stockbroker with a much younger and attractive wife. They both appeared ill at ease and some prevarication ensued until the avuncular Lewis managed to put them at their ease and get Mr Esdaile to reveal the purpose of their visit.

Mrs Esdaile, it transpired, had visited Madame Rachel's New Bond Street salon to buy some perfume, where Rachel's clever sales patter had quickly ensnared her. She had agreed to a course of her costly Arabian Baths and these had taken place, assisted by an attendant in suitably Arabic-style dress, over the course of the last six months. On a recent visit, three weeks previously, she had left her diamond rings and earrings in a changing room as usual, only to discover them missing when she returned from her bath. She called the attendant and asked to speak to Madame Rachel. When Mrs Esdaile told Rachel that her diamonds had disappeared Rachel had flatly refused to listen, insisting that she must have left them at home. She called her attendant in, who confirmed that Mrs Esdaile had not been wearing her diamonds when she arrived. By now perplexed and highly distressed Mrs Esdaile continued to insist she had left her jewellery in the changing room, upon which Rachel had turned on her and had threatened to have her thrown out. On returning home Mrs Esdaile had told her husband and he had insisted on taking the matter to a solicitor.

Something did not ring true about the story as the intuitive George Lewis heard it that morning; he sensed Mrs Esdaile was being economical with the truth and that she wanted to speak to him alone. She indicated this by deliberately placing her gloves on his desk. Recognizing the signal, Lewis told her husband he would need time to ponder whether the case could be pursued in the courts. As the couple left, Mrs Esdaile deliberately forgot her gloves. Later that afternoon, as expected, she returned unannounced to retrieve them, upon which, under the persuasive influence of Lewis's genial manner and penetrating gaze, she confided in him a rather different story.

The truth was that Mrs Esdaile had been using the Bond Street premises (or rather Madame's Arabian Baths, at Mrs Hick's bathhouse in nearby Davies Street) as a meeting place with her lover. Here, twice weekly, she admitted, she had met up with an out-of-work music hall artist called Raikes, where they had enjoyed sexual encounters in a private cubicle. Madame Rachel had demanded additional fees for providing these facilities and, as the six months wore on, had steadily increased them to cover her 'expenses'. The hapless Mrs Esdaile had struggled to pay and in the end her diamonds had been taken by Rachel who apparently had been far more intimidating than Mrs Esdaile had described to Lewis that morning. 'It's no use you giving yourself airs here,' Rachel had rounded on her, 'I know who you are. I have had you watched. I know where you live.' How would Mrs Esdaile like it if her husband knew the real reason for her visits, in order to take advantage of 'something young Raikes has got which your husband hasn't?'

At Lewis's gentle prompting Mrs Esdaile went on to tell him that whilst there were those who went to Bond Street for the cosmetics and beauty treatments, a number of other women took similar advantage of the premises as she had – as a discreet, high-class house of assignation where they could meet their lovers. Madame's Arabian Baths thus operated along the lines of the disreputable eighteenth-century *bagnios* – the houses of prostitution that masqueraded as Turkish baths. Apparently Rachel was a very able procuress who could oblige her rich lady clients by providing handsome and virile young men – stable boys, out-of-work footmen, even army deserters – for a price, although Mrs Esdaile herself, she insisted, had met Raikes 'at a concert'. Lewis didn't believe her. There was also another class of men, according to Mrs Esdaile, who frequented the Bond Street salon – these were the better off stage-door Johnnies and men about town, the kind who haunted the up-market brothels and supper rooms around the Haymarket. They liked to come to Davies Street to watch through a Judas hole as Madame's rich ladies took their Arabian baths. Amazingly, Mrs Esdaile herself admitted to having known that these peeping Toms had been lurking when she took her own baths.

What Lewis heard that afternoon did not surprise him but it did shock him. He had by now already heard a rather different version of the recent Carnegie story: that Rachel had written to Mr Carnegie – another husband with a much younger wife – demanding she be paid and alleging that her treatments had really been for curing his wife of 'scabies' caught as the result of a sexual encounter at a house of assignation, but this part of the story had been withheld from the court case. Lewis knew that to reveal the true extent of the goings on at New Bond Street would rock the very foundations of Victorian society. But no client, least of all Mrs Esdaile – for all her candour in the privacy of his office – would be persuaded to go into the witness box and destroy her reputation at a stroke. They were all terrified of publicity, which is precisely why Madame Rachel had such a hold over her clients and why so many of them presented her with the lavish 'gifts' on display in her salon. There was therefore nothing Lewis could do to get Mrs Esdaile's diamonds back without exposing her to ruin. After consulting with legal counsel, Montagu Williams, he reluctantly wrote and advised her husband that it would be too potentially damaging to take the case to court.

It is highly likely that this was by no means the first case of its kind relating to number 47a New Bond Street to be confided at a solicitors' chambers but go no further because of the prospect of scandal. Leading counsel Serjeant Parry, who was often hired by Lewis, later told his son as much, though Lewis, scrupulously discreet to the last, never betrayed any of his professional confidences in print. Parry also later claimed that the 'the police kept a watch on the shop', whilst George C. Boase the first Victorian biographer to offer any concrete details of Rachel's life in 1894 suggestively remarked that 'it would not do to enter into the particulars of the various services which Rachel rendered to some of her clients, in addition to selling them enamels and perfumes.' The proximity of Burlington Arcade, a covered walkway of exclusive shops some of which operated as discreet houses of assignation only a short walk from Bond Street, conveniently situated Rachel's cosmetics business in range of the regular promenades of the prostitutes who worked there particularly in the early evening when the military men who made up the bulk of their clientele went out walking before dinner.

And so the rumours of procuration and blackmail at New Bond Street circulated unabated over the port and cigars in London's clubland and at society dinner tables. Rachel, it would seem, also offered her services as a marriage broker; there were plenty of desperate and aging middle class widows and spinsters with money in London anxious to find husbands. One such had been a plain woman of thirty or so named Alice Maynard, who had ventured through Rachel's door desperate to be made beautiful in order that she might find a husband. When Rachel offered to help, Miss Maynard had handed over seven hundred pounds for beauty treatments and the promise that Rachel would find her a suitable candidate, complete with title. The Hon. George Sylvester was duly introduced and after a decidedly cursory courtship, proposed and was accepted. Having married Miss Maynard, he promptly borrowed fifty pounds from her and disappeared. It was only then that his abandoned wife checked her husband's credentials in Burke's Peerage to find that there was no such titled family of the name Sylvester. Subsequent investigation by a solicitor revealed that the man Alice had married was nothing but a bookmaker's tout who had made it a practice to marry rich ladies and desert them soon after; Rachel had recruited him for £5 to do the same for Alice Maynard. The police went in search of him but the betrayed and broken hearted Alice died only a few months later. Like many in the now accumulating trail of Rachel's victims there was no redress for Alice Maynard; such was the sensational and salacious way in which these gullible women were conned that it seemed highly unlikely that anyone would ever be brave – or foolhardy – enough to go to court as a complaining witness against Rachel, either as a bogus beauty practitioner or in any other respect. She had been far too clever for them, constructing her own immunity by capitalizing on the pathological fear of publicity among her lady clients. To try to best Rachel would be to expose their own use of cosmetics – and perhaps also of the other facilities on offer at her salon – not just to their husbands, but worse, to society at large.

George Lewis could not have been more surprised therefore to encounter Madame Rachel's nemesis in his own offices shortly after Mrs Esdaile's visit, in the unlikely figure of the widow of an officer in the British Army in India, Mrs Mary Tucker Borradaile. Early in April he had received an impromptu visit from the lady's brother-in-law, Alexander Cope, a poor law guardian and local magistrate who had come up from his family home in Flintshire, North Wales, upon hearing that his sister-in-law had been carted off to Whitecross Debtors' Prison. Discovering that Mrs Borradaile's creditor was Madame Rachel, her respectable family in Wales had been horrified and Cope immediately enlisted Lewis to obtain her release on bail. Cope, it transpired had in fact come up from Wales before – as long ago as September 1866 – when he had first got wind of the fact that his sister in law, who had insisted on cutting herself off from her family and staying in London after being widowed, had fallen into 'bad hands' and was being systematically milked of vast sums of money.

Mary Tucker Borradaile came to see Lewis with Cope shortly after her release from Whitecross Street and told her story. She had first seen Madame Rachel's advertisements in *The Times* back in 1864; she had paid two visits to her salon that year in the hope, after years of being ravaged by the hot Indian sun where she had lived till widowed, that she too 'might be improved'. At the time, Rachel had merely sold her 'some powder and two or three bars of soap'. Borradaile returned twice in 1865 and then 1866, spending in all £170 in the first two years. But after that Madame, on the promise of making the vain and silly woman beautiful enough to be the bride of a rich nobleman whom she, Rachel, claimed was in love with her, had proceeded to drain her, slowly and inexorably of everything she possessed. On the promise of marriage to a certain lord, Mary Tucker Borradaile had been reduced to destitution, but when Cope had confronted Rachel at the Bond Street salon she had denied his accusations of extortion and fraud and had sent him away with a flea in his ear. This time he was determined to see justice done.

Lewis's initial response was far from optimistic. Rachel's colossal swindle had been so cleverly orchestrated that he doubted there would be any hope of winning a civil action against her. The only option therefore was a criminal prosecution which, he warned, could bring with it the destruction of Mrs Borradaile's good character. Nevertheless, she and her brother in law were determined to pursue the case in court and instructed Lewis to proceed with the evidence gathering and an application for a remand.

On 8 June Montague Williams QC, on instructions from Lewis, appeared before Mr Alexander Knox, one of the best metropolitan magistrates of the day, who had presided at Marlborough Street Police Court since 1862, to apply for a warrant for Rachel's arrest. The charge was threefold: of obtaining goods to the sum of £600 by false pretences; of obtaining a further £550 as part of a sum of £1,000 by false pretences, and of conspiracy with others to defraud Mary Tucker Borradaile of £3,000. For the defence, Rachel's barrister Mr Edward Lewis (no relation) said there was no proof of a conspiracy. His client feared nothing and indeed 'had nothing to fear'. She had, he insisted, a complete answer to the case. Mr Knox duly issued a warrant against Rachel, setting her bail at two sureties of a crushing £1,000 each.

Rachel, who had immediately been locked up at Newgate, had no difficulty finding volunteers to stand bail in Mr Kingswell, a coach-builder and Mr Richards, the publican of the Thistle & Crown – both of St Martin's Lane. Kingswell stated that he had known Madame Rachel's husband for twenty years and believed he lived at 50 Maddox St and was an 'independent man living on the earnings of his wife'. Mr Richards's wife knew Rachel too and Phillip Levison had guaranteed him against any loss by standing bail. These statements are something of a surprise as Rachel only recently in court had asserted that she and Phillip were estranged and no longer lived together: Levison certainly did not offer so much as a shilling towards her bail. An objection was immediately made by Montagu

Williams, who claimed that Madame Rachel might try to abscond to Paris where she was rumoured to have 'lodged all her property', but nevertheless Mr Knox accepted the bail, the house in Maddox Street being noted as security worth £4,000, and Rachel was released from Newgate on 10 June pending her trial.

That should have been the end of it, for now at least, but the press soon got wind of the fact that the nobleman who had supposedly been the object of Mrs Borradaile's romantic and marital aspirations was none other than famous man-about-town, Lord Ranelagh. He had turned up at the hearing, having, as a member of the aristocracy, been forewarned that he might wish to ensure that nothing in any way discreditable was said about him. Ranelagh, who had lounged disdainfully in court, complained vigorously about his name being dragged into things and emphatically denied any connection with the case, bar receiving some rather deranged letters from Mrs Borradaile. But tongues were soon wagging, for Ranelagh had a far from spotless reputation.

***

Thomas Heron Jones, 7th Viscount Ranelagh and Baron Jones of Navan, cut a fine soldierly figure strutting around Mayfair with his aquiline nose and ferocious, wedge-shaped beard. Born in 1812, he had succeeded his father as Viscount in 1820 and had served as a volunteer in the Carlist War of the Spanish Succession, fighting at the Siege of Antwerp in 1832, a fact on which he dined out for many years afterwards. He had then served as an officer in the Life Guards before becoming an early promoter of the Volunteer Movement in Britain. In this capacity he had been made Lieutenant Colonel of the 2nd South Middlesex Volunteers in 1860. From his residence at no. 7 New Burlington Street, where he shared rooms with fellow officers, he was well known as an arbiter of London fashion and the stage, a man who drank champagne from the slippers of women he admired at Bertolini's smart restaurant. Like other military men he also frequented the eateries of the Haymarket – the Raleigh Club, The Cremorne and Mott's, for their champagne and oyster suppers before going on to find a willing young whore at one of the late night cafés and supper rooms such as Sally Sutherland's, Rose Young's and the most notorious of them all, Kate Hamilton's (now run by Rachel's old friend Mary Belasco). One of his favourite prostitutes, Annie Miller, later became a celebrated Pre-Raphaelite model and the lover of the artist William Holman Hunt. Ranelagh and his group of 'parasitic satellites', known as the Corinthians, in their frilled shirts and flowered waistcoats also haunted London's theatres where they set themselves up as the criterions of taste, making or breaking the careers of young actresses and dancers.

In the 1840s Ranelagh had famously humiliated the would-be 'Spanish' dancer and 'Señorita of Madrid and Seville', Lola Montes at her debut performance at Her Majesty's Theatre. As the exotic young dancer had stood there taking her bow to a shower of red roses, Ranelagh's loud and supercilious voice had drawled out from one of the boxes: 'Why, if it isn't Betty James'. Lola, it turned out, was a fake, an Irish girl from Limerick and the former wife of a lieutenant in the Indian army who had divorced her for adultery. At a stroke, Ranelagh succeeded in ruining Montes's London stage career for good and all. He thereafter preened himself on his disclosure, but in fact it had been driven by sexual jealousy. As a notorious rake, he had always thought he had a way with women but his charms had not extended to Montes, who had rejected him not long before. For the next twenty years his reputation followed him, as the ageing roué lived out his life in London's clubs and theatres and the supper rooms of the Haymarket where he was well-known to the prostitutes who worked them.

As the press got hold of details of the Borradaile court case to come, headlining their coverage with strap lines such as 'Madame Rachel Again' and 'Madame Rachel in Trouble', a lurid tale of infatuation and fraud beckoned, with talk of secret admirers spying through peepholes as ladies took beautifying Arabian baths. 'Offensive', 'abominable' raged papers such as the *Era,* in righteous indignation at the salacious aspects of this forthcoming saga 'subversive of all morality and virtue', knowing full well that its – and every other newspaper's – circulation would shoot up once the trial was on. With talk of love letters and clandestine courtship, of diamonds and carriages and lavish trousseaus for a bride; of lotions and potions that had promised to transform Mary Tucker Borradaile into a thoroughly 'enamelled' beauty in time for her wedding night, the public imagination was set racing in anticipation of this age-old story of the spider and the fly, as well as a moral tale that promised to be illustrative of the 'extraordinary credulity in high life'.

Press coverage was also already laying the ground for a more deeply disturbing, racial undercurrent to the trial. Anti-Semitism had been rippling through London society since February, when the Jewish-born Benjamin Disraeli who had converted to Christianity in his teens, had succeeded Lord Derby as prime minister. His rise to prominence on the heels of that of Lionel Rothschild, the first Jew to be admitted to parliament in 1858, had given expression to a mounting irrational fear of the powerful and cultivated Jew that would grow more vocal over the next decade. It was most tellingly summarized in the remark of Lady Palmerston, wife of a former prime minister, who observed with withering disdain, 'We are all dreadfully disgusted at the prospect of having a Jew for our Prime Minister.' Similar hostility was expressed against Rachel in the run up to her trial by an anonymous observer, who wrote to the *Pall Mall Gazette* on 12 June that he had noted that one of the best boxes in the pit tier at the Royal Opera House in Covent Garden had her name on it: 'We know of course that wherever music is the god, Israel is to be found at the shrine. But is the money taken and no questions asked with regard to the letting of these chief places in the synagogue? It may no doubt be only a curious coincidence of name, or it may be something quite the reverse.' Clearly it was not just Rachel's disrepute that would be on trial – but also her Jewishness.

The preliminaries also raised another issue much preoccupying the public since the recent scandalous case in April of Mrs Lyon and the medium Daniel Dunglas Home. In a direct allusion to an article by Eliza Lynn Linton of March that year denigrating 'The Girl of the Period', *Lloyds Weekly* ran a story entitled 'The Widow of the Period', which told how seventy-five year old wealthy widow Mrs Lyon had been stripped of £60,000 by fake society medium Home, who had promised to make contact with her dead husband on the other side. The article expressed growing public concern at the way in which women of means were now attempting to take control of their lives – not just with regard to personal choices about wearing makeup and dyeing their hair as raised in Linton's article – but also in terms of the financial power of the well-off widow and her ability to fritter away her money as she pleased. Give woman any kind of freedom in either respect was the inference, and her common sense appeared to desert her. Drawing comparisons between Mary Tucker Borradaile and the widow Lyon, the only difference *Lloyds* could find between the two women was the extent of the gullibility of the victim and the amount of money stolen from her. Both cases were unfortunate examples of the 'intellectual calibre of the female half of the upper ten thousand'; Mrs Borradaile's case would demonstrate what some women's vanity induced them to go through in the cause of beauty and would prove the folly of the 'ever-increasing love of display and … passion for admiration which has marked the last quarter of a century.' Whilst such women were the exception to the modest rule, 'The sooner other foolish women were put upon their guard the better.'

Only a week after the committal hearings had begun, Rachel turned up again in Mr Knox's court like a bad penny. This time, he wearily had to listen to a garbled accusation from her of assault on herself and Leontie (now back from Paris) by two men who had come to Maddox Street, so she claimed, in an attempt to extort money from her. Albert Crabbe an accountant and John Houston, clerk, both of Kentish Town had knocked on Rachel's door, claiming to have a letter implicating '50 people in a conspiracy' to damn her with far more serious charges than the fraud that she was currently indicted for. Crabbe was a trained lawyer, in fact claimed to be a Queen's Counsel, and asked for a bribe of £500 to negotiate on Rachel's behalf and ensure that the matter was 'set to one side'. When Rachel refused, she claimed that Crabbe had backed her up against a door and hit her and likewise hit out at Leontie as she came to her mother's defence. Leontie and their servant Rosanna Molloy confirmed the assault in court; her mother had the marks to show how she had been manhandled, she asserted. However, Rachel who was clearly ill and in an unstable mental condition, proved so confused in giving her evidence that Mr Knox found it totally 'unintelligible', as did her defence Mr Sleigh, who threatened to withdraw from the case. Knox gave Rachel short shrift and threw the case out. He was, he said, 'presiding over a farce' and Madame Rachel had seemed little short of deranged in the witness box. Quite what she had hoped to gain by yet more press exposure, other than to attempt to milk a little sympathy when all the cards were now so well and truly stacked against her, is difficult to fathom. Perversely, she seems to have clung to the British justice system that was about to haul her over the coals as her last and only resort.

During the Crabbe case Leontie had described how exhausted from stress and insomnia her mother was. Still suffering the after effects of the Paris accident, as well as poor health since her attack of rheumatic fever, Rachel it would seem was not in a fit physical state to be tried and on 22 June an application was made for a postponement. She had now quarrelled with her solicitor Edward Lewis, and Phillip Levison had appointed a new one, William Henry Roberts, who immediately deposed that the trial be adjourned till the following session. He had not had sufficient time to receive instructions from his client, who since her release on bail had been too ill and was now laid up in bed. Two doctors in Saville Row signed a letter to that fact, confirming she was suffering from 'great mental and bodily excitement'. A top London medical man, Sir William Fergusson, who had recently been appointed Sergeant-Surgeon to Queen Victoria, was also called in at considerable expense to examine Rachel and sanction the need for a postponement: 'I have just seen Madame Rachel' he wrote to the court from his George Street practice, 'and hereby certify that she is in such a prostrate condition of body and mind as to be unable to undergo an examination in a public court.'

Mr Knox was unimpressed and threw the letter out; Rachel was, he felt, 'feigning indisposition to prevent the ends of justice'. She had haunted his court almost every day the previous week and he would only postpone the case if she were certified insane. She could just as easily come and sit in a chair and give her evidence at the hearing. Word was sent to Rachel in Maddox Street, which apparently 'restored her to such purpose' that ten minutes later she promptly arrived at Marlborough Street Court in a cab. Her counsel, Mr Digby Seymour, nevertheless still insisted that his client was not in a fit state to give him 'intelligible information'.

Knox ignored all the protestations on Rachel's behalf. On 24 June he committed her for trial at the Central Criminal Court.

***

As counsels for defence and prosecution went about their evidence gathering, in the days long before the gagging order prevented discussion of a case before it came to court, exploitation of the comic and satirical content of the forthcoming Rachel trial became a free for all in London's clubs, pubs, music halls and the press. At the Judge & Jury – a drinking den and club on Leicester Square which staged vulgar mock trials based on society scandals of the day – a week-long run of 'Rachel in the Witness Box' was announced. For the shilling entrance fee men-about-town were entitled to 'a cigar and a glass of rum or gin and water, or beer' whilst simultaneously enjoying tales of the 'Israelitish enameller's' escapades, 'Mrs Bothertaile's Indian pickle' and the trial to come under the headlines.

'Is a thing of beauty a joy for ever?' Query answered without going to Bath! Showing how the daughters of Israel French polished the "vidder". Poses plastiques (without enamel) before and after the trial.

Allusions to Rachel's Jewishness prevailed in all the highly prejudicial pre-trial press coverage, the most hostile being that of the *Tomahawk*, which referred to her as a 'Jewish spider', a sorceress and a Jezebel. At the end of June it alleged that it had received anonymous letters with regard to the goings on at Madame's Arabian Baths, and talked of how Madame Rachel had not been idle. As soon as adverse circumstances permitted, it wrote, she would produce the following 'adjuncts to the toilet':

'The Lily of the (Borro) dale' – a refreshing perfume for ladies anxious to marry

'Blanc de Whitecross Street' – a preparation that will lead to whitewashing one for ever

'Cosmetique de Ranelagh' – a preparation to be used on empty heads

'Savon de Marlborough Street' – a soap peculiarly adapted for dirty hands

'The Noble Lover's Enamel' – a preparation for ladies with barren faces whose vanity is more than skin deep.

Public antipathy was mounting in the form of a popular street ballad now on sale:

> I will stand my trial like a brick
> And to my business I will stick,
> I will all the silly old ladies nick,
> My name is Madame Rachel

and this parody after a poem by Lord Byron

> Madame Rachel, ere we smash,
> Give, oh give me back my cash;
> Or, since that has left my chest,
> Let me have a little rest.
> Hear my vow before I go –
> Upon my life, I'll sue you!

Rising above the grossly biased press reporting, the *Pall Mall Gazette* could not resist drawing the public's attention to the fact that the Bond Street shop still had emblazoned over its doorway 'Purveyor of Arabian Perfumery to the Queen'. Was this simply 'an audacious and impertinent falsehood', it asked, or was there really 'within that mysterious and discreditable temple of Venus a warrant – framed and glazed – declaratory that the priestess of the temple had received the royal sanction to make Her Majesty "beautiful for ever"?'"

In the end, Rachel's trial had to be postponed until the August sessions because her new solicitor Roberts once more pleaded, quite rightly, that he had not been given sufficient time to properly prepare the defence. Nor was Rachel malingering; she was indeed 'suffering from a painful malady which required rest', which appears to have been inflammation of the gall bladder. Her state of nervous anxiety and ill health was further aggravated when her original sureties suddenly withdrew their bail; substitutes were found in Thomas Stack, a boot and shoe manufacturer from the Edgware Road who had known Rachel for many years and had served her and her family when she had her first perfumery shop in Bow Street. Henry Lacey, manager of the Royal Marylebone Theatre, also offered bail at his friend Stack's request. However, on the 9 July these new applications were rejected by the court. Swathed in black and clearly weak and ill, Rachel was taken back to her stuffy eight by twelve foot cell at Newgate.

Meanwhile, as Rachel's several applications for bail were all rejected, the levels of sycophancy accorded to Lord Ranelagh, who was a key witness – if not the decoy duck in it all – were the obverse. The grovelling assumption that as a peer of the realm he was above reproach was equal only to the venom with which Rachel was openly damned. *Reynolds's Newspaper* was an almost lone voice in pointing out what it called the obnoxious 'Flunkeyism of the Bench and Bar' towards Ranelagh during the hearing at Marlborough Street. His behaviour and the legal profession's toadying had been a sickening illustration of 'magisterial sycophancy and subserviency' of the kind familiar already from the Milton and Carnegie cases. Ranelagh was well known to all the press for his line in refined dissipation and yet almost to a man the newspaper editors indulged in a blanket whitewashing of his reputation whilst simultaneously blackening Rachel's.

Such blatant bias aroused 'an unpleasant suspicion in the public mind,' observed *Reynolds's*, 'that impartial justice is not always meted out to all class of persons'.

The editorial's words were prescient, for a couple of days later Lord Ranelagh found himself in a spot of bother when he least would have like it. Out on Piccadilly late on the night of 23 June he was accosted by a young street walker named Louisa Gould, one of his regular girls whom he had known for several years. Gould had heard all about the allegations relating to Madame's Arabian Baths and propositioned Lord Ranelagh: she knew two pretty little 'milliners' who would be happy to entertain him likewise; wouldn't he like to come with her now and see them? Ranelagh had refused and had tried to get away from Gould but she had then reminded him of some money he owed her. The last time she had obliged him he had given her only half a crown on account and she now trailed after him down Piccadilly demanding in a loud, drunken voice that he settle up – or at least give her a shilling for a glass of wine. When Ranelagh had consistently refused, she took a swipe at him, knocking off his hat and the cigar from his mouth.

The following morning Ranelagh brought a charge of assault against Louisa Gould. In the dock at Marlborough Street she remained unrepentant, claiming that she and he had been 'on the best of terms' and she had been to his house often. 'I've been a good friend to you, Lord

Ranelagh,' she declared, 'when you have been short of money'. He might be a lord, she continued, but she knew he was hard up. In court Louisa's all too familiar fourteen-year career of prostitution, drunkenness and disorderly conduct went against her. She had been up before the magistrates on several occasions and had already served eighteen months in jail. Mr Knox could do little more than order her to keep the peace, but as Louisa Gould, the tart with a heart, was carted off, her plaintive voice rang out across the court in a parting shot to Ranelagh: 'Why don't you pay me that seven and six you owe me? It's not much and you know that you owe it to me.'

The odour of respectability that till then had surrounded his Lordship – whose solicitors of course immediately wrote to the papers denying any association with Gould or any debt to her – now began to take on a decidedly less fragrant character. At Gould's hearing he had said that the Madame Rachel affair had been 'the source of endless annoyance to him'. It was about to get considerably more annoying.

CHAPTER SIX

A Charlatan and
Her Willing Dupe

IT HAD BEEN A while since a much-talked about female criminal had stood in the dock at the Central Criminal Court. Twenty thousand people had turned out to see the ruthless serial poisoner Catherine Wilson hanged at Newgate after her sensational trial in 1862 and the notorious baby farmer Charlotte Winsor, twice sentenced to hang but reprieved in 1865, had equally monopolized news coverage. Although Rachel's offence was not a capital one, the promise of a powerful, magnetic woman criminal once more holding centre stage ensured that her trial in August would have maximum pulling power.

Female criminals such as Madame Rachel had long been on display in effigy in the Chamber of Horrors at Madame Tussauds, beginning with Maria Manning – the most notorious of a spate of murderesses whose stories had filled the papers during the 1840s – and continuing to Constance Kent, who in 1865 had finally confessed to the Road Hill House murder of her brother in 1860. A whole industry had, for decades, been tied to such trials through the medium of popular street ballads, broadsides, tracts, books, penny pamphlets, religious tracts, as well as the much sought after, but often fictionalized, accounts of the final hours and execution of the condemned written by chaplains and prison officials. The new generation of sensation-novel writers had further exploited the insatiable demand for salacious descriptions of hideous murders already being fed by cheap crime fiction and the advent of the daily penny newspapers in the mid 1850s. The price of newspapers had steadily fallen since the abolition of Stamp Tax in 1855 and the extension of the franchise with the Second Reform bill of 1867 had further stimulated public interest in politics and the press. Demand for reading matter grew as elementary education spread and literacy levels rose. The *Telegraph* led the field with a circulation of 142,000, *The Times* with 65,000 and the *Standard* – their most serious rival by the late 1860s – following with 46,000. Some papers, such as *Lloyds' Weekly Newspaper,* were heavily accented towards crime stories and both *The Times*, with its tradition of law court reporting, and the *Daily Telegraph* ran extremely lengthy verbatim accounts of trials.

But by the 1860s the illustrated newspapers were beginning to steal a march on the market; from 1865 the *Illustrated Police News* carried sensationalist front page engravings of criminals and their crimes. Indeed, crime news had by now become the bedrock of the new mass-circulation Sunday papers. Reports of trials tended, however, to be all of a piece – taken down verbatim and syndicated across regional newspapers with a mass of tedious peripheral detail and very little variation in comment It was in the editorials and debates that followed high-profile trials that interesting and often highly contentious argument emerged. The newspaper column effectively became what Wilkie Collins called the 'amateur court of Justice', with the press according itself the power of judge and jury. How it presented a particular criminal was critical to how the trial proceeded – and most of the press during the Victorian period was heavily biased against women convicted of serious crimes.

On 27 May 1868, shortly before Madame Rachel was locked up at Newgate to await her trial at the law courts nearby, London had witnessed the final enactment of what for many had been the most popular form of mass entertainment for centuries – the public execution. That day, the Irish nationalist Michael Barrett who had been convicted of a bomb outrage, had met his maker in front of a crowd that had been up all the previous night drinking and carousing, singing hymns and music hall songs by flickering torchlight and becoming increasingly unruly as they swelled in numbers around the foot of the gallows. A great roar had greeted the tolling of eight a.m.

on the nearby church tower of St Sepulchre when the condemned man had been brought out. Barrett, his face white as marble, died in silence without a struggle. The event was something of an anti-climax: the crowd who had booed and jeered and sung 'Rule Britannia' as the trap was pulled, had been a small one – only 3,000 or so, perhaps reflecting the lack of interest in Barrett as a far less glamorous criminal than Maria and John Manning whose execution at Horsemonger Lane jail in 1849 had pulled in an audience of up to 50,000. Nevertheless the crowd made the most of this last act of collective voyeurism, lingering at the foot of the gallows to eye Barrett's hooded corpse hanging there. After the statutory hour had passed, the ageing and increasingly incompetent public hangman, William Calcraft, tottered out to take down the body, which was then buried in quick-lime inside the walls of Newgate. From now on the next best spectator sport that could be got for free was the criminal trial. And everybody wanted to get into Madame Rachel's.

Detailed press coverage of the hearings at Marylebone had already set up a voracious appetite for the case. Across London Mrs Borradaile's accusations had enlisted 'a degree of interest wholly disproportionate to their merit'. Rachel knew that she would need the best barrister that money then could buy. Mr Serjeant Ballantine was the man everyone wanted, a celebrated criminal lawyer, known to be formidable in cross examination. Back in 1852, as defence counsel, he had managed to get Rachel's friend David Belasco's murder charge reduced to manslaughter. Unfortunately Ballantine had already been hired – by George Lewis for the prosecution. Rachel therefore paid fifty guineas for the next best man, the eloquent and charismatic Mr William Digby Seymour. The August Sessions of the Central Criminal Court were to be held as usual at a building on Old Bailey; at that time a thoroughfare between Snow Hill and Ludgate Hill. The court was a precursor to today's of the same name that was built on the site of the demolished Newgate prison in 1907. The sessions looked set to be very busy, with 120 criminals on the Calendar of Trials, but it was clear from the outset that Madame Rachel's was the trial that would 'probably excite the greatest amount of public interest'. Realising this, Rachel did not stop at hiring Digby Seymour but spared no expense in employing three additional top barristers in her team: Mr Serjeant Parry, Mr Serjeant Sleigh (who had prosecuted the Milton case) and Mr Butler Rigby. All in all, she had at her disposal 'perhaps the cleverest quartet of criminal lawyers then in practice'. How she found the money to pay them all was never made clear, but it was some indicator of the kind of profits she had been coining.

On the opening day of the trial, 20 August, the approaches to the Old Bailey and the court itself were jammed with people – many of them were women, some of them ladies of conspicuous fashion and social status, eager for a place in the gallery. This in itself disgusted some of the legal profession and press present, who considered the presence of women in court – and outside the domestic sphere where they belonged – as distasteful in the extreme. But such had been the demand for admission, despite a murder trial running concurrently in another court, that the prosecution had feared that some of their witnesses would not even be able to get to the court, which itself was far from adequate for such a high-profile trial. All three small courts in the building in fact sat in fairly cramped conditions. But word was out that Lord Ranelagh would be in attendance and expectations were high that 'some scandalous revelations would be made'. After all, it wasn't often that 'they get hold of a lord at the Old Bailey', as journalist, James Hogg remarked.

The trial was to be heard by the Recorder of London, the Right Honourable Russell Gurney, QC. Rachel, looking stout and stony faced, was brought up from the holding cells below the dock, swathed in black widow's weeds of bonnet with lace streamers, a mantle heavily edged in expensive lace and a black satin dress tied with a large bow, all no doubt deliberately chosen to project an image of herself as a venerable dowager in the mould of HM the Queen. She looked a little pale and tired but otherwise fearless and indomitable. Her age was given as forty-three, but most of the press noted that she looked much older. She clearly was not well, so was allowed to remain seated, prisoners at the bar normally being required to stand.

The entire body of the court had gathered ready to start promptly at 10 a.m. but were kept waiting by Mrs Borradaile, who finally arrived an hour late. Serjeant Ballantine opened by laying out the case for the prosecution, observing that there was no doubt that it was 'one of an extraordinary character, probably unprecedented in the present century'. He was only too familiar with the rumour and gossip attaching to Madame Rachel, having defended Viscount Milton over the diamond earrings incident in 1862. Despite the fact that he was acting for Mrs Borradaile he was forced to admit that his client was a person 'of an enormous quantity of folly and of a credulity hardly to be believed in the present age'. Throughout his opening address Ballantine found it hard to disguise his contempt, though he did his best to defend his client's virtue and respectability as being something on which 'no imputation could rest'. He had to admit that Mrs Borradaile was well past the first flush of youth, but he did so in a roundabout way. She had 'undoubtedly got into that period of life when beauty of the person is not the most remarkable thing to be discovered about a woman'. Nevertheless she had persisted in believing in her own 'powers of fascination', which is what had taken her to Madame Rachel's salon after she had first seen advertisements for her products in 1864. Rachel's subsequent entrapment of his client had, continued Ballantine, played on her inordinate vanity.

When she had demanded the enormous sum of one thousand pounds for a course of treatment in order to 'improve' her client, Mrs Borradaile had prevaricated. But then Rachel had added an irresistible inducement, by telling her that she had a mysterious admirer. A certain nobleman of high rank and large fortune, she told her, had fallen in love with her. Such was Mrs Borradaile's self-delusion that she swallowed the bait with the utmost alacrity. Rachel's domineering presence, her smooth words and persuasive powers promised she would make her client beautiful in order to take her place alongside her lord, from which point she had proceeded, with alarming rapidity to strip Mrs Borradaile of every penny she possessed.

Having summarised the case he was to put before the court, Ballantine called Mary Tucker Borradaile, who entered from a side door and 'tottered into the witness box' where she was allowed to sit. Everyone craned their necks to catch sight of her. She cut a rather pathetic figure: 'the quondam beauty, a skeleton encased apparently in plaster of Paris, painted pink and white, and surmounted with a juvenile wig', as Ballantine himself later recalled. His fellow prosecutor, Montagu Williams concurred; Mrs Borradaile was 'a spare, thin, scraggy-looking woman, her hair was dyed a bright yellow; her face was ruddled with paint; and the darkness of her eyebrows was strongly suggestive of meretricious art'. If her appearance undermined her credibility (and there were audible gasps of horror at her painted face when she appeared), Mrs Borradaile's manner also alienated any who might have been disposed to sympathise. 'She had a silly, giggling, half-hysterical way of talking', recalled Williams; her conduct was a far remove from the traditional heroine of a secret romance. Yet there was something about this faded beauty that still suggested, in the view of James Hogg, that she knew how to play the coquette: if her 'chin had not fallen in', Mary Tucker Borradaile might still be 'flirtable'.

Mrs Borradaile was actually fifty and had been born Mary Emma Tucker Edwardes, at Sealyham in Pembrokeshire into a good family of the minor Welsh aristocracy. She was well-educated and highly accomplished. In 1845 she had married Colonel Alfred Borradaile of the 5th Regiment of the Madras Light Cavalry. After living in Brompton, London, they had spent seven years in India, where she had given birth to a daughter, Florence (a previous daughter had died at birth). In India she had lived the good life of the British Raj, appearing in society 'attired in semi-oriental style, in gorgeous silks and gossamer shawl, and fanned by her Indian maid'. In those days she had been looked upon as 'an exquisitely bewitching and dazzling beauty, known especially for her long golden hair'. It was immediately clear to everyone in court when this was mentioned, that Madame Rachel's efforts to restore that particular aspect of Borradaile's lost beauty had been a dismal failure. Colonel Borradaile had died at Agram in India in 1861 leaving her comfortably off and with an army widow's pension. Now back in London after years of colonial seclusion, Mrs Borradaile had appeared unused to its sophisticated ways and thus had been an easy victim.

Her first visit to Madame Rachel's salon in 1864 had been prompted after she had suffered a 'little eruption' on her face. She had spent a modest amount there over the next two years but was not satisfied by the results and expressed her dismay that Rachel's potions had still not done anything for her skin. One day in May 1866, she had visited the shop when Rachel junior was present in the company of a 'Russian lady named Valeria' (another cosmetician, who sold her Neolin Hair Wash for 'infallibly restoring grey hair' from 46 Wigmore Street) sitting in her back parlour with a gentleman whom Rachel announced as Lord Ranelagh. The couple were introduced and Ranelagh gave Mrs Borradaile his card. She saw him once or twice more at the shop, she asserted, but there was little or no contact between them bar a passing courtesy. Yet, astonishingly, she believed Madame Rachel when shortly afterwards, Rachel announced to her that Lord Ranelagh had fallen madly in love with her and had sworn to marry her. Mrs Borradaile was not so entirely witless that she did not demand some kind of proof of Ranelagh's passion, to which Rachel responded by telling her that he was currently caught up in urgent family matters; his estates required his attendance and management and so their courtship would have to be conducted pseudonymously by letter, leading to a marriage by proxy, all in order to preserve their privacy and his position. Rachel had, she claimed married two parties by proxy in this way before. In his letters to her, Lord Ranelagh would sign himself William (short for his code name of 'Captain William Edwards') in order to protect his identity should the letters fall into the wrong hands.

Convinced of Lord Ranelagh's undying adoration, Mrs Borradaile now entered into a lavish series of treatments, visiting New Bond Street almost daily and spending around £1,000 – an astronomical £65,000 today – in a very short space of time. Madame Rachel told her that central to her beautifying process were her exclusive 'Arabian baths' and so she took a course of them at Mrs Hicks's baths in nearby Davies Street. It was here, Rachel later confided, that Lord Ranelagh had first seen Mrs Borradaile and fallen in love with her by spying on her when she was taking her bath. In the eyes of the Almighty he was therefore as good as her husband for he had seen her a dozen times, through the Judas hole.

One of the first letters to arrive from her admirer 'William', via the intermediary of Rachel (who passed all letters back and forth between the couple and whom the letter writer referred to as 'Granny') was written on suitably convincing monogrammed notepaper and accompanied by gifts of a perfume box and a pencil case that he claimed had belonged to his 'sainted mother':

She died with them in her hand. When she was a schoolgirl it was my father's first gift to her. Granny has given the watch and locket to me again. Your coronet is finished my love. … Let old Granny arrange the time as we have too little to spare. My adored one, what is the matter with the old woman? She seems out of sorts. We must keep her in good temper for our own sakes. She has to manage all for us, and I should not have had the joy of your love had it not been for her, darling love. Mary, my sweet one, all will be well …. Bear up my fond one, and I shall be at your feet, those pretty feet that I love, and you may kick your ugly old donkey. … With fond and devoted love, yours till death, William.

The letter when read out in court provoked considerable laughter and the prosecution unwittingly piled on the humiliation of its client, by reading out a series of others, all handed to Mrs Borradaile in the box to identify. There was, however, an alarming irregularity about them that she, much to her counsel's dismay seemed to have accepted without question. Some were clearly written in different and sometimes illiterate and ungrammatical handwriting; others were, puzzlingly, signed 'Edward'; yet others 'Tommy'. The variation in handwriting had been explained away by Rachel as being by Lord Ranelagh's servant Edward, who had written them at his dictation because Ranelagh had 'hurt his arm' and who had even sometimes 'inadvertently' signed them Edward. Mrs Borradaile had little opportunity to press home her objections to such inconsistencies, for, she claimed, she was kept in check by constant exhortations in the letters not to offend or upset 'Granny' as go-between. In addition, she had barely had time to digest their contents before Rachel whisked them away from her, later providing her with copies. Confused she may have been by such inconsistencies, the lovestruck Mary Tucker Borradaile was somehow kept in thrall by an outpouring of sugary effusions:

> My Own Dear Love – My sweet darling Mary … I tell you again and again that you are the only woman I love. There should be no disguise, my sweet pet. I love you madly, fondly. Why do you trifle with my feelings, cruel one? Your ever loving and most truly devoted, and ever affectionate William.
>
> My sweet love, I will devote my love and all my life to you. I cannot express my love to you. I cannot find words to do so. My devotion in years shall tell my heart's fond love for you. Darling sweet one, I will tell all at your feet…

Meanwhile, the inducements from Rachel to spend, spend, spend were unceasing and reached the point, where, having exhausted her ready capital, Mrs Borradaile was put by Rachel in the hands of her own shady solicitor, Joseph Haynes of Palace Chambers, St James's Street, who made arrangements to raise money against her property, charging high fees for himself in so doing. During the unravelling of the case, even Serjeant Ballantine could not be sure exactly how much of his client's money had fallen into Rachel's hands or was siphoned off by others including the dubious Haynes, who was clearly out to line his own pockets. Soon Mrs Borradaile was obliged to go with them both to the city, to sell out money she had in stocks and shares at the Bank of England worth £1,300, against which she raised £963 2s. 11d. She already owed £800 of this to Rachel for her beauty treatments. She was given a receipt written in Haynes's presence on which Rachel had put her mark:

> Receipt: Wednesday, June 6, 1866. Received of Mrs. Borradaile the sum of 800 pounds, the balance of 1,000 pounds, for toilet requisites, bath preparations, soaps, powders, sponges, perfumes, and attendance and personal appearance, and enamelling, to be continued till Mrs Borradaile is finished by the process.

Having read this out, Serjeant Ballantine couldn't resist adding, and to considerable laughter, that in one respect at least Madame Rachel had certainly kept her word, 'for Mary Tucker Borradaile 'had been well and truly finished'. Rachel in fact did not receive all of this £800, for she owed Haynes, as mortgagee of the New Bond Street premises, £125 for two quarters' rent which he withheld, plus an additional two quarters on account. Mrs Borradaile herself never saw a penny of the paltry £160 that was left. Constantly bullied and browbeaten by Rachel she claimed that she 'used to sign things which I did not understand'. Such was Rachel's ascendancy over her by now that she could make her victim believe anything: 'I really think she bewitched me and that I wrote under fascination'. It was the best explanation the increasingly distressed and bewildered Mrs Borradaile could offer to the court.

Yet still the exploitation continued, with the pathetic Borradaile an inexplicably pliant victim: slowly but surely every last thing was extracted from her, from ready cash to material possessions. Through it all Mrs Borradaile remained convinced that Rachel was minding everything for her in preparation for her marriage. And so she handed over £1,260 for a tiara and necklace for her trousseau, to be made by Mr Pike the jeweller of New Bond Street. This extravagance was paid for in August 1866 by the sale of the reversion on a property in Streatham for £1,340 organized by Haynes. The order was later cancelled when word apparently came from Lord Ranelagh that he had his own mother's diamond coronet to present to his betrothed after it had been remodelled, but Mrs Borradaile did not get her money back and was forced to pay Pike a £100 forfeit for not taking up the order. In addition she paid out £32 for hair ornaments, £160 for dresses from Proctor the Linendraper of Brompton and £400 for expensive lace for the wedding gown from a dealer named Bower. She never saw the lace or any of the items, which had all been sent direct to Rachel's salon. Rachel later informed her that the lace had had to be pawned to provide funding for Lord Ranelagh's volunteer regiment, the Middlesex Rifles. In the end, Mrs Borradaile was induced even to take her own silver tea service to New Bond Street in a cab. Rachel would pack it all up ready for her wedding day, she assured her. By now utterly brainwashed to Rachel's demands, Borradaile handed over a quantity of her own jewellery – rings, trinkets, family seals – even her marriage settlement, her dead husband's letters written from India during his last illness and a pair of studs taken out of the shirt he was wearing on the day he died. Meanwhile, Rachel kept up the fantasy of Mary Tucker Borradaile's wonderful life to come as a Viscountess, by taking her to a coach builder's in New Bond Street to select a carriage, upon the side of which the Ranelagh family crest would be emblazoned.

With the insistent demands for money continuing to help fund his Volunteers, it soon became apparent that 'Dear William', far from being a well-heeled lord, as street walker Louisa Gould well knew, was rather hard up. Nothing, it would seem, could satisfy the constant demands for money backed up by wheedling letters, even when Mrs Borradaile had none left to give:

My own darling Mary – Why do you not do as Granny tells you? Why do you put obstacles in the way of your own happiness? Sign the paper; I will pay everything, my own darling love. If you marry your pension will be stopped; therefore it will not matter if you sign the paper, my own heart's life … Why do you doubt my honour and sincerity? .. If you wanted my life, I would lay it down at your own beautiful little feet. Mary, you are my joy. …I place your letters with your likeness in my bosom every night….

William told his beloved that he was now giving way 'under this dreadful suspense' especially with the threat of Mrs Borradaile's sister and brother-in-law, who had got wind of things, interfering in the matter.

May, my heart's love – Is it your wish to drive me mad? Granny has my instructions. Do as she tells you. Four letters, and not one reply. What is the meaning of this delay at the eleventh hour? Granny lent me the money. You shall pay her, my own sweet one. Get the lace today and fear nothing … Your sister and her husband have behaved very badly towards you if you knew all. I tell you, love, if you are not careful they will divide us for ever. … Leave all to me my own and fear nothing. If you have lost all love and confidence in your ugly old donkey, tell me; but this suspense is terrible… Mary, beloved one of my heart, do not trifle with me; I love once, I love for ever….

Throughout, Borradaile was kept in line by assurances from William that 'Granny loves you as though you were her own child' and that she must do as she was told, combined with a series of further passionate inducements, none more absurd than the occasion on which, at the Bond

Street salon, Rachel brought Mrs Borradaile a lighted cigar saying that Lord Ranelagh had just visited and that his love was as hot as the cigar he had left behind.

Ballantine did his best to avoid reading out in court the letters his client wrote in response, so incredulous was he at their muddled and delusional content. Did she never question the logic of the replies that she claimed Rachel had dictated to her? 'I frequently asked Mme Rachel what her object was in inducing me to write such silly letters,' admitted Mrs Borradaile, but all she could offer was that Rachel 'had immense influence over me'. She had been obliged to do as Rachel told her because she insisted that 'that was the only way that I should be able to get on.'

Knowing only too well that she had invested her last hopes and her rapidly fading looks in this highly desirable match – and with it a title and a supposedly wealthy husband – she had allowed Rachel to stand over her as she wrote them in the back parlour at New Bond Street. Rachel would then put them in envelopes and seal them saying she would deliver them in person. In her letters Mrs Borradaile repeatedly assured 'William' that she would never deny him a favour; she sent him gifts of clothing and solicited news of his well being: 'If you have not taken the cough mixture, take it, and put a little flannel on your chest. You are always angry when I tell you you are not getting younger. You have had no wife to take care of you, but this time you have.'

With time Mrs Borradaile's confidence finally became

rattled and she began to ask for the goods supposedly bought on her behalf or her money back. She was told 'Dear William' had them all safely put away and she must ask him for the money. When she asked for her letters to be returned she was refused. In the end, Mary Tucker Borradaile was left with nothing: 'She was not made beautiful for ever,' Ballantine told the court, 'All she got was a packet of powders which she put into the water of the baths she took.' And then, insult had been heaped on injury when, in, December 1866 Rachel had had her client thrown into Whitecross Street debtors' prison for non payment of a bond for £1,600 owing to her for various goods obtained for her wedding trousseau. Whilst languishing here for five weeks, Borradaile was visited by Rachel in January 1867. She remained nearly a whole day, during which she browbeat her into signing away the last thing she had left to cover the debt – her army pension of £300 a year; otherwise she would not get out of jail. She was also induced to distance herself from her sister and brother-in-law, the Copes, and prevent them from interfering in her affairs. When Alexander Cope had subsequently confronted Rachel she had turned the whole of the William story around, as her defence now did in court, claiming that 'Dear William' was in fact a real-life paramour on whom Mrs Borradaile had been lavishing money, against her, Madame Rachel's, advice, and that all the large IOUs to Rachel had been for money loaned to

Borradaile to fund this affair. The endgame in this whole sorry saga came in February 1867 when Mrs Borradaile was induced to sign an additional bond for £1,400 direct to Lord Ranelagh, alias 'Captain William Edwards' – against various bills and IOUs from Rachel. In the space of about six months the whole of her property and assets to the tune of £5,300 had been systematically stripped from her.

It was now Rachel's counsel, William Digby Seymour's turn to cross-examine, and he did not spare the by-now traumatised Mary Tucker Borradaile. He opened by asking her age, to be told in no uncertain terms that it was a 'very rude question'. She would not be pressed on the subject nor admit to how much of her personal charm was down to mother nature and how much to artifice. Her outraged response to Digby Seymour's insinuation that her hair, which she wore curled girlishly over her forehead, was not all her own, sent the court into hysterics. She might, she admitted, have used 'a little of Madame's Arabian Wash' on it but as for the rest and the extent to which her hair was the product of Rachel's 'scientific appliances' she refused to be drawn. However, she would take off her bonnet and prove it if need be – an assertion which provoked further roars of laughter in court.

Rachel might be on trial for fraud but as Digby Seymour proceeded to cross- examine it was clear that Mary Tucker Borradaile's virtue, character and integrity were about to be hauled over the coals. Her sad little withered figure in the witness box, where she was publicly condemned by her own evidence, reduced her to a pathetic rag doll for whom no one had any sympathy. Rachel, meanwhile, had revived and grown in confidence. Convinced that the trial was going her way, she now took on a more haughty attitude, 'reclining in the dock like a tragedy queen, and sniffing scornfully whenever any damaging statement was made by a witness for the other side'. James Hogg thought her statuesque sitting there in a comfortable arm-chair, 'with her finger to her face, tired but attentive, a picture of repose and immobility: intelligent, well-bred, well-dressed, it was difficult to believe that she was so illiterate that she could not write and could hardly read'.

After an exhausting day in the witness box, Mary Tucker Borradaile was finally allowed to stand down. The whole attention of the court the following day focused on the next witness, Lord Ranelagh. He was once again accorded a position of privilege, as he had been at the remand hearings, sitting in the body of the court alongside the judge, where he appeared to be enjoying the spectacle of Mrs Borradaile's ritual humiliation along with everyone else. In opening his cross- examination, prosecutor Ballantine made no bones about insinuating that Ranelagh was 'occasionally, if not frequently, at 47a New Bond Street', though quite what his purposes were, short of the already widespread inference of being a peeping tom, were not alleged in court. When pressed on this point Ranelagh was rather sheepish about his connection to Rachel. It so happened that he lived very near to her premises, he said, and, yes, he occasionally went to her salon because Rachel also dealt in china and other articles of *vertu* on commission, and he had bought things from her: 'If I found the door open in passing up the street, I went in and had a chat with her,' he told the court. More recently, once the case had been sent to trial at Marylebone with his name dragged into it, he had gone back to Rachel's out of morbid curiosity, to see this woman who had managed to 'get such large sums out of a lady'. But he stood, he said 'in rather an unenviable position,' for he too had been 'enamelled by this public scandal.'

Ranelagh admitted to having met Mrs Borradaile at New Bond Street once, as she had described, but denied having ever presented her with his card and could not remember meeting her there on any other occasions. He had indeed received about ten letters from her and clearly thought her delusional and in need of being taken in hand by her family, and had instructed his solicitor to write a letter to that effect to Mrs Borradaile's aged mother in Pembrokeshire. But he denied he had ever received a penny of her money, nor had he written any letters to her, or for that matter entertained any thoughts of her. When shown the evidence in court – the monogrammed letterhead used on some of the William letters – he made it clear that the monogram was not his, but a poor imitation.

The confusion over the true identity of the writer of

the William letters so cleverly orchestrated by Rachel, had played into the ambiguities that now littered the entire correspondence and which neither the prosecution could adequately prove, nor the defence disprove. Despite the court hearing the testimony of a sixteen-year-old boy named James Minton, who from time to time was engaged to deal with Rachel's correspondence and who alleged that he had written some of the 'William' letters at Rachel's dictation, the jury and the court at large remained puzzled by whether William was real – i.e. Lord Ranelagh – or a clandestine unnamed lover, or perhaps even a figment of Mary Tucker Borradaile's deranged imagination. Was the illiterate Rachel really clever enough to invent a long and convoluted series of letters describing a supposedly bogus intrigue – or was Mrs Borradaile trying to shift the blame for an illicit affair of her own on which she had squandered all her money? All the letters had supposedly been written by her at Rachel's salon to 'Captain William Edwards care of Madame Rachel' yet some of them were addressed to 'My dear Tom'. The defence now played on the fact that Borradaile in fact had a cousin called Colonel Edwardes about whom she perhaps entertained amorous intentions. The letters often at times implied by their content to have been written to someone far more familiar to her than Lord Ranelagh. Did Rachel, knowing of the Edwardes connection, deliberately use this as Ranelagh's nom de plume in order to muddy the waters and create a bogus lover that Mrs Borradaile could later be accused of throwing her money away on?

But if not, what was the logic in Rachel dictating so many letters to achieve her ends? It only needed a few surely, argued Digby Seymour, for Rachel to extract money from her client. He insisted that a woman such as her who could not write (but who could read a little as he failed to clarify) was not capable of dictating the letters. They were nothing but Mrs Borradaile's own silly 'effusions'. He made much of the fact that in one of her letters to William, she had, at Rachel's dictation written

> You know there are such things as talking birds. I feel better now since you told me we shall leave Charing Cross next morning. Will that morning ever come? ... But you seem to know the overland route to my heart.

Was it really credible, asked Digby Seymour, that Rachel could have come out with such clever words? In her own testimony Borradaile had talked of going the overland route to India when first married – a fact which she could easily have imparted to Rachel in conversation. And illiteracy, of course, has nothing to do with a lack of natural intelligence. There were many similar such fanciful phrases in the 'Beautiful For Ever' catalogue, written by her clever daughters, that Madame Rachel could have drawn on.

Digby Seymour chose not to introduce any witnesses

for the defence but relied on his considerable oratorical skills in a lengthy summing up. There was, as far as he was concerned, only one witness who could throw any light upon the subject 'and her mouth was closed by being in the dock', for up until the Prisoners' Evidence Act of 1898 prisoners in criminal cases were not allowed to give evidence on their own behalf. Digby Seymour also complained about the lurid reports about the prisoner that had been circulating in the press, which had been prejudicial to a fair trial. Trying to play the sympathy card he alleged that his client had met this case 'at the hazard and risk of her health and strength'. As to the prejudice against traders such as her professing to make women Beautiful For Ever – if women were dissatisfied with their looks and sought to change them then they were the ones to blame, not his client. There was scarcely a newspaper that did not carry advertisements making exaggerated claims for every kind of lotion and cosmetic, hair dye or elixir. Rachel openly advertised her processes and her charges so why must she be made the centre and focus of so much indignation? His client was, asserted Digby Seymour, 'no better and no worse than scores of other advertisers in the columns of the press who appealed to the weakness and folly of the age'. He challenged the prosecution to produce any corroboration of Mrs Borradaile's evidence; no witnesses had been called to confirm the alleged purchases made under false pretences. Where was the proof that Rachel had stolen or kept these goods bought on Mrs Borradaile's behalf? In his final appeal to the jury he asked them to consider 'the probabilities of the truth' of Mrs Borradaile's story. If Madame Rachel was the author of the letters why had Mrs Borradaile so willingly written so many patently false statements that might reflect on her own virtue?

In the end the case stood or fell on whether the jury believed Mary Tucker Borradaile. Rachel's enforced silence in the case was to her advantage, for in legal terms, the whole case rested on Mrs Borradaile's 'uncorroborated assertion' that Lord Ranelagh was the object of her letters. The inconsistencies in her evidence did not, argued Digby Seymour, 'point to dictation', but to the aberrations of her own mind. Either way, it remained utterly incredible to everyone in court that Mrs Borradaile should surrender all her cash and property so freely and to the point of self-destruction, on merely the dubious promise of marriage to Lord Ranelagh.

Serjeant Ballantine in his summing up for the prosecution asked for a verdict 'that would cleanse London of one of its foulest stains', but the Recorder in his directions to the jury appeared to favour Madame Rachel, in that stronger evidence from the prosecution was required to justify a conviction. He admitted that he was 'utterly unable to understand a great many of the curious things which had been imparted into the case'. The labyrinth of contradictions of the William–Mary letters clearly confounded him as it did most of those in court and he for one was far from convinced that the prosecutrix had told the truth.

At 6 p.m. on 22 August the jury duly retired, anxious to reach a verdict that day rather than have to return the following morning. However, at 11.10 that night, after twice returning to ask questions of the Recorder, they still had not reached a verdict and stated that there was no likelihood of it. 'Sensible men,' Rachel was heard to mutter under her breath, 'let them send their wives to Bond Street. I'll beautify them and prove I'm no fraud'. Despite the late hour, the court had remained crowded all this time in anticipation of the verdict. With the jury unable to agree (one lone juryman having 'sturdily resisted' a conviction) the Recorder discharged them, ordering an immediate retrial the next morning. Rachel's exhausted counsel Digby Seymour immediately objected: he was, he said, physically incapable of proceeding with a new trial after such a lengthy speech for the defence that day and asked for a postponement to next session. He also applied for bail for Rachel, 'who had already suffered a long imprisonment'. The Recorder agreed to this, reducing her previous bail of £4,000 by half.

In the interim the hope in Rachel's camp was that Mrs Borradaile and her friends would 'take the advice tendered by the whole press of the country, and withdraw from the prosecution', in order to save her from further humiliation in court. For such had been the shocking extent of Mrs

Borradaile's self-deception that she clearly had 'no claim on public sympathy'. The general feeling was one of huge relief that there would now be a brief respite from the case. 'We were all becoming tired of this squabble between a charlatan and her willing dupe', observed the *Pall Mall Gazette*.

CHAPTER SEVEN

Mrs Plucker Sparrowtail

DESPITE THE PATENT world-weariness of the legal profession, the British press was by no means prepared to give its readers a break from the Madame Rachel scandal. An inevitable post-mortem followed the collapse of the trial for several days in the press. *The Times* was amazed that the jury had not immediately acquitted Madame Rachel; there was no logic to her having dictated so much 'amorous verbiage' to Borradaile, if her only objective had been to get her money. It was a waste of the time and ingenuity of a good swindler. Mrs Borradaile's story could not be accounted for, because it flew in the face 'of the very constitution of the human mind'. The *Glasgow Herald* concurred: whilst the trial had 'far exceeded anything Miss Braddon or any other of the more courageous sensation novelists had ever dared to put before their readers' there was clearly insufficient evidence to warrant a conviction.

The best legal outcome would have been the Scottish one of 'Not Proven', leaving the case of both ladies to rest with public opinion. Whilst being far from sympathetic towards Rachel, many journalists agreed that whatever her culpability, she was perfectly open in her professional dealings and no criminality should attach to what she charged for her beauty treatments or of what they were comprised. Even if Madame Rachel 'could not beautify at all' argued the *Scotsman*, 'still less for ever, it does not necessarily follow that she practised wilful deception.' There was nothing new in the making and selling of cosmetics, observed the *Saturday Review*, it had taken place since the days of the Empress Poppea in ancient Rome. 'If women, old or young, want to be beautiful, "repaired" and "finished" they must pay the price demanded by the painter, varnisher and decorator, or leave it alone.' Venus was always a mercenary dame'. But it was *The Times* that got to the heart of the matter: 'The jury must have wanted to play the part which too many juries have a disposition to play – that of a little PROVIDENCE – and to punish the prisoner, not for her particular guilt on this charge, but for her supposed immorality.' Charging high prices was not a criminal offence but effectively Rachel was condemned for doing so. The *Penny Illustrated Times* put it more bluntly: Madame Rachel had been 'the subject of a great amount of much that we should call prejudice'.

All of the papers were greatly exercised over the issue of the 'Dear William' letters. Could any sane person write letters implicating her own good name, and believe at the same time that she was securing an eligible husband? Mrs Borradaile had either been extraordinarily foolish, possessed of a childishness 'that would have been inexcusable in a schoolgirl barely out of her teens', or Madame Rachel's influence over her had been akin to that of 'an expert electro-biologist over his patients'. With the *Daily News* alleging that the whole proceedings had been 'shrouded in a twopenny mystery' Rachel went quietly back to Newgate, leaving everyone guessing, to await her release on bail. She knew full well the impact the trial would have; despite all the public outrage to the contrary, it had played into her hands, for soon she was receiving dozens of letters from women convinced that she did indeed possess some mysterious power that could make them beautiful for ever. All they wanted to know was how they could get hold of her cosmetics. Nor was Rachel averse to engineering some of her own publicity. Whilst the press continued to argue over the ramifications of the trial, a couple of penny pamphlets giving a partial account of it were rushed out by William Swift of the Strand. They were clearly produced at Rachel's behest to counter the deluge of adverse publicity and were an unapologetic promotion of her business.

From the opening sentence of the first, 'The History and Trial of Mdm Rachel', it is clear that it was written much in the same florid vein of the 'Beautiful For Ever' pamphlet of 1863. No doubt the clever Rachel junior and Leontie were once more at work, going by the resounding opening claim that 'the magic efforts of genius' – i.e. their mother's – were indeed capable of staving off the ravages of time. The proof was there in the succession of titled and wealthy ladies of the 'fashionable world' who had for years now been flocking to Madame Rachel's 'Temple of Renovation' – even as recently as the latest London season, during which 'the beautifying art of this great *artiste* had caused many high-born dames to command admiration for their borrowed beauty in the grand Court of the Sovereign and in the brilliant *salons* of the aristocracy.' It was clear that Rachel was intent on brazening it out, insistent that she was indeed the inventor of a 'marvellous art'. What is more, as the author of the pamphlet was anxious to show, the calumny hurled at her was unjustified, for Madame Rachel in fact had a heart of gold. Her old neighbours from Clare Market were solicited for their opinion and vouched, with 'warm approbation', that Rachel was 'one of the most kind-hearted, compassionate women that ever breathed' and dispensed charity with a liberal hand. In high Dickensian style the pamphlet painted a portrait of how one night she had seen a half-naked beggar and her child cowering in a storm outside. She had brought them in to the warmth of her fireside, shared her only loaf of bread with them and wrapped them in part of her bed curtain. Even whilst on remand at Marlborough Street during the Carnegie case, the compassionate Rachel had paid the 40 shilling fine of the cabman who had intimidated her daughter, rather than see his wife and children starve. In addition she was a 'devoted and honourable wife' and 'the 'affectionate mother of an amiable and highly accomplished family'.

The pamphlet concluded by announcing that after Rachel's acquittal – 'for most assuredly she will be acquitted by any intelligent jury' – the public would have an opportunity of hearing her give public readings (of what exactly was not specified), which would prove that 'she is quite the reverse of illiterate'. More intriguingly, it also titillated readers by alleging that the 'Dear William' of the letters really did exist, that he was a certain 'W– S–', 'one of the gayest and handsomest men, moving daily about the fashionable locality of the West End', who had had numerous romantic escapades and whose appearance was 'well calculated to fire the heart of any amorous widow of fifty and induce her to hazard all on being made 'beautiful for ever'. What is more, the mysterious William, so the pamphlet claimed, had had the temerity to sit out the whole of Rachel's trial incognito. The only thing was that apart from the mention of his age as being 28 the rest of the description of this mysterious personage perfectly matched the appearance and track record of Lord Ranelagh. Rachel was playing a clever game keeping everyone guessing and manipulating it all to her own ends.

But meanwhile, the whole sordid business would have to be aired again at the next sessions in September. So far things had gone Rachel's way; as one shrewd old lawyer observed after the first case: 'If that woman keeps her mouth shut, no judge or jury in this country will convict her upon Mrs Borradaile's evidence and those letters.' In the five weeks that followed, Rachel's solicitor made repeated and unsuccessful attempts to obtain bail for her. For all her notoriety, she was not short of offers, but they were all rejected by the court. Meanwhile, rumours abounded that the juryman who had held out for acquittal at the first trial had been a friend of Rachel's and had supplied himself with refreshments in order to sit out the long deliberation – a fact most strenuously denied by the juror in question in a letter to *The Times*. After the sixth attempt at bail, and with the press circulating rumours that Rachel was planning to abscond to Paris, it was decided to abandon the application. And so Rachel languished at Newgate, now only used for holding prisoners committed for trial or those awaiting the death penalty, though she spent most of the time in the relative comfort of the prison infirmary.

In the interim, there was no let up on public allusions to the Rachel case. A set of popular *cartes de visite* of Rachel, Borradaile and Ranelagh were put on sale by the Stereoscopic Company of Regent Street and sketches in court by E. M. Ward were also available. At a party political hustings in Guildford it was observed that Toryism had been to the Temple of Beauty, and, like Mrs Borradaile, had been made Beautiful For Ever. Mr Disraeli was Toryism's Madame Rachel in that by giving it 'an abundance of false hair, by enamelling and skilfully dressing it out, he had sent it to woo the working man. But it would share the fate of the bride who fell to pieces on the wedding night. Amidst all the disguises and enamel, the features of the old lady persistently shone through.' Meanwhile, a rising young playwright and parodist, Frederick Hay, had produced two short comedies *Hue and Dye* and *Beautiful For Ever* that were doing the rounds of British theatres. At the Star Music Hall in Bermondsey Mr Fred Albert was offering his own 'Beautiful For Ever Entertainment' and the Surrey Theatre was resounding to roars of laughter nightly with the production of George F. Hodgson's farce which included a character named Mrs Botheremwell and where the music hall comic Mat Robson took on the part of Madame Rouge Cosmetique in drag. But of all the music hall stars, none could equal the inimitable Arthur Lloyd, who toured with his own song, 'Mrs Plucker Sparrowtail or Beautiful For Ever', the sheet music for which became a resounding hit across Britain. Dressed in drag as one of Rachel's victims, and having managed to soap over his considerable moustache and hide it from view, Lloyd would bring the house down each evening with the song's rousing chorus:

Ladies, I pray, take example by me,
Can I forget Madame Rachel, no, never!
Altho' she got from me a very large fee,
In return I got beauty for ever.

On 12 September, publication of an official account of the aborted first trial was announced in the press by G Purkess of the Strand. Produced in conjunction with the *Illustrated Police News* it came with portraits of the major protagonists Rachel, Mrs Borradaile and Lord Ranelagh. Any chance Rachel might have of a fair retrial thus evaporated when this penny pamphlet hit the news-stands, containing as it did a sequence of savagely anti-Semitic cartoons of a rapacious Rachel with hideous hook nose fleecing a scraggy and bald Mrs Borradaile. Elsewhere the *Tomahawk* could not resist dredging up the story of Rachel's friendship with Jewish brothel keeper David Belasco and her testimony at his 1852 trial, running it under the heading 'The Persecuted Jewess!'

Rachel's solicitor, William Roberts, in response to the extensive press coverage and growing public antipathy applied to the courts for a writ of *a certiorari* for the case to be tried at the Court of the Queen's Bench with a special jury, 'in consequence of a prejudice existing against the defendant among the class of persons from whom common jurors are selected'. It was, insisted Roberts, impossible that his client would get a fair trial at the Old Bailey. Although the application was refused, the tide of publicity – negative and racially prejudiced though it was – had, paradoxically, been very good for business. Back at 47a New Bond Street, Rachel junior and Leontie were doing a roaring trade. 'The sale of the celebrated Arabian dew,' remarked the *Hull*

Packet, 'seems to have been stimulated by the discoverer's misfortunes.' Business, it told its readers, had been far from harmed by the trial: 'Women who are not lovely, and who long for loveliness, will cling even to a Rachel, as drowning men catch at straws' and even now their carriages were blocking the thoroughfare down Bond Street.

CHAPTER EIGHT

The Bond Street Mystery

THE SECOND TRIAL of Sarah Rachel Levison, when it opened on 21 September before Commissioner Kerr, would drag its slow length along five wearisome days in an airless, packed Central Criminal Court at the expense of both prisoner and accuser. Mary Tucker Borradaile had been warned that yet another high profile criminal case would damage her reputation beyond repair and expose her private life to ridicule, and for almost two days solid in the box, she had to endure the consequences. Her cross-examination by Rachel's clever and exhaustingly persistent barrister Digby Seymour reduced her to a quivering, self-contradicting wreck. However, the difficulty with this retrial, as prosecutor Serjeant Ballantine, observed in opening it, would be for the jury to ignore all the gossip and rumour that they had heard about the first and listen only to the evidence presented.

That Monday, Rachel had 'made her way into the dock

with the same air of extreme lassitude and exhaustion' as she had during her August trial. She looked very ill but was nevertheless still opulently dressed and still possessed of an imposing presence and a cynical contempt for those sitting in judgment on her. Dressed in a black lace mantilla arranged 'not ungracefully' over her head and 'grouped so as to throw the shadows more deeply over her heavy, hueless face' she sat there passively, rarely communicating with her counsel.

Mary Tucker Borradaile for her part, arrived in court looking as demure as she could, dressed in plain black silk, with a white worked collar across her shoulders, and with the stereotyped black cotton gloves which were the distinguishing mark of genteel British middle class widowhood. She still displayed the 'same grizzly yellow ringlets' and was heavily veiled, stubbornly refusing to expose her face to the searching test of full daylight. Digby Seymour began his cross-examination by insisting she raise her veil as he could not hear her speak through it. Borradaile refused, but at his insistence relented, though she persisted in half-covering her face with her hand throughout his cross-examination. Her testimony was punctuated by the constant half-hysterical giggle as before and 'the same odd mixture of natural shame at her position and pride in her momentary notoriety, the same incapability of giving a plain answer to a plain question, the same querulous impatience if the question had to be repeated'.

During the second trial Digby-Seymour went vigorously on the attack, by proceeding to mercilessly demolish Mrs Borradaile's good character, suggesting that she had been willing to prostitute herself by carrying on with another man – the real object of the 'Dear William' letters – for months. Further, the money she gave Madame Rachel as go-between was for this William figure and not Lord Ranelagh. Borradaile's own letters now became the focus for the defence at the retrial, with the pathetic widow being subjected by the unforgiving Digby Seymour to a protracted and extremely searching six-hour cross-examination. In one of the most ludicrous turns in the evidence, he produced several additional and highly erratic 'Dear William letters' written by her, that for his own reasons he had withheld from the August trial. Incomprehensibly, although addressed to 'Dear William', many of them proceeded to refer to Lord Ranelagh in the third person:

My Own Dear William – If you knew what I have suffered since Saturday night on your account, one unkind word would never have escaped your lips to me. My brother-in-law went to The Carlton to see Lord Ranelagh. They told him he was out of town and they said he would not be back for a week … You would have been amused at the frantic manner in which he was running about town looking for the invisible person who could not be found, thanks to our lucky star. Mr Cope and my sister made me promise I would not see Rachel again as I led them to suppose she had been the promoter of His Lordship in intriguing with me.

Under cross-examination, Mrs Borradaile swore on oath that she had thought she was writing to Lord Ranelagh at the time. She could not explain the illogic of their content. That, she insisted, was what Madame Rachel had told her to say. Even more bizarre was the statement in a letter read out soon after:

One of your kind friends and your bosom companions has informed me that you have been and now are keeping a woman. Not one member of my family will hold any intercourse with me for forming such a degraded connexion, as it is well known in Pembrokeshire that I have been living with you for some months. When I receive a letter from my daughter it is full of insults. You cannot be, and are not surprised at this, considering the life we have been leading. Am I to believe that the woman you travelled with, and whom you introduced to me as your sister, is your mistress?

Again, Mrs Borradaile could offer no explanation as to why she agreed to write such bizarre things. When pressed, all she could do was glare at Digby-Seymour and insist that Rachel was 'a vile woman and you are as bad as she is.' Altercations of a similar nature peppered the whole of her cross-examination, such as when Digby Seymour challenged her over her authorship of: 'It is very kind of you to take care of my comb and frisette; it is my own hair. The man who keeps the hairdresser's shop at the corner of High Street, Cheltenham, made it for me – the man who used to shave you when you were there', a statement which provoked much laughter. Throughout, Mrs Borradaile seemed extremely unwilling to discuss her own letters, let alone even look at them, steadfastly refusing either to acknowledge or deny the genuineness of those purporting to bear her signature or to be in her handwriting. To her counsel's annoyance she frequently rambled at length about the harshness of the treatment she had received, constantly volunteering statements about her own virtue and integrity. Digby Seymour, for his part, managed to contain his frustration during the cross-examination and although he never took unfair advantage of the many openings she offered him with her interjections, he did make the most of exposing her admission that she had bought a photograph of Lord Ranelagh at a shop in Regent Street and taken it to bed with her. But in the end he remained perplexed by the 'astonishing indistinctness' of Mrs Borradaile's memory in regard to the letters and the way in which she clung to her version of the story, and her insistence that she wrote whatever Rachel told her, no matter how nonsensical. 'I cannot make out how I ever came to write the letters that have been produced,' she insisted. They were, she admitted, the letters of a 'self-confessed idiot'. All she could offer in mitigation was a new allegation – that Madame Rachel had fed her whisky at the time she wrote them assuring her that whisky had done her, Rachel, a great deal of good.

Digby Seymour could not resist pressing home the levels of Mrs Borradaile's idiocy. In another letter, supposedly written by her to William, she had told him 'your sister ought to see that your stockings are mended. I cannot see why she cannot mend them herself, and put some buttons on your shirts…. Send all your clothes that want mending to me.' Did Mrs Borradaile really write such things at Rachel's behest?', asked Digby Seymour. Did she honestly think a nobleman such as Lord Ranelagh should send his mending to her? 'I ask you on your solemn oath,' Digby pressed her, 'did you, when you wrote that letter to this shirtless, buttonless, stockingless, bootless, flannelless, hatless individual, think that you were writing to Lord Ranelagh?' And, in reference to another letter talking of an assignation, did Mrs Borradaile wish the jury to believe that 'you, the widow of a colonel in the English Army, expected to meet Lord Ranelagh to whom you thought you were going to be married, at a *coffee shop*?'! Worse still, in an allusion in one letter to William that she had given her lover 'all that woman holds dear', Digby Seymour could not resist the insinuation that Mary Tucker Borradaile was a loose woman.

Mrs Borradaile was adamant: it was all down to the evil influence that Madame Rachel had over her and that was the best explanation she could offer. However, when put under pressure by Digby Seymour she was forced to admit that, when writing the letters, sometimes, where the grammar was poor, she had improved on a sentence here and there and put in words of her own. She had written most of them in the back parlour at 47a, at Rachel's dictation, after business, or in the house round the corner in Maddox Street – sometimes in Leontie's presence. Indeed, Mrs Borradaile now insisted that, come to think of it, some of them looked very much like Leontie's handwriting; she was often at the house and she saw her writing letters for her mother. This statement immediately roused the accused from her till-then listless indifference in the dock and she called out that she wished Leontie to be called to the witness box.

Once the subject of Rachel's two eldest daughters was brought up it was clear that there was much confusion in Mrs Borradaile's fuddled brain as to their true age and relationship to her. Commenting on her initial reluctance to prosecute Rachel, she had remarked: 'I told the prisoner in a letter I wrote to her, that she was better than she was made out to be and that she behaved well to her grandchildren.' She had always thought the children – Leontie and the fourth daughter, Elise (Elizabeth) – that she had seen at the shop to be Rachel's grandchildren 'because she always told me so'. But this had all been part of Rachel's business hype – to allege to clients that she was in fact much older than she looked. With this in mind, she had made out that her younger children were Rachel junior's, claiming that she herself was really eighty years of age but that her secret arts had kept the years at bay. Borradaile could not tell for sure how old the two eldest daughters were, she said in court, as they were 'so made up'.

The novelty of Rachel's two daughters being called as witnesses brought a new dimension to the second trial. The press did not fail to note how self-possessed both appeared to be and that Leontie in particular had 'a singularly handsome face and a very pleasing manner'. Once on the witness stand, the two young women were primed by Digby Seymour's praise of their education, beauty and propriety of manner, but in the cross-examinations that followed both were clearly and charmingly lying through their teeth to protect their mother. Rachel junior denied writing any of the letters and said that the young lad Minton who claimed to have written some of them had often 'been turned out of our house' as he was very impertinent. They did, however, have a shop boy called William and she thought some of the William letters were in his hand. Mrs Borradaile used to stop in the shop and the parlour for a very long time and, claimed Rachel, 'she used to give us a great deal of trouble'.

For the prosecution, Serjeant Ballantine chose to take a different tack and cross-examine Rachel junior about the authenticity of her mother's highly-priced and exotic products. In so doing he introduced an element of comic relief that broke the monotony of the trial. Did Madame Rachel, he asked her, really bring water all the way from the River Jordan, for which she charged the outlandish prices

1. RIGHT: Sarah Rachel
Levison, the notorious
Madame Rachel

2. BELOW LEFT: New Bond
Street in the 1860s

3. BELOW RIGHT: Lord
Ranelagh, rake and man-about-
town, who was unwittingly
implicated in Madame Rachel's
1868 prosecution

4. Madame Rachel's victim, Mrs Mary Tucker Borradaile

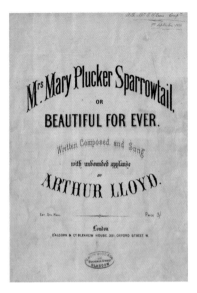

5. Arthur Lloyd's famous music hall song about the 1868 trial

TRIAL OF MADAME RACHEL AT THE OLD BAILEY.

6. Madame Rachel's trial at the Central Criminal Court, 1868

BEAUTIFUL FOR EVER

7. TOP LEFT: A typical anti-Semitic cartoon relating to the Borradaile case

8. TOP RIGHT: Madame Rachel's nemesis, the solicitor George Lewis

9. LEFT: A popular penny pamphlet about the 1868 trial

10. Cartoon depicting the sale of Madame Rachel's house contents after her conviction in 1869

11. ABOVE: Women prisoners in the laundry of Woking Invalid Convict Prison

12. RIGHT: 1860s advertisement cataloguing Madame Rachel's outlandish beauty claims

13. The rue de la Paix, Paris where Léontine Rachel set up a salon at no. 10 in the 1870s

14. The Paris Morgue in the 1870s

A BATH AT MADAME RACHELS

MADAME RACHEL or BEAUTIFUL for EVER.

Mᴿˢ PEARSE in the WITNESS BOX

MADAME RACHEL EXAMINING the SKIN

15. Madame Rachel's second high profile victim, Cecilia Maria Pearse, at the time of the 1878 trial

16 and 17. Two of Madame Rachel's aristocratic clients, the Countess of Dudley (left) and the Countess of Cardigan (right)

18. Madame Rachel demonstrates the 'before and after' effects of her beautification process to clients

19 AND 20. The opera singers Hélène Crosmond (left) and Alma Verdini (right) who both debuted at Covent Garden in the late 1870s.

21. The grim surroundings of Millbank Penitentiary on the banks of the River Thames

22. Women prisoners exercising at Woking Invalid Convict Prison, where Madame Rachel died in 1880

of ten and twenty guineas per bottle? 'We have it for more than that,' replied Rachel boastfully. But Ballantine would not let it go at that, nor would Rachel junior desist from giving him sly and taunting answers to his questions:

Q: Now I ask you, Miss Leverson, did you believe this Jordan Water was a reality or a sham? A: I believed it to be a reality.

Q: You mean to tell the Court and jury on your oath that you believe that water came from the River Jordan? A: I believe it is brought from the East.

Q: From the East! Well, but that is very indefinite, for the East may mean Wapping. What I ask you is, do you mean to say it came from the river Jordan? A: Yes. Of course, I did not see it brought.

Q: How do you know that? A: Because it was consigned to us.

Q: By whom? A: Oh! I cannot expose our professional secrets. If you will come to our shop and buy a bottle, I may tell you.

Q: Where is the river Jordan? A: Is it not near Jerusalem?

Q: And you say you have an agent there? A: I don't know whether he is at the Jordan, but I say he consigns the Jordan Water to us.

Q: Who is he? A: I will not tell you.

When questioned about the Beautiful For Ever brochure, it was, said Rachel, she and her sister Leontie who had written it; in fact Leontie generally wrote her mother's letters for her as they had, she claimed 'a vast number of customers besides Mrs Borradaile'. She, Rachel, had assisted her mother in the shop in 1866 and 1867 before being sent to Paris to run the establishment there, and helped prepare the articles they sold. When it came to Leontie's turn in the witness box, she also alleged that Mrs Borradaile was constantly in and out of the shop and 'had been in the habit of borrowing money from my mama for a very long time'. Throughout her cross-examination she proved equally capable of holding the clever Ballantine at bay, parrying his questions by innocently 'not being able to recollect' certain key facts. Her mother certainly lent Mrs Borradaile notes and gold, indeed, she was in the habit of lending money to other ladies; she did not use a banker but kept her money in a little cabinet in the back parlour. As for the written assignment to Rachel of Mrs Borradaile's pension, she and her sister had both thought this was in their younger sister's handwriting (it was not specified whether she was referring to Hannah or Elise) – and she was now 'in Paris'.

In the end, the calling of the two daughters as witnesses for the defence did nothing to further Rachel's case, and by 24 September, the newspapers were observing that the Rachel trial was becoming ever more arduous and complicated as it proceeded. The heat in the courtroom, which was packed with women, was intolerable, but the general consensus was, as before, that Rachel would be acquitted. Digby Seymour opened his summing up for the defence by commenting on all the adverse publicity that had prejudiced the case. Mrs Borradaile, he claimed, seemed throughout to have been 'walking in her sleep – drugged, subdued, captivated, enamoured of some man named William'. Was it all the 'invention of a disorganised brain'? There seemed to be so many lapses and oddities in her effusive letters to William that she must have written some of them. They had been poured out on a wave of increasing delusion – with her now and again switching to 'Dear Tommy' in letters such as one in which she talked of an assignation: 'I will go to the baths at the Argyle Rooms this evening; I will then wait for you at the public house at the back of Regent Street, and will ask for a private room for us there'. Would a woman of Mary Tucker Borradaile's social standing and in her right mind write such things? It would, he argued be far easier to account for her many eccentricities if one knew that she was suffering 'under some affliction of Providence'. In the end, he could only conclude that 'If the case rested solely upon her evidence, the jury would not hang a cat'. After eight hours and five minutes on his feet in his final powerful and impressive speech for the defence, Mr Digby Seymour QC finally sunk to his seat exhausted, to the sound of considerable applause.

In summing up for the prosecution, Serjeant Ballantine said the whole case was a 'trumpery affair'. It was a very 'dirty story' but one which had run to enormous expense, the cost of the two trials later being estimated in the region of £2,000 (£130,000 today) – all this, to get to 'the merits of such a miserable transaction'. The case presented the jury with 'a labyrinth of vice and lying of all kinds'; it was one of 'idiocy on one side supplemented by forgery on the other'. But, as in the recent case in Chancery of Lyon v Home, Mrs Borradaile was not the first woman to be so systematically duped. As to the practices carried out at the New Bond Street salon – aside from the particular case of fraud, Ballantine made dark allusions to 'other acts' which were perpetrated there, no doubt based on popular rumour and his own personal knowledge, but that these had 'better not be more particularly mentioned now, except to add that the sooner such dens were rooted out of London the better'.

Toward the end of the trial Madame Rachel collapsed into an hysterical fainting fit in the dock and the proceedings had to be temporarily stopped. By this point, as the *Illustrated Police News* observed, of the two women 'who are virtually on their trial' it was 'hard to say which looked the more worn and exhausted.' When it came to the judge's summing up, Commissioner Kerr asked the jury, by now as weary as everyone else, if they would like the trial to be concluded that evening, as it was now 8 p.m. They insisted that they did; but the unseemly haste with which they arrived at their verdict – just twenty minutes – had a great deal to do with the firm direction in which Kerr's summing up steered them. During this, Kerr produced his own supposed 'evidence of guilt' – an early stab at amateur forensics – by unexpectedly making much of the appearance of a particular water-mark on the paper used for the letters between Mrs Borradaile and 'William'. A notepaper manufactured by Joynson & Co., he concluded that this was strong evidence of the same hand being complicit in both sets of letters. It was, as even a reader of *The Times* was quick to point out after the trial, naïve in the extreme to draw this conclusion, for the notepaper was extremely common and widely available. It had turned out to be 'rather a dangerous experiment in dealing with the impressionable minds of a jury to lay stress upon circumstantial evidence of this kind'. The notepaper proved nothing at all, but it had clearly influenced an exhausted jury in their decision, as too had the widespread speculation in the press, all of which had been highly prejudicial against Rachel. This time it was clear that the judge was for a conviction, and made no bones about it. But which of these two equally repellent women would the jury believe? For in truth, the baffling content of the letters, combined with the succession of witnesses, most of them repeating their evidence from the previous trial almost verbatim, plus the presence of Rachel's daughters, had left them little the wiser about the truth of the case.

Commissioner Kerr's undisguised bias and his failure to criticize Mrs Borradaile's inconsistent behaviour in his summing up, rankled with legal traditionalists who felt that however great a rogue Rachel was, she had not been proven guilty of the actual offence for which she was charged. In the event, the unseemly haste of the jury's deliberation resulted in a verdict of guilty. Before sentence was passed Madame Rachel asked Commissioner Kerr to read a sworn affidavit from her solicitor Haynes and then said, from the dock: 'I have been defended by most able counsel and I have nothing to complain of. They have done all in their power for their client. … Far be it for me to make any speech or create any sensation,' she continued, before adding darkly, 'but that which is known as the Bond-Street mystery will remain a Bond Street mystery still'. And with that she offered her stony face to the judge: 'Pass the sentence upon me if you please.'

As the courtroom held its breath, Commissioner Kerr responded by throwing the full weight of English justice at Madame Rachel – not for the crime committed, but effectively for perpetrating a moral sin that had outraged Victorian society. When sentence of five years in jail was pronounced – an unusually harsh one for the crime of fraud – Mrs Borradaile, now sitting in the body of the court, rose and 'endeavoured to get a good view of Madame Rachel, evidently with a desire to gratify her morbid curiosity'. But 'Madame had turned away and, with a smile to the judge, defiantly walked out.' That, at least, was the *Glasgow Herald*'s version. Other papers reported that when sentenced,

Rachel had tried to speak but had been unable to do so and had dropped a written statement from her hand. Others wrote that she had fainted and was carried out of the dock; still others that one of her daughters had let out a scream of agony.

***

No sooner was the sentence passed than the British press rushed into an orgy of lurid demonization of Rachel. 'Here is sensation quite as thrilling as *Lady Audley's Secret*,' remarked a penny account of the trial, with the papers describing Rachel as a 'vile old hag', a witch and a crone, as well as more racially specific terms of abuse. Reviled for practicing 'hocus-pocus and broomstick fascination', Rachel and her daughters were collectively condemned as the 'Bond Street nest of Jewesses'. Insinuations about her supposed past fraudulent history as procuress and even abortionist also inevitably wormed their way into the papers. *Reynolds's Newspaper* led the gutter press in its rabidly sensationalist tone. 'The spider has been caught in the web she has woven to entrap others', it proclaimed, describing Rachel as 'the old harridan'. The shop in Bond Street was a painted sepulchre and Rachel herself 'the high priestess of all the foul and filthy doings that transpired within its gilded doors'. The *Saturday Review* whilst finding the whole trial tiresome, was one of the few voices of balance, pointing out that the whole of the case for the prosecution had been deliberately geared to cast doubt on Rachel's 'Englishness' and accentuate her nefarious arts as 'a Jewish purveyor of feminine charms' who dabbled in an exotic Eastern mysticism that was alien to Englishness.

But even Madame Rachel deserved justice, and the general consensus among the legal profession was that, in point of law, Rachel had been condemned contrary to the evidence. Papers such as *Trewman's Exeter Flying Post* protested Kerr's line of observation in the summing up. 'It was the charge of a sharp *Nisi Prius* lawyer [of a lower level court], not the grave and well-considered charge of an English judge.' From its position as paragon of journalistic integrity, *The Times* considered the verdict satisfactory but not the manner in which it had been obtained. It found fault with Serjeant Ballantine's unfair appeals to the powerful prejudice against Madame Rachel's high prices and 'equivocal business' – a prejudice which had had nothing whatever to do with the points at issue in the trial. Many of the newspapers were far from convinced that Mary Tucker Borradaile had been telling the truth, such had been her ludicrous and inconsistent testimony in court. 'The dirty linen of which Mrs Borradaile appears to have accumulated so much, ought not to have been washed in public', opined the *Preston Guardian*, adding that the unidentified 'William' of the letters 'promises to become as immortal as the man in the Iron Mask'.

The *Daily Telegraph* along with other papers remarked on the unaccountable silence of Madame Rachel on the existence or not of the William of the letters – though she had of course already insinuated that he was real in her own penny pamphlet – the inference being, in support of the guilty verdict, that he did not exist at all otherwise he would have been called to give evidence. The simple fact was that nobody had told the truth in court: not Rachel's daughters, not her crooked lawyer Haynes, not Mary Tucker Borradaile, not the boy Minton, nor Lord Ranelagh. In the end, the trial had been 'a very long and considered advertisement for 'Beautiful For Ever'. 'The only result of the *affaire* Borrodaile, the *Saturday Review* concluded, 'will be the doubling of Madame Rachel's "fees"'.

Aspersions continued to be cast also on Commissioner Kerr's role in it all. How had he been allowed to sit at the Old Bailey on the Rachel trial when in reality he was only a county court judge? Concern among the heavyweight press was expressed at the rigorous maintenance of the rule of English law and the right to a fair trial and it began to call into account Kerr's tendering of the 'proof' over the William letters. Their authorship was the crux of the case. If it could be shown that both parts of the correspondence had been written by the same hand, or concocted by the same brain, then all subsidiary evidence of fraud would have to be discounted and it would have buried the case for the defence. Kerr had taken it upon himself to decree that conclusive proof of the authorship of the letters lay in the use of watermarked paper and instead of allowing the defence and prosecution to argue the case between them he had withheld this until after they had both rested their cases, 'keeping it, like a stone in his sleeve, to throw at the head of the jury' as conclusive evidence of Rachel's guilt. 'Mr Commissioner Kerr committed as grave an error and as great a fault as we have for many years been compelled to record,' wrote the *Examiner*. 'We are bound to uplift our voice against an act, which, were it tolerated by public opinion, would be the first step in an innovation wholly subversive of all popular confidence in the administration of criminal justice.'

At the end of this five-day gladiatorial show, many people came away with the lingering feeling that they had not heard the whole story, this in large part because the law had prevented Rachel from giving evidence on her own behalf. Mr Serjeant Parry for the defence team later told his son that he was convinced there had been an actual 'William' on whom Mrs Borradaile had spent her money but that when faced with exposure in court she had made up the Ranelagh story, knowing that the real William would never reveal himself. Rachel had thus assisted her in her deception and had connived in using Ranelagh as a blind to deceive Borradaile's family about the true identity of her paramour. Either way, the unspoken feeling among the legal profession was that a conviction was probably just as well, for Rachel clearly knew far too much about the private lives of the many rich and influential people who made up her clientele – and the only way to ensure her silence was to lock her up. Prosecutor Ballantine was more than satisfied with the sentence, in his later memoirs condemning Rachel as 'one of the most filthy and dangerous moral pests that have existed in my time'. The suggestion was made that the charge on which Rachel was convicted would have paled into insignificance compared with other 'worse' offences in which she might have been implicated. But nobody was willing to talk; among Madame's rich and titled clientele there remained a conspiracy of silence.

Mary Tucker Borradaile meanwhile, was now reduced to beggary, with her reputation in tatters and at the mercy of the benevolence of her family back in Wales. She had been left everything her husband possessed and, as she had proudly declaimed in court, 'the right of doing what I thought proper with it'. Yet the whole of her combined assets – her plate, jewels, clothes and pension to the tune of £5,300 (about £350,000 today) – were gone, a fact which had proved, if proof were needed, that women, in the minds of the male Victorian law-makers, were incompetent at managing their own financial affairs, thus fending off the passing of the Married Women's Property Act for another twelve years. Worse, as Borradaile's solicitor George Lewis was only too well aware, the trial had fatally compromised her previous position of 'gentility'; *The Times* had condemned her as a 'Senescent Sappho' who would now be a laughing stock wherever she went.

As for Lord Ranelagh, his reputation, if he ever really had one, was permanently damaged too. His sexual predilections might have been well known among his own social circle, but they were now common knowledge and thereafter he would never be able to live down the popular nickname of 'Peeping Tom' or having the finger pointed at him in the street as 'Madame Rachel's man'. Soon after the trial he was obliged to salvage his reputation in the eyes of the South Middlesex Volunteers, who even now were being referred to as 'Mrs Borradaile's Own'. He wrote a letter to *The Times* that was syndicated across the national press in which he talked of 'the personal annoyances' to which he had been subjected in the Rachel case; it was greatly to his regret that these had been 'indirectly felt' by his regiment. He was an innocent victim, of course, having been 'singled out of a great number of gentlemen' who 'for the idlest of curiosities strolled occasionally in to Madame Rachel's shop'. He denied having heard so much as a whisper of the 'slightest immorality' attaching to no. 47a. He strongly denied prosecutor Ballantine's suggestion that improper motives had sent him to Bond Street, but by slinging mud at Ballantine he did nothing but further damage his own now grubby reputation. The press was of the opinion that he should have done the decent thing and resigned his colonelcy.

Rachel herself was, not surprisingly, very much affected by the outcome of the trial, for she had not expected so severe a sentence. She was sent immediately to Millbank Prison to pick oakum for nine months, after which the rest of her sentence, under normal circumstances, would be completed at the Female Convict Prison at Brixton. At the end of three years she would be eligible to apply for a ticket of leave. From a box at the Royal Opera House to a cell in Millbank was indeed a cruel change of circumstance, but criminals such as her, alleged the *Express* 'do not acquire the deep cunning and terrible proficiency in evil … without having served a long and painstaking apprenticeship'.

In summing up the facts of the case, the *Penny Illustrated Paper* expressed the hope that the public had 'heard the last of both Mrs Borradaile and Rachel'. But Rachel wasn't done yet, and nor, for that matter was Mary Tucker Borradaile. No sooner had the doors of Millbank slammed behind her, where even now she was receiving letters of sympathy from former clients, than word filtered out that it was the intention of Madame Rachel's solicitor Mr Roberts to 'appeal to a higher tribunal in reference to the summing up and sentence of Mr Commissioner Kerr'.

CHAPTER NINE

Closed During Alterations

IN THEIR FIGHT to take her case to appeal, Rachel's team
of lawyers, whilst already deliberating an accusation of bias
against Kerr's summing up, which might have been harder
to argue, settled instead upon a clear technical breach in
the case. At the end of October they moved for a fiat
for a Writ of Error from the Attorney General, Sir John
Karslake. The breach boiled down to a legality about the
judicial status of Mr Commissioner Kerr and his right to
sit as a judge at the Central Criminal Court, on the ground
that the court that tried Madame Rachel was not properly
constituted during the trial. English Law required that
during a criminal trial, in addition to the judge sitting on
the bench, there must be another commissioner within the
precincts of the court at all times. During Rachel's trial Kerr
was present throughout, but the second commissioner – in
fact only an alderman – had not been there continuously
but on occasion had left the precincts of the Old Bailey.

After considerable bureaucratic delays the application was finally heard on 5 December 1868 and a fiat to apply for a Writ of Error – which if won would order yet another retrial – was granted. But the case would have to wait until the new term, after Christmas.

During these protracted proceedings Rachel continued to be vilified on all sides. On 29 September her waxwork went on display at Madame Tussauds in a costume identical to the clothes she had worn at her trial. Not to be outdone, over in Ireland the Dublin Rotondo rushed to put its own waxwork on display. So popular was the Tussauds effigy, that it was temporarily moved to the Smithfield Cattle Show in December to maximize on public viewing. By the end of October 'Beautiful For Ever Waltzes' by W. Godfrey, 'superbly illustrated and perfumed by Eugene Rimmel's patent process' and based on Arthur Lloyd's popular music hall songs were on sale, free for 24 stamps from D'Allcorn at 351 Oxford St. George F. Hodgson's *Beautiful For Ever* farce was playing to packed houses every evening at the Royal Surrey Theatre and Herr Schutze at the Philharmonic Music Hall was doing likewise with his 'Masks and Faces' in which he presented satirical portraits of the personalities of the Rachel trial. Over in St Clement Danes, on 5 November, despite the earlier protestations of loyalty to Rachel from some of her former neighbours, the butcher boys of Clare Market indulged their age old annual tradition and burned two monster effigies – those of Rachel and Mrs Borradaile – on Guy Fawkes Night. Had Rachel's trial been in 1768 rather than 1868 she would undoubtedly have been persecuted as a witch.

The language of newspaper reporting was now increasingly peppered with the language of the trial with words such as 'enamelling', 'beautiful for ever' and 'Madame Rachel' widely used as a shorthand for any allusion to artifice or deception of any kind. The term 'to enamel' had already been absorbed into the language; the *Girl of the Period Miscellany* presenting a parodic 'Miss Polly Glott's Dictionary of the Future' in which the word 'enamelled' was defined as 'fleeced, cheated, deluded, swindled'.

***

Madame Rachel herself was now languishing in Victorian Britain's first National Penitentiary – Millbank – the largest prison in London, built to house 1,120 inmates. In response to a campaign for prison reform at the end of the eighteenth century, it had been opened in 1821 on the banks of the River Thames near Vauxhall Bridge (a site now occupied by the Tate Gallery). It was intended to be a model prison, but had the appearance of a forbidding, windowless fortress cum madhouse, its design presenting a geometric puzzle of an outer octagonal perimeter wall containing six pentagonal blocks laid out likes spokes in a wheel, converging in the centre where the guards and governor's house were located. The intention of the new design was to prevent the spread of disease, but unfortunately the authorities had chosen one of the worst locations in London – a dreary, sixteen-acre area of marshland close to the river which Dickens had described in *David Copperfield* as a 'melancholy waste'. Here the stench from the garbage-strewn mud of the Thames and the constantly encroaching river-damp rapidly made Millbank as gloomy, fetid and wretched as any other older prison and a place where scurvy and cholera regularly reared their head. By the 1860s it had already been superseded by the new model prison at Pentonville and had been reduced to the status of a clearing house for convicted prisoners before they were sent on to other establishments. Women were held in the third of the prison's six pentagons, which collectively covered three miles of serpentine passages in which even the warders sometimes got lost. The cells, located far from daylight and fresh air with only a feeble gaslight, contained a small table, a hammock rather than a proper bed, a coarse rug, a wooden slop tub with a lid and, of course, a Bible. Prisoners spent their days here picking oakum and making clothes and mail bags, stopping only for a meal of beef and potatoes at midday or simply plain bread and gruel in the evenings. For the first four months of her sentence Rachel was to be held in solitary confinement in the Third Pentagon, prior to a transfer to the more liberal regime of Brixton Women's Prison, south of the river.

In a story aimed at edifying its readers about the work of the Victorian correctional system, the *Illustrated Police News* in December sent one of its reporters to spend 'Two Hours in Millbank Prison'. His article began as a homily on this supposedly state of the art prison, describing the regime and expressing confidence in its industrial training programme as being reformative of those unfortunate creatures now incarcerated there. Within Millbank he saw women prisoners 'scrubbing like charwomen, or industriously engaged in needlework ... or in the laundry'. But, 'How are the mighty fallen!', the reporter proclaimed, for here, 'surrounded by a perfume of soapsuds instead of the fragrant "waters of Jordan"' was that 'arch-prisoner', Madame Rachel. 'Shorn of chignon, unenamelled, and attired in a costume rather different from that in which she flaunted in her box at the opera a few seasons back', she was now clad in the regulation prison garb of dull brown woollen dress, check apron and plain cotton cap. The reporter took great delight in celebrating the fact that Rachel was obliged to wash her own dirty linen in the Millbank laundry – 'a task she would possibly now be only too happy to perform at home in Bond-Street'.

Madame Rachel was allowed out of Millbank on 22 December 1868 to hear yet another application for bail. She appeared visibly weak and was assisted by Rachel and Leontie and allowed to sit in a room nearby from which the public were excluded. Her friend Thomas Austin Stack, the boot manufacturer, once more offered to stand bail, having been implored to do so by Leontie, this time with a Mr S. L. Solomon, a picture dealer of 39 Old Bond Street, who also had known Rachel for some years.

This time the judge accepted the bail, thus immediately defusing the *Illustrated Police News*'s triumphant leader article of a few days earlier, which had revelled in Rachel's reduction to prison laundress. Just before Christmas 1868, pending the hearing of her appeal on the Writ of Error, and just as the pantomime season was gearing up to satirize her mercilessly, Rachel was released. She enjoyed barely a month of untrammelled freedom before, at the end of January 1869, she was once more back in the news when Rachel junior submitted a lengthy affidavit to the court of the Queen's Bench for an order against her mother's solicitor and financial agent James Haynes. In it she alleged misconduct and the misappropriation of Madame Rachel's money during his representation of her business interests since 1862, as well as conspiring to procure her conviction. During that time Madame Rachel had made considerable amounts of money; Haynes, it was alleged, was a 'designing attorney' who had taken advantage of Madame Rachel's inability to write in order to siphon off some £6,000 during his various monetary transactions of her behalf. Aside from risking her money in worthless investments such as the 'Horse Island Mining Company' in Ireland, he had also appropriated some of the monies received from Mrs Borradaile that had been due to Madame Rachel. A request was now made by Rachel's solicitor Mr Gibbons that Haynes be struck off the rolls. When her affidavit was read out in court on 30 January, it contained a surprising revelation: Mary Tucker Borradaile had not been a stranger to her on that first visit in 1864. She had first become one of Madame Rachel's customers twenty years previously when, in her business as a wardrobe dealer, she had sent articles of clothing out to Mrs Borradaile in India. She also now tried to distance herself from her 'husband' Phillip Leverson, claiming that he was an 'imbecile' and that she had not known where he lived 'for some years'. In response, George Lewis arranged to interview Leverson and found him to be a 'nice, intelligent man' who exhibited, so he said, 'a marked activity of the mind'.

When questioned in court about the details of her income and her customers, Madame Rachel declined to name any names, as her daughter had in previous court appearances: 'My ladies are ladies of the world, and it would ruin me and my family to expose their names,' she said, adding that she refused to do so 'from motives of delicacy'. Suffice it to say, however, that one lady in 1862 had spent £1,000 with her; Countess – had paid her £1,000 in notes and gold for beauty treatments; there were several other ladies from whom she had earned £500-£1,000, in addition to which she 'also took thousands over the counter' in her day to day sales of beauty products at the salon. When again pressed to give the names of these ladies she adamantly refused: her children, she said, 'must live after her'. In the run up to the hearing of the Writ of Error it was clear that the intention of this latest case was to show that Rachel had not received the money she had been sentenced for feloniously receiving, in a bid to set up a favourable attitude to her appeal. The case against Haynes was adjourned till 21 February. But it was not until 6 May that the Chief Justice finally dismissed the charge, stating that there was much evidence during the years when it was alleged that Haynes had been fleecing Rachel (1861–66) that she and her family were in fact in straitened circumstances and not making as much money as she claimed.

In early January that year several newspapers had noted that the famous shop in Bond Street was now locked up but that Madame Rachel's two daughters were busy transferring the business to Paris. When Rachel came out on bail rumours abounded that she was about to resume business in Bond Street herself. Meanwhile, a notice had been posted over the door of no. 47a announcing that the premises was 'closed for alterations', in response to which a street boy had chalked up 'Beware of the Paint'. And then, in early March, even while Rachel's solicitor was still arguing in court over the summons against Haynes, Londoners were surprised to be told of a great and impending event:

the 'splendid contents' of Madame Rachel's residence at Maddox Street and her shop at New Bond Street were to be sold off at auction by Messrs George and Whitehead of Kilburn. Placards went up around London announcing the fact. Madame, it transpired, urgently needed to raise funds to pay her continuing legal bills.

The shilling catalogue – nothing came free with Rachel – claimed to offer purchasers an extraordinary range of fine furniture: the drawing room at Maddox Street contained 'a superb carved and gilt suite covered in crimson ... console glasses, girandoles [ornamental candlesticks], needlework, carpets, inlaid centre and occasional tables of the rarest excellence and unparalleled beauty, rare and costly Sèvres tables on ebony stands, Indian, Japanese, and Chinese tables – all exquisitely made and rare.' The dining room offered more fine pieces: 'a matchless oak sideboard, artistically carved with lofty plate glass back, a handsome set of carved oak chairs, a very rare and valuable clock, and a pair of massive candelabra formerly belonging to the Emperor of the French, and a very valuable and magnificent pair of incense burners, on costly ebony stands, formerly the property of the King of Delhi.' The list went on and on, offering works of art, articles of vertu 'many of them being presentations from Madame Rachel's distinguished patronesses' ... a 'brilliant toned piano', a compass by Kirkman, 1,000 volumes of books, a cellar of the finest wines,' all giving a clear indication that Rachel had spared no expense in impressing her clients with her exclusivity and wealth.

The viewings were crowded out at Maddox Street and the sale which began on Monday 15 March attracted large numbers of buyers and spectators, with crowds of the hoi polloi outside on the street attempting to gain entry, which was permitted by programme only. The police had to be called in to prevent a riot. Inside, at the downstairs front room-room window sat Madame Rachel herself and her two daughters, 'all gracefully attired' in dark but very rich dresses for the occasion and each 'paying the closest attention to the traffic in catalogues', piling the money up on the table in front of them as they took it. Many of those inside at the auction, whilst amazed at the sheer amount of objects crammed into a relatively small house, noted that some of them were cheap nick-nacks and fancy articles of Parisian or English manufacture. They doubted the authenticity of some of the more outlandish pieces on offer, which seemed positively tawdry; the gold and crimson furniture in the 'drawing room' was, it was claimed, 'tarnished and dingy'. It was clear from the detailed itemising of the lots that sales to souvenir hunters were anticipated, with 'Lot 215, Madame Rachel's dinner bell', and Lot 250, her 'pen wiper, ink stand and blotting case' – no use to Madame herself of course, but no doubt the source of some of the infamous 'Dear William' letters scribbled by Mrs Borradaile – being among the most desired items. In the end, however, the public weren't duped by the inflated claims of the catalogue and the prices paid were well below those expected.

Even as Rachel and her daughters were counting the money made at the contents sale disaster struck. 'Once again the Rachel case is pressed upon the public,' intoned the *Birmingham Daily Post* gloomily, announcing that Thomas Stack having seen the sale of Rachel's house contents going ahead, became convinced that she was about to take her money and abscond to Paris, leaving him liable. He withdrew his bail, even though Rachel denied that this was the case; the property being sold was her daughter Rachel's she claimed, she having started the business in Rachel junior's name The sale had raised £500 of which she had given £100 to Mr Stack towards her bail. Nevertheless, Madame Rachel was immediately arrested at Maddox Street. In court she 'implored' that she be sent to Newgate – rather than the inhospitable Millbank, where her poor health had been seriously undermined – pending judgment on the Writ of Error, and she thanked the judge for his 'kind consideration' when he agreed. Soon after, a fresh application for bail by Rachel's solicitor, opposed by George Lewis on behalf of the Crown and instructed by the Treasury, was immediately rejected. Two more sureties went before the judge on 31 March, upon which Lewis objected to one of them and they too were turned down. By 13 April, with all her bail applications rejected, it seemed likely that Rachel would have to remain in Newgate till her case was heard, but the next sessions was already very busy: of 53 cases due to be heard at the Court of Queen' Bench, hers was number 42. On 22 April an application was therefore made to advance the date of her hearing. The Chief Justice agreed that her case, which had already dragged on far too long, should be given special priority within the next few days. Meanwhile, a succession of people with names similar to those who had offered to stand bail and had been rejected, hastened to disassociate themselves from the case. It prompted *Punch* to observe that 'the world is divided into three classes: men, women, and people who have written to the papers to say they didn't give bail for Mother Rachel.'

Punch had had more than enough of it all. It's editor didn't mince his words in expressing a highly misogynist, anti-Semitic line in ennui: 'Will no one abolish, eliminate, improve off the face of creation, or otherwise get rid of that horrible old convicted swindler, Sarah Leverson *alias* Rachel and her very offensive brood?', it asked on 24 March, complaining that 'this notorious, animated pestilence … will persist in coming before the public, either on her own accord or that of others.' It was time to put an end to things: 'this libel on womanhood should no longer be thrust down the throats of newspaper readers already utterly nauseated with the loathsome mouthful.'

In the same week, *Punch's* sister journal, *Judy*, followed up with its own personal plea:

> Madame Rachel, Madame Rachel,
> Cease your applications, pray,
> Let's be spared your wretched name, ma'am.
> If it's only for a day.
>
> Your appearance in the papers,
> Ev'ry morn, and ev'ry night,
> We have borne with too much patience,
> We must quench your *baleful* light.
>
> Rows with lawyers, Bond-street auctions,
> Show you in your colours true;
> And believe us when we say, now,
> Ev'rybody's sick of you.
>
> Mother Leverson, remember,
> Your disguise at best was thin;
> The enamel has worn off, and
> Underneath we see the skin.

Most of the papers were gratified when Rachel was locked up again in Newgate and once more out of sight and hopefully out of mind, but they had not reckoned on Mary Tucker Borradaile who suddenly reappeared on the scene, this time as the defendant in a case called on the Home Circuit at Kingston Assizes, Surrey on 30 March.

She was taken to court on a summons by her 'literary agent', a Miss Sarah Sutton, who had met and befriended her when they had both been in Whitecross Street debtors' prison in 1866. Sutton, who claimed to have taken pity on Borradaile at the time, had offered to help her prepare her case against Rachel when she had said she felt unable to do so. She claimed to be a 'literary and monetary agent', formerly editor and proprietor of the *London Review* (a fact soon denied in *The Times* by its current manager) on which she had lost money and had landed up in Whitecross Street in June 1866 after standing security for a friend who had defaulted on a debt. In jail Mrs Borradaile had been only too glad to avail herself of Sutton's 'superior ability' in drawing up her case and 'making it intelligible for the court', though Sutton was vigorously contemptuous of her lack of common sense and told her 'hundreds of times' what a fool she was. Mrs Borradaile in her opinion was profoundly unsophisticated and would only have made a good wife for a 'country clergyman'. The two women had, claimed Sutton, agreed on a fee of a guinea a day, plus a percentage of any money won or recouped from Rachel in court. But Sutton now claimed in court that Mrs Borradaile had failed to pay her for services rendered, to the tune of £160 18s, which included her best efforts in 'releasing Mrs Borradaile from the toils of the serpent Madame Rachel',

Rachel having 'so mystified everything' that Mrs Borradaile had been unable to make anyone understand her story.

Having assisted her through these tortuous preliminaries, and having spent £25 of her own money in travelling about by omnibus, cab and railway on her behalf, Sutton had forwarded her bill for settlement. Mrs Borradaile's solicitor claimed the costs were absurd and inflated; his client had never agreed to pay anything to Sutton who had appeared to be offering help as a friend. She had foisted herself on the gullible Borradaile and had kept no proper accounts to prove her expenditure. The jury were out for a good two hours, no doubt pondering whether the witless Borradaile deserved any pity for a display of yet more unconscionable folly, or if the predatory Sutton, as much of a swindler as Rachel, should be believed in her extortionate claim. In the end they awarded Sutton a mere £5 in compensation. A few days later she moved for a new trial on the ground of misdirection by the judge but it was promptly rejected. She and the penniless Borradaile were both left to cover their own costs.

As Mary Tucker Borradaile at last finally faded from view and from the newspapers, to live out the remainder of her life in obscurity till her death in Paris in 1899 at the age of 80, Madame Rachel's appeal for a Writ of Error now came before the Court of the Queen's Bench at Westminster. A long and legally tortuous hearing was held on 1 May before the Lord Chief Justice and two other judges, the deliberations reported in agonizing detail by *The Times*, but the legal technicalities and jargon of the case were clearly beyond the comprehension of the ordinary public. Ten days later, in the case of Leverson v The Queen, a judgment for the Crown was delivered. Madame Rachel's conviction was upheld and she was now transferred from Newgate back to Millbank to serve out the remainder of her five-year sentence.

Her return to jail coincided with a final coda to the Borradaile case when Rachel junior went back to court on 18 and 21 June on her mother's behalf in pursuit of their erstwhile friend Mr Stack who had withdrawn his offer of bail back in March. Litigation was now clearly in the blood of the Levison family and with it an instinct for performance in the witness box. Rachel junior appeared in court looking appropriately solemn and dressed in black, her features partially covered by a thick veil, her objective to recover the £100 in money and goods that the family had advanced to Stack towards the cost of her mother's bail. As additional security for the bail, Rachel junior had handed over various documents and deeds as well as, at Stack's insistence, a valuable leather travelling trunk, cigar case and some expensive lace. In court, she was adamant that her mother had had no intention of fleeing to Paris after the house sale. True, 'she fretted much to see her children who were at school in Saint Cloud' but she would not do so, for fear of 'what would be said about it,' she alleged. Meanwhile, she Rachel junior, was still in the process of pawning and selling her possessions to pay for her mother's now enormous legal expenses. The case may for once have gone in favour of Rachel and her mother but she had no sooner left court with a judgment for £120 in damages against Thomas Stack than her own solicitor, Mr Wilding, slapped an immediate summons on her for professional services owed amounting to £18.3s. In court Rachel junior was given fourteen days to pay.

The last gasp in the long running Madame Rachel saga, which had now dominated the press for fourteen months solid, came in early August 1869 when the *Irish Times* reported that another 'lady of good family and position in the north of Ireland' had announced that she was anxious to 'slap a claim' on Rachel. But by now the entire legal profession as well as the prison authorities had had enough. The lady concerned – a Mrs McNeil, who was, it transpired, 'connected by marriage to a member of the House of Lords' – had finally plucked up the courage to lodge a claim against Rachel for restitution of £2,000 supposedly advanced to her against various beauty treatments. To do so she would require access to Millbank being granted for her solicitor to serve the writ personally on Rachel. The authorities deemed that there was nothing to be gained from such a futile exercise. The application was refused and Madame Rachel was at last left to ponder the error of her ways in jail.

***

By December 1869 the signs had come down at the salon at no. 47a New Bond Street which had become the premises of Mr Tibbey the green grocer. It might no longer be possible to be made beautiful forever there by Madame herself, but Rachel junior and her sister Leontie had nevertheless been busy all year keeping the cosmetics franchise alive. It was, after all, the only living they knew. After the auction in March, Rachel junior had advertised herself as 'Mlle Rachel' in *The Times,* still citing the famous 47a New Bond Street address for the recognition value it held, but announcing that her 'Guinea Box of Preparations for the Season' was now available by post from Vere Street, Oxford Street, where she could be consulted daily between ten and four. A few months later she was offering ladies her personal attendance 'at their own residences', no doubt because her own premises were not up to her mother's former expensive standards. The prices had come down and so too had the upmarket address – in London at least – but the claims remained the same for the various exotic beauty washes and preparations. And now, in Paris, Mlle Rachel was pleased to inform her lady patronesses, her sister 'Mlle Léontine Rachel' was also available for consultations – at 25 rue de Choiseul.

The Paris venture, however, was short-lived. For, barely

a year later, in July 1870 the Franco-Prussian War broke out, making Paris a dangerous place to be, particularly Saint Cloud, a popular upmarket suburb, where Rachel's three youngest children were being expensively educated. The war was a catastrophe for Louis Napoleon's government and after a crushing defeat by the Prussians at the Battle of Sedan in September he was deposed and a Third Republic declared. During the Siege of Paris that followed until the end of January 1871, the whole city was subjected to heavy artillery shelling. The French government had retreated to Versailles in the south-west of the city – beyond Saint Cloud, which was directly in the line of fire and was half reduced to ruins by the artillery fire. It may well be that Madame Rachel's house there was damaged or even destroyed at this time. After the armistice with Prussia the new French government had had to take on the Paris Commune of rebellious workers and socialists who had barricaded the city in protest at the new government and held out until crushed at the end of May 1871.

The war clearly disrupted David Levison's medical studies and the business on rue de Choiseul, too. With their mother now in jail, he and Rachel junior took responsibility for their younger siblings who all returned to London. The 1871 census taken on 2 April recorded David, now studying medicine at University College, living in Burghley Road, Kentish Town, with his brothers Arthur (Aaron) and Harry (Abraham) and younger sister Elise (Elizabeth);

Rachel junior, no longer the celebrated enameller of ladies faces, now described herself as merely a 'housekeeper'. Young Arthur, aged seventeen, and – no doubt through Madame Rachel's Drury Lane connections – was working as a limelighter in the theatre. Hannah had married the previous year and left home. But there was no sign of Léontine. Had she remained in Paris by choice or been trapped by the war?

***

Over at Millbank Penitentiary, at some point between September 1869 and her release, Madame Rachel's health once again took a turn for the worse and she was transferred to the female wing of the new Woking Invalid Convict Prison, situated thirty-six miles south of London at Knaphill in Surrey. It was the first prison of its kind, specifically opened in 1860 for prisoners suffering from mental and physical illness. Built on sixty-four acres of heathland bought from the London Necropolis Company which owned nearby Brookwood Cemetery, it had added a female wing in 1869. There had been, according to Inspector of Prisons, Arthur Griffiths, universal rejoicing the day Madame Rachel was transferred from Millbank. She had had no friends there, he observed, 'and this in spite of her profuse promises to make the matrons "beautiful for ever"'; nor had she done a good job when, with her experience in cosmetics, she was asked to take a plaster cast of a prisoner's head, when she had put the wax on too hot and scalded him.

During her time at Woking, Rachel would have been put to work in the prison kitchens or given sewing – prison and school uniforms – or knitting and even gardening. But for much of the time she was unwell and unable to undertake arduous work. Now reduced to the prison uniform of poke bonnet, plaid shawl and blue serge gown, she may again, when health permitted, have worked in the laundry. As at Millbank, the work was arduous and involved handling soiled clothes and bedding from the prison infirmary that had come into contact with all kinds of contagious diseases from chronically sick prisoners. It was also done in perpetually damp and steamy conditions. This meant that inmates returned to their cells at the end of each day in wet clothes which had to dry overnight on a nail or be worn again, still damp, the following morning. But at least conditions here were more tolerable – the cells being larger, lighter and more airy. Indeed, so comfortable was Woking compared to other prisons, that it was nicknamed the 'Thieves' Palace' and had a recreation room, providing 'draughts, dominoes, sofas, and paintings on the wall, (not to mention an aviary)'.

A further perk at Woking was a craft specialism to which some of the women were put to work: the making of black and white mosaic tiles. The work was overseen there for a while by its most adept female inmate, Constance Kent (convicted of the Road House murder in 1865), who spent part of her sentence at Woking. Women inmates could earn as much as 1s. 2d. a day breaking up and shaping pieces of discarded marble to be used in mosaic floors for churches, museums and other public institutions. At some point, because her health was rated 'delicate' by the prison surgeon, Rachel was put to work at this less arduous work, during which she crossed paths with Kent, who later remarked that she had been a 'hopelessly bad pupil'; Madame Rachel had, it appeared, 'failed as signally in her efforts to embellish a floor as she had to beautify her numerous and credulous customers'.

As a result of her good conduct in prison and also her failing health, on 20 April 1872 Madame Rachel was released from Woking on licence after serving just over three of her five years in jail. But there was no return to Mayfair. This time she retreated to her son David's house at Kentish Town, expressing her intention to leave for Paris as soon as she could in order to regain her health. She had not of course accounted for the terms of her ticket of leave, under which she was obliged to report in person to a district police station once a month and was therefore forced to remain in England.

Nothing was heard of her for a while. And then, one day, Madame Rachel made an impromptu visit to William Morrish, governor of Millbank, one of the few prisoners ever to voluntarily return to their place of incarceration. She never explained the purpose of her visit but turned up 'dressed in satin and ostrich feathers', was shown into Morrish's office and 'sat and talked idly for some time'. The prison authorities assumed it was her way of cocking a snook at them all, out of a desire to 'astonish her former gaolers by her splendour'. She clearly had no intention at all of playing the part Victorian society demanded of her – that of the reformed sinner.

Eight months after her release from Woking, an advertisement appeared, almost unnoticed, in the *Era*:

> Madame Rachel's Royal Arabian toilet preparations which render the Hair, Teeth and Complexion beautiful beyond comparison, can only be obtained at her sole agents, Mr T. Arthur (from the rue de la Paix Paris and New York), 33 Russell Street, Covent Garden, opposite the Royal Entrance of Drury Lane Theatre. Arabian Perfumers to the Royal Courts of Europe. By Special Appointment.

An unrepentant Madame Rachel was back in business.

CHAPTER TEN

Gone to Ground

MADAME RACHEL MAY have been once more peddling her beauty products in London, but it clearly was in considerably restricted circumstances that she attempted to regain her lost credibility and clientele at the end of 1872. 'Madame Rachel is at large once more,' noted the *Belfast News-Letter*, 'and following some branches of her trade,' but for a while no one knew exactly where or how. Many of Rachel's old customers – and some new ones – apparently had 'welcomed her with open arms', but her former experiences had taught Rachel this time 'to confine her business within what admirers style "legitimate bounds"'. She might be once more making ladies beautiful for ever, but that, it seemed, was as far as it went. Previously, Rachel's advertisements had been a regular feature of *The Times*, but this time, with no talk of expensive Mayfair premises, she eschewed its small ad columns, operating from a series of temporary addresses. In 1874 she was briefly listed in the London directory as a perfumer, based at 35 Russell Street, Covent Garden, having deemed it more sensible – and probably more lucrative – to return at first to her old network of contacts in her former stomping ground of Drury Lane.

One thing at least had not changed with Rachel and that was her absolute conviction – as she projected it to her clients – that *her* preparations were the best. As far as she was concerned, she was still sole master of the mysterious art of enamelling and on leaving jail she expressed her disgust 'and in no measured terms either' at the 'vulgar imitations of her art' that had 'sprung up on all sides during her temporary retirement from public life.' She was shocked, she said, at the 'daubed specimens' she now saw on the streets whenever she went out. Nevertheless her business operations remained very low key for some time. She didn't advertise at all between December 1872 and November 1876, no doubt relying on word of mouth and her old clientele. Then, from November 1876 to April 1877 a new series of advertisements, offering the old familiar Madame Rachel nostrums – of Youth and Beauty Enamel, Peach Blossom Wash, Alabaster Powder, Armenian Liquid, Sultana's Cream, Golden Hair Wash and Arabian Soaps – appeared in the *Era*, announcing that she could now be consulted at 29 Duke Street (by her aristocratic and wealthy clients), whilst 'the Theatrical Profession' should apply to her agent, Hartnoll, at 76 Tichbourne Street,

Haymarket. Rachel clearly intended to set boundaries of respectability between her old clients and hoped-for new ones. Duke Street, a few blocks east of New Bond Street, and to the north of Grosvenor Square, was not quite as upmarket as her previous premises but it was in the right area for the better class of person Rachel now needed to give new credibility to her revived cosmetics franchise. She clearly had ambitions for rebuilding the business, for her advertisements also announced that 'Agents' were required 'everywhere'. But whilst she may have thought she had lived down her notoriety at last, she had not quite been forgotten. At Smithfield Club Cattle Show that December a prize cow named Madame Rachel won in the Hereford Heifers class.

One of the reasons Rachel seemed so preoccupied with achieving a degree of respectability and avoiding scandal at this time was in order to protect the burgeoning career of her third daughter Hannah, who had, from an early age, shown a talent for singing. While Rachel had been in jail, Hannah had married at the age of only twenty; her husband was a silk merchant named Edward Cooke Turner who was fifteen years older than herself. She had till then been living with her brother David and the other children in Kentish Town. Léontine, back in England during the Franco-Prussian War, was a witness at the wedding. But Hannah had not had a Jewish ceremony; the couple had married by licence at St Thomas's parish church in

Camden on Christmas Eve 1870. Rachel junior followed her sister into wedlock in 1871 – marrying out of the faith like Hannah, by licence, in a civil ceremony at St Pancras Register Office. Her husband, Llewellyn George Pritchard, was a civil engineer, born to a British officer and circuit judge in Madras, India.

Perhaps both marriages were a conscious step by Hannah and Rachel towards a degree of respectability, loosening themselves from the bonds, if not the social stigma, of their Jewishness and with it their mother's pernicious influence. After her 1871 marriage Rachel appears to have adopted a new given name of 'Ursula'. As the uncontroversial Mrs Lewellyn Pritchard, she disappeared into obscurity. Hannah might have done likewise had she not set her heart upon a career as a professional singer. On 18 September 1872, as 'Mrs Hannah Turner', she auditioned for the singing class at the Royal Academy of Music, whose teachers noted that she had a 'nice voice'. At the academy's original premises in Tenterden Street, off Oxford Street, she studied for the next three years under Signor Alberto Randegger, an Italian-born composer, conductor and singing teacher, who had been appointed professor of singing at the Royal Academy of Music in 1868. Whilst there, she met and befriended a fellow student, Thekla Fischer, from Baden in Germany, who in 1876 married her brother David and gave birth to a son, Harold, a year later. Hannah graduated with a silver medal in the July graduation examinations of

1877. She had by then already taken her first professional steps by joining William Carter's choir at the Royal Albert Hall; but her solo professional debut was not to come until the end of 1877.

***

After Hannah's wedding, and with the rebels of the Paris Commune now defeated, Léontine had been eager to return to France to resume her side of the cosmetics business. If her mother's London franchise was in temporary decline, the Paris end of things seemed to be very much on the ascendant. Like her mother, the ambitious Léontine never thought small. After briefly renting premises at 18 avenue du roi de Rome, she transferred to a *boutique* at the very chic address of no. 10 rue de la Paix, in the most fashionable part of Paris, equivalent to London's Bond Street and full of highly desirable milliners, dressmakers and jewellers. From here she supervised the continuing Parisian education of her youngest sister Elise, now aged sixteen (it is not known whether the two boys Abraham and Aaron were with them). Léontine had plenty of Levison *chutzpah* when it came to self-promotion: in 1872 she took a high profile advertisement in the famous *Galignani's New Paris Guide*, promising to restore 'youth and beauty' to ladies 'whose complexions have been spoilt by the application of Cosmetics'; a similar advertisement appeared in the

April number of *Paris Mode*. Under her French persona of 'Léontine Rachel' she offered her 'celebrated alabaster wash and powder' prepared by her own fair hands at the rue de la Paix, adding with a now familiar, brazen flourish that she was 'Perfumer to the Courts of Europe'. By 1874 the premises was listed in the Bottin de Commerce in Paris as a *Parfumerie Anglaise*; Léontine Rachel's salon was the talk of the town.

It was then, in April 1874, that word came from Madame Rachel in London that Elise should return to England. Now eighteen, she had spent much of the last three years in France and dreaded the thought of going back; she was happy and settled and England only had unhappy associations with the scandal surrounding her mother. But there was another more pressing reason that made her resist her mother's call: she was in love and did not want to leave Paris. Clearly Rachel was adamant, for on 10 April Léontine escorted her sister to the Gare du Nord in good time for the train for the French coast and the ferry to England. Six days later word reached Léontine from England that Elise had never arrived.

There was only one place people went in those days to report or seek out a missing person – and that was the Paris Morgue. Located behind Notre Dame Cathedral on the quai de l'Archevêché, it was where all of Paris's anonymous dead were taken until, hopefully, identified. The Préfecture de Police deemed it useful in determining the speedy identification of corpses to put them, naked (except for a discreet smoked glass screen covering their genitals), twelve at a time, on public display. The corpses lay there on black marble slabs sloping towards the onlookers behind a glass window, with a constant stream of water playing over them to keep them fresh. Behind them, the pathetic remnants of the clothes they had been wearing when found hung on hooks on the wall. By the time of Elise's disappearance the Paris Morgue was the number one tourist attraction – a place of voyeuristic theatrical entertainment, visited by the young and old of every profession and social class, and, like public executions, affordable to all.

Here, on 16 April, Léontine's description of her sister and the clothes she had been wearing the day she left were carefully entered in the 'Registre des Disparues' (Register of the Disappeared) pending either her reappearance or the discovery of her corpse. Elise was slender, 5 foot 2, with chestnut hair, a straight nose and large brown eyes. She had one distinguishing feature – a missing tooth in the front of her upper jaw. She had been wearing a fringed alpaca coat, a black dress and buttoned boots, finished off with a small round hat of green silk and with black lace around her neck. The only other thing she had had on her was a ticket for the train to London.

Five days later, the white and bloated corpse of Elise Levison was pulled out of the Canal Saint Martin near the Gare du Nord, from where she should have got on the train that day. It was taken to the nearby Hôpital Saint Martin and from there to the morgue to await identification. But it was not till 10. a.m. on the morning of 24 April, two weeks after Elise had drowned, that Léontine discovered her sister there. The register lists the last pathetic details of Elise's short, sad life and, most plaintive of all, records the presumed cause of her suicide in that inimitable French phrase – 'chagrins d'amour'.

The *Jewish World* broke the news of Elise's death in England – having identified her to its readers as the daughter of the 'well-known Madame Rachel'. She had, apparently, thrown herself into the river 'within an hour or so of her contemplated departure from Paris'. As soon as the body was released for burial it was interred, despite official Jewish disapproval of suicide, with all the customary funeral rites, in the Jewish cemetery at Ivry outside Paris. But whether Madame Rachel or any of Elise's siblings other than Léontine were there to bid her farewell we do not know.

The family had barely had time to come to terms with this terrible blow than another struck them. Rachel junior, now Mrs Pritchard and living comfortably near Regents Park, died unexpectedly on 1 September – only five months after her sister Elise – of peritonitis, possibly the result of a burst appendix. She was only thirty-three. Her brother David, still studying medicine, was at her bedside when she died suggesting that her husband, who was now working as a journalist, had been away on business at the time.

***

The horrifying suicide of Elise followed so soon after by the tragic loss of Rachel junior explains the absence of Madame Rachel from the advertising columns of the newspapers for the next couple of years. Her health and mental state were devastated by their loss and she was ill for some time, able only to maintain the business intermittently. The one consolation in her grief must have been the promising career of her third daughter Hannah.

Just after Christmas 1877, and now newly incarnated under the professional name of Hélène Crosmond, Hannah Levison stepped out on to the stage at Her Majesty's Theatre in the Haymarket as the heroine Betly in Adolphe Adam's operetta *Le Chalet*. The part was a fairly insignificant one that did not stretch her vocally, but the music critic of the *Graphic* noted, of the debutante soprano, that she had clearly studied 'with care' and although nervous was someone 'from whom a great deal may reasonably be expected'; her performance had won the 'unqualified approval of the house'. Hélène's first important part in a major opera followed in February 1878, taking the lead as Marguerite in Gounod's then extremely popular opera, *Faust*. Here she sang to great effect in a much more difficult role, thought the *Daily News*, especially excelling in the 'Jewel Song', which was 'given with much brilliancy and impulse'; not only that, but 'Mdlle Crosmond' had that rare gift in a

singer: 'an aptitude for dramatic expression'. She had greatly distinguished herself both as vocalist and actress agreed
the *Pall Mall Gazette*. The critic of *The Times* thought that
as Marguerite she had shown herself equal to the occasion
with her 'good stage presence and unquestionable intelligence'. Soon afterwards, Hélène was snapped up by the
English impresario, James Henry Mapleson, for his Grand
Italian Opera Company. On tour, she reprised her role in
Faust and took the part of Donna Anna in *Don Giovanni*
at the Theatre Royal, Edinburgh, where again her performance was singled out by the critics; at the end of the tour
she returned to London for the opera season, to play the
lead in Balfe's *Il Talismano*.

By now Hélène, who was living with her husband in the
smart London suburb of St John's Wood, had top billing
in newspaper advertisements for Mapleson's Company
as a 'principal artiste'. Everything boded well for her
professional future. And then, at the end of February 1878,
her promising career was rocked overnight by scandal.

The old adage that the 'burned child fears the fire' had
evidently had no effect on her mother. Experience had
taught Madame Rachel that, once back in business, sooner
or later 'the flies would come to the web of beauty.' And so
they had, and with it, inevitably, Rachel's magpie-like love
of jewels had been reawakened, leading her once more
to overreach herself. Having purloined the jewels of her
latest victim in lieu of unpaid bills, she now found herself

again on a charge – of deception and fraud. All the socially crippling and embarrassing past history that the Levison family had spent the last eight years trying to live down had come back to haunt them.

CHAPTER ELEVEN

A Show for Idle Women

CECILIA MARIA DE CANDIA PEARSE was no silly, twittering Mary Tucker Borradaile. The latest in the long line of Madame Rachel's disaffected clients, she was twenty-four years old, a noted beauty and a woman of some social standing, respected for her extensive work for charitable causes. She and her husband were members of the same artistic circles as the cultured George Lewis and his socialite wife Elizabeth, numbering among their friends the artists Whistler, Singer Sargent and Burne Jones and the writer Oscar Wilde.

Something of an amateur singer herself, Cecilia had impeccable, top drawer connections in the world of opera. She was the daughter of Mario – probably one of the greatest tenors of the nineteenth century. An Italian marquis, Giovanni Matteo de Candia was already a star of opera in France and Italy when he had gained his greatest triumphs at the Royal Opera House Covent Garden during 1847-67 and again in 1871 the year of his retirement. In 1856 he had married the equally famous Italian soprano Giulia Grisi, another great favourite with London opera goers including Queen Victoria, who regularly attended her performances at Covent Garden as a young woman. Cecilia's friend, the painter Louise Jopling, whose artist husband Joseph had painted her portrait, thought her 'one of the most charming of women'. She had an exquisite singing voice and although she had 'inherited in no small degree the fascination' of her parents she had decided against a professional singing career, Jopling of the opinion that her voice was 'too delicate for public life'. But in private, among friends, she enchanted all her listeners.

By 1878 Cecilia was comfortably married to a city stockbroker, Godfrey Pearse and lived in Ebury Street, Pimlico, with a second residence in Brighton. She was prompted, so she later claimed, to first visit Rachel's salon at Duke Street, because her doctor happened to have a surgery nearby in the same street. She had noticed the sign 'Arabian Perfumer to the Queen' above the front door – though she denied ever having heard of Rachel prior to her first visit – and dropped in one day to take a look. She continued to visit occasionally thereafter, and after spending time in Rome in 1877, visited her again that December at her new premises at 153 Great Portland Street. Here Rachel, still with the same domineering manner and dressed as ostentatiously as ever in black silk, occupied the first floor and kitchen downstairs, using the upstairs front room as a salon; the back rooms were a bedroom and sitting room.

The pattern of entrapment that followed Cecilia Pearse's first visit was a familiar one. When Cecilia expressed concern about her 'poor complexion', Rachel had offered to 'finish' her, suggesting a course of treatments guaranteed to 'renovate' her appearance – and of course, as usual extended credit. Her beauty treatments would make Mrs Pearse look as young as she was now, even at 60. How old did she think Rachel was? Eighty-five, she claimed – and thus a living testimony to the efficacy of her own face washes and creams. In any case, Rachel confided to Cecilia, being herself related to the great tragedienne, Mademoiselle Rachel – whose bust even now graced her salon as well as a portrait in the window – she would be more than proud to enlist her finest arts in beautifying the daughter of the legendary Signor Mario.

On her second visit to Rachel at Great Portland Street, Cecilia Pearse had met Hélène Crosmond who had been there visiting her mother. It's possible the two women may already have had a nodding acquaintance from their association with the musical world; on meeting Cecilia that day, Hélène had asked her to take part in an amateur concert for the Turkish Compassionate Fund (for victims of the recent Russo-Turkish War). When the Turkish concert fell through Hélène informed Cecilia that she and her sister-in-law, Thekla, who was also a singer were using all their

influence with theatrical managers and professional singers
to set up a benefit concert for Cecilia's father, Signor
Mario, who since his retirement had been in some financial
difficulty. Madame Rachel claimed later to have used her
own personal influence to obtain the Queen's patronage
for the benefit from clients who were ladies in waiting at
court.

Like all Rachel's apprehensive patronesses, Cecilia was
adamant that her visits to her should be kept 'quite dark'
from her husband. But, once started, when she had hesitated
over the ongoing cost of the treatments Rachel agreed, as
Mrs Pearse was 'a friend of my daughter', to drop her price
from her usual £1,000 to a mere £200 – which for her was
extremely cheap. But even this amount, in comparative
terms today, was equivalent to some £14,000. Nevertheless
Cecilia had been pleased with the initial results: 'my face
improves every day' she wrote to Madame Rachel … 'I am
pretty well and much admired, thanks to you'. Inevitably
the debts had mounted. Cecilia went to money lenders but
they would not help her without her husband's permission.
So, as had happened with other Rachel clients in the past,
Cecilia Pearse had found herself obliged to offer her finest
jewellery as security. The majority of it had come down
to her from her opera singer mother Grisi: 'a diamond
and pearl locket; one pair of diamond and pearl earrings;
two bracelets; one gold necklace; two other lockets; one
gold eye glass, a turquoise brooch, one pair of turquoise

earrings and one thimble' – Rachel had promptly pawned the lot for £50 with Mr Sheldrick of Attenborough's at 40 Duke Street, even though, like all property of married women, it actually belonged to Cecilia's husband Godfrey Pearse, under the law as it then stood.

Not long after using several of Rachel's face washes in the winter of 1877, however, Cecilia Pearse complained that her face had broken out in a rash. Rachel looked her all over 'with a sort of small microscope' and said this was because the treatment was opening up the pores of her skin; she then induced her to pay £5 for an Arabian bath at her house to 'take away the rash'. When Cecilia continued to complain about the state of her skin, Rachel had terrorized her into continuing, with sinister warnings that she would do nothing more for her until her money was on the table. Mrs Pearse's complexion would be 'ruined for life' if she did not finish the process and she must use nothing else but cold water, when not using Rachel's products.

The situation rapidly became untenable and Cecilia Pearse was forced to tell her husband what had happened. He had gone straight to Rachel's premises and demanded the letters his wife had written to Madame Rachel, as well as the money she had got for pawning her jewels. When Rachel refused he accused her of extortion; he would put the matter in the hands Mr George Lewis. At this point Rachel had rounded on him quite violently making threats. 'There was nothing she desired more than to meet Mr

George Lewis in a Court of Law,' she had said. Mr Lewis wanted to 'hang her' – she knew that only too well – but if Godfrey Pearse dared to do anything against her she would 'make the whole city ring with it and subpoena every friend he had in the world'. The next day Rachel went to Pearse's office and tried to beard him in his den with further threats waving a clutch of letters at him written to her by his wife which she claimed 'incriminated her' by showing she had voluntarily hired Rachel's services at the agreed amount. More sinisterly, she added that he might not find his wife 'all he supposed her' to be. Rachel's daughter Hélène however, by now anxious that her mother faced yet another prosecution that would by association also damage her own respectability and growing professional reputation, tried to persuade her to relent. Her husband, Edward Turner was also dragged into things; Godfrey Pearse visited him some days later asking him to intercede and persuade Madame Rachel to return the money and all Mrs Pearse's letters if he would withdraw the summons. Rachel refused to cooperate and George Lewis was instructed to go ahead with the prosecution.

On 15 February 1878, Madame Rachel was called to answer the charges against her as Sarah Rachel Leverson – though some of the press described her as Rachael Levison, thus perpetuating confusion about what her real name was. She appeared before Mr R. M. Newton at Marlborough Street Court, the indictment charging her with obtaining money and jewels by false pretences and making demands with menaces. Several male members of the aristocracy were visible, seated in the body of the court like Ranelagh before them – no doubt there to ensure that their names – or rather the names of their wives – were not dragged into things. Many fashionable women came to observe the proceedings from the gallery, and, after several days of long drawn-out cross-examination of the Pearses and various witnesses, on 23 February, Rachel was committed for trial. The judge agreed bail of one surety by Rachel herself of £2,000 and two additional sureties of £1,000 each, but no one came forward this time and she spent the intervening weeks once more within the old familiar walls of Newgate.

Meanwhile the news had filtered out in the press that Mrs Pearse was the daughter of the celebrated Mario. She was, it was noted, a very beautiful woman and 'one of the last persons in the world' whose complexion needed improving. It was therefore a puzzle to her friends that a young lady whose personal appearance was said to be 'very engaging', should have had 'the least temptation to subject herself to the hideous experiments which were made upon her by the veteran destroyer of female beauty'. Nevertheless, the Pearses deserved 'the gratitude of the public' for having come forward to 'protect other ladies against the fraudulent acts of Madame Rachel'. They had a large circle of friends and were, after all, 'cognate persons in society'. The old familiar pattern of media kow-towing to the presumed integrity of the upper classes once more was the order of the day.

***

In preparing their case against Madame Rachel, the Pearses decided to marshal all the available ammunition they had against her, irrespective of the scandal it might provoke. This included dragging the name of another of Rachel's clients – the Countess of Dudley – into it, as further evidence of her penchant for purloining the jewels of eminent ladies. During the remand hearings, Cecilia Pearse revealed that as part of her wheedling sales patter, Rachel had boasted to her about how she had 'enamelled' the Countess of Dudley with great success. What is more, in the next room,' she told Cecilia that day, she had something that would 'astonish' her – Lady Dudley's jewels ... one diamond among them being 'as large as the top of her thumb'. It turned out that having run up a bill with Rachel for £2,000 the Countess, finding herself in a little financial difficulty, had been prevailed upon to send her maid round with some of her favourite jewels – though fortunately not the celebrated Dudley diamonds that had been exhibited at the 1867 Exposition Universelle in Paris – as security.

The reporting of the Dudley story during Rachel's remand hearings immediately set everyone in London talking. But surely Rachel's possession of the Countess's jewels was a lie? The beauteous Georgiana had no need of Madame Rachel's treatments. And anyway, hadn't she reported her jewels stolen back in December 1874?

The Earl and Countess of Dudley were one of the most high-profile, fashionable couples of their day, and therefore had more than enough reason to do all in their power to suppress a prospective scandal. Fifty year-old William Ward, 1st Earl of Dudley had married his second wife, Georgiana Elizabeth Moncrieffe, in 1865. She was almost thirty years his junior, one of the most celebrated professional beauties of the day, painted by Millais, and a favourite of the Prince of Wales, (Lilllie Langtry being the prince's current inamorata in 1878; the Countess finally got to share his bed in 1896). The couple lived in a fine house on Park Lane, from where Georgiana attracted enormous attention wherever she went, particularly when driving through Rotten Row in nearby Hyde Park.

Back in December 1874, a newspaper story had broken in which the Dudleys claimed that when they had recently gone to Paddington to catch the 6.30 p.m. Worcester express, on their way to their country seat of Witley Court, the countess's jewels had been stolen. During the melee of servants loading the luggage on the station platform, a dressing case containing upwards of £15,000 of jewellery, including a pearl and diamond bracelet presented to the countess by the inhabitants of Dudley, had gone missing. While the servants were organizing things, the countess's maid claimed to have kept her foot on the dressing case, but when her attention was temporarily diverted she took it off and, hey presto, it had suddenly and mysteriously vanished. Quite how any maid worth her salt would have let such valuable jewels out of her sight for a second was never questioned; but a reward of £1,000 for their safe return was immediately advertised by the Earl of Dudley in all the papers.

It was patently obvious now, in April 1878, that the entire story about Lady Dudley's stolen jewels had been bogus – a desperate cover-up to save her from the embarrassment of being publicly pilloried for having been foolish enough to let Madame Rachel purloin them. Nor did she and Lord Dudley appear to have any conscience about the fact that the case inevitably provoked the asking of questions about the honesty of Lady Dudley's innocent maid. *The Times* had not approved of Lord Dudley's offer of guaranteed anonymity to the 'thief' for the safe return of the jewels, which was tantamount to kowtowing to blackmail. It is not surprising therefore that four years later when the Pearse case broke, the Dudleys were once more forced into frantic acts of damage limitation, furiously denying Pearse's statement in court through their solicitor. Indeed, Lord Dudley wrote a letter to George Lewis in which, in no uncertain terms, he 'stigmatised the assertion that his wife had ever been to the house of the defendant, as a base calumny and as having no foundation whatever, direct or indirect.'

On the advice of her solicitor Madame Rachel now denied ever having said anything about the Countess or her jewels to Mrs Pearse, or indeed ever having had Lady Dudley as a client. She didn't have much option – Lord Dudley was sitting there in court during the remand hearings waiting to hear her say so. Rachel might be damned but she had to make one last attempt at saving herself from yet more litigation by denying the story. During the hearing, Isabella Scott, the Countess's unfortunate maid who had 'lost' the diamonds at Paddington station, was obliged to play the role of fall guy, prevailed on to perjure herself on her mistress's behalf. No, she did not know Madame Rachel; she had never been to her salon with her mistress, who had had positively no association with her. Indeed, her mistress had never 'used any wash or compound for her face in any shape or form'.

***

As the public waited eagerly for the trial to come to court, the press was once more gearing up for an orgy of Madame Rachel character-assassination. On 2 March her engraved portrait appeared on the front cover of the *Illustrated Police News* and a week later the paper again featured her on the front – this time in the form of the particularly nasty anti-Semitic cartoons of Rachel taken from the popular pamphlet produced after the 1868 trial.

The trial was due to start on 13 March but the day

before, Rachel's solicitor Robert Williams applied for a postponement. He was still awaiting copies of the three indictments against Rachel, an additional charge of assault by her on Cecilia Maria Pearse now having been added. The gist of this was that she had caused her actual bodily injury by administering to her 'a poisonous and noxious lotion' which had brought her skin out in a rash. Rachel's counsel argued that he and his client would need time to gather 'scientific evidence' in respect of this additional charge, for which they were as yet unprepared. It had also been intimated that the prosecution was preparing to call additional witnesses to those who had appeared at the remand hearings and thus, Williams contended, it was only fair that Madame Rachel should know 'what they were about to prove'.

The trial was therefore adjourned until the new sessions in April, but already it was causing 'an immense sensation in fashionable quarters' according to the press (no doubt in an allusion to the fact that many of the titled and wealthy ladies of London were once more running scared at the thought of being named as Rachel's clients). The Sheriff's office had been inundated with applications for seats at the trial, particularly from women, so much so that 'several thousand ladies whose names are well known in the West End had been refused admission'. So far, observed the *Western Mail*, Mrs Pearce's photograph had been kept out of the shop windows, unlike that of Mrs Borradaile before her, but it was 'pretty certain to be on sale before too long' – either that or a 'swift fingered artist' would soon grab the opportunity of sketching her. Meanwhile, the trial would go ahead within the cramped confines of the Central Criminal Court at Old Bailey – a fact which no doubt resulted in 'much lamentation and tearing of dyed hair in the West End' by those ladies unable to gain admission.

The new sessions for April 1878 had fifty-seven male and nine female prisoners listed for trial, representing a typical cross-section of everyday crime in Victorian London: wilful murder, manslaughter, forgery, highway robbery, attempted murder, administering poison, letter-stealing and rape – plus thirteen 'Chinamen' on a charge of riot. But the star attraction was, even ten years on, undoubtedly the ubiquitous Madame Rachel.

***

Across the Atlantic Ocean in New York a woman of equal notoriety to Rachel was also preparing to go on trial that very same month. Ann Trow, better known by the French sobriquet of Madame Restell – or, more popularly, 'Madame Killer' – was an English emigrant to New York who had started out selling patent medicines and moved into peddling 'female antidotes' and 'relief to married ladies'. Despite much campaigning against her dubious practices in the New York papers during the 1840s, she had prospered.

Fashionable ladies in trouble had beaten a discreet path to her door, prepared to pay anything between $500 and $1,000 for her infallible French pills and abortifacients. Restell had quickly moved up-market on the proceeds, spending as much on her annual advertising as Rachel in London, and taking a grand residence on Fifth Avenue, with servants, carriages and fine horses. Several attempts to prosecute her had been withdrawn out of similar fears of scandal; considering herself impervious to prosecution, Restell had continued to flaunt public opinion much like Rachel, and also much like her was repeatedly attacked for her ostentatious and unrepentant manner. Finally, in 1847, Restell had been prosecuted for procuring an abortion and spent a year in jail on New York's notorious Blackwell's Island. She returned to her old tricks after her release and built a large four-storey brownstone mansion at the corner of 5th and 52nd Streets, from where she operated as a 'lady physician'. But, just as Rachel had been isolated amid her plush and gilded Second Empire furnishings at Maddox Street, so Restell remained a pariah and her wealth could never buy her social acceptance. A raid on her premises in 1878 under the new anti-obscenity Comstock Law, which was heavily targeting abortionists, had produced an enormous haul of abortifacient pills and powders. Restell was indicted for trial on 1 April 1878 – just nine days before Madame Rachel. But even as the courtroom in New York filled with spectators on that first day of the trial, Madame

Restell's lifeless corpse was discovered in her bath on 5th Avenue. She had cut her throat with a carving knife. All the press concurred that it was a fitting end to an 'odious career' and no doubt now, the British press hoped that the end was finally in sight to Madame Rachel's. The *Washington Post* later that month was not the only newspaper to compare the downfall of Madame Rachel with that of Restell: two 'unscrupulous hags' who had flouted the 'moral restraints of social life' and exploited the weakness and vulnerability of other women, brazening it out in the face of public antipathy and making considerable amounts of money in so doing. Madame Restell had mercifully organized her own exit in order to be spared the ignominy of a very public trial and a stiff prison sentence, but on 10 April, a sick – and, as it would appear to many in court, mentally distressed – Madame Rachel had to face her third and final trial. She was only about sixty but, plagued with ill health for years now, she looked much older.

***

The Central Criminal Court was once more full of women on the opening day of the trial, 10 April 1878, with society ladies even taking the seats usually reserved for military officers. The court was presided over by a suitably fashionable judge to match: Mr Baron Huddlestone a former QC, married to Lady Diana de Vere Beauclerk, a daughter of the 9th Duke of St Albans – a man whose sympathies would clearly be on the side of the rich and titled and protecting their interests. Mr Harry Poland, who appeared as prosecutor for the Crown in many important criminal trials, was assisted by Mr Douglas Straight (who had acted for Mrs Borradaile at the 1868 trial). Rachel's defence this time was somewhat down-market from the brilliant team assembled in 1868, led by Mr Day QC, with the assistance of Mr Robert Williams who had appeared at the remand, Mr Besley and Mr Bennett.

At the opening of the trial it was announced that only the first charge, of fraud, was now to be proceeded with against Rachel – not as a private prosecution by the Pearses, but on behalf of Her Majesty's Treasury. Rachel once again pleaded Not Guilty. 'Well do I recall her appearance on that occasion,' remarked an observer, 'muffled up in black, and casting tiger-like looks at the inmates of the court.'

Cecilia Pearse was the first to be called into the witness box. Mr Straight for the prosecution took her through an almost precise reiteration of the evidence she had given at the remand hearings. An innocent purchase of tooth powder at Rachel's salon had led to her buying some violet powder (a kind of talcum powder used after bathing). Both these powders had, she admitted, been 'very good' which had led her to try Madame's expensive washes 'from the East' at a guinea a bottle. She had also bought powder recommended by Rachel to put on her arms and neck when going to a ball, which she admitted had made her look quite 'lovely' in the opinion of her friends and had 'made a great sensation'. She trusted to the endorsements of other clients quoted to her by Rachel, including the name of Lady Dudley, and had bought the washes in the belief that they would clear her complexion. By the time she left for Rome to visit her father in February 1877 she was so hooked that she had written to Madame telling her she would like to 'be made beautiful for ever' before her departure. Once in Rome she had sent letters asking Rachel to send more creams and powders to her – she preferred to buy her cosmetics from Rachel because she had assured her they were 'harmless'. Rachel never responded, probably through illness, but on her return Cecilia Pearse had gone straight to her new salon at Great Portland Street, to buy more washes for applying to her skin as well as putting in the bath.

During Cecilia's visits, Rachel had spent many hours bending her ear about the campaign of persecution she had suffered since 1868 and the 'conspiracy' against her. She had told her that 'people wanted to get £30,000 from her,' but that the Home Office was taking up her case to 'prove her innocence'. She had, said Mrs Pearse, expressed 'very strong feelings' against Mr George Lewis; she now claimed she would rather meet the devil than face him. But her daughter was on the stage and for her sake she did not wish their business dealings to be known or Hélène's name brought into them.

At the end of December 1877, when the rash had appeared on Cecilia's face, arms and neck, Rachel had assured her that, having studied the skin 'for more than 50 years' she alone knew the cures for such rashes and how to prevent her being 'disfigured for life'. Eventually, when Cecilia had found herself unable to keep up the payments, Rachel had reduced her charge to £50, and even suggested she could draw the money from 'her father's fund at Coutts'. A hard-pressed Cecilia had offered her jewels in lieu of the £50 cash Rachel now demanded, but when she later discovered that she could have pawned them herself for more than that, she was furious and asked for them back. (At this point an uncomfortable Mrs Pearse was forced to admit by Rachel's counsel that she had on occasion pawned her jewels before.) Rachel refused; Mrs Pearse was making an awful lot of fuss about jewels worth only £50, she told her; she had jewellery worth many thousands more than that in her charge, and she browbeat Mrs Pearse into writing a letter to the pawnbroker endorsing the transaction. When Cecilia Pearse later accompanied her husband on a visit to Rachel to persuade her to return the jewels, Rachel had 'abused us all the way downstairs, calling us names'. They had then gone straight to Lewis.

Godfrey Pearse followed his wife into the witness box to corroborate her story, during which he confirmed that he had handed over the remains of one of Rachel's bottles of face wash to his family chemist, Mr Saunders of Charles Anderson & Son of Lower Belgrave Street, for analysis. Another bottle was taken to Godfrey & Cooke's, chemical analysts of Conduit Street.

The final witness called on the first day of the trial was Madame Rachel's former maid, Sabina Pinney, who had been in her service at Great Portland Street from August 1877 to January 1878 and was now a domestic servant in Kentish Town. She it was who first gave the court an inkling of what actually was in the face washes that she had helped prepare at Madame's behest: nothing but 'starch and fuller's earth and something out of a paper' – she didn't know the name – to which water from the ordinary domestic tap downstairs was added. Madame's hair wash, which again cost a guinea a time, consisted of pearl ash and water – if it did no good 'it at least had the merit of doing no harm'. She had filled the Arabian bath for Mrs Pearse the day she took one at Rachel's – a less than glamorous tin hip-bath pulled out from under the table, to which was added nothing but bran and water. Rachel had warned Sabina that her face washes sometimes brought ladies out in a rash but that it made them good looking in the end. She, Sabina, didn't use any of them – just helped to mix them and stuck the labels with Rachel's name and address on the bottle. Not all of Rachel's products were harmful by any means, and she clearly knew the values of the cosmetics she used. She gave Sabina cream for her chapped hands which made a great improvement and her own hair washes were 'generally used in the family' – including her small grandchild (probably David's son Harry) who visited from time to time – and found to be 'very beneficial'. After receiving Mrs Pearse's jewels, Madame had paraded around in some of them, telling Sabina they were a 'Christmas present' from her grateful client.

On the second day of the trial, the rain fell in torrents. Rain was a great leveller where fashionable society was concerned; it deterred 'ladies clad in gorgeous apparel, and with trailing robes of costly material' from setting foot outside their doors and so attendance on day two of the trial fell off somewhat, aside from those resolute ladies of the elite who had come especially to hear 'all about their dear friend, Lady Dudley, and the wicked stories that had been told about her.' Indeed, there were still so many women in court, ogling the defendant in the dock through their opera glasses, remarked the correspondent of the *Examiner,* that one might have imagined one had stumbled inadvertently not into 'a tribunal of public justice, but into a fashionable morning concert, or some other entertainment largely frequented by "the quality".' In deference to this, the aldermen at the Central Criminal Court had gone out of their way to cater for the aristocracy present by laying on a 'substantial civic repast of soup, joint and sundries', as well as glasses of sherry, during the lunchtime break from proceedings.

Cecilia Pearse's Italian maid, Orsolina Palmieri, was the first to be called that day, giving evidence through an interpreter, although she spoke fairly good English. Rachel had claimed to her that Mrs Pearse came to her salon 'out of respect to her daughter Hélène'. Madame had had a powerful influence over her mistress, had dictated letters to her as she would 'a child at school' (just as she had Mrs Borradaile before her) and made her mistress 'sign her name in a book' where she kept accounts of all the monies owed to her by her clients. Mrs Pearse had bought several bottles of wash, but Orsalina had thrown their contents away after her mistress had come out in a rash. She had tried it herself and a rash had come out on her arm too. One of the servants Mary had also tried the dregs of the lotion left in bottles discarded by her mistress and had had the same allergic reaction. But she had kept the bottles and then sold them.

The time now came for the relatively recent, Victorian equivalent of forensic evidence to be brought into play with the calling of expert witnesses. Mr Harold Senior, FCS, of the pharmaceutical chemists Godfrey & Cooke, was called to confirm his analysis of the washes supplied by the defendant to the complainant. He confirmed that the sample he had been given contained organic matter – possibly the result of a dirty bottle. The contents were as follows:

lead compound – 100 grammes

clay-like earth, probably Fuller's Earth – 50 grammes

starch – 160 grammes

hydrochloric acid – 15 grammes

the remainder, 2,400 grammes of water

in all 2685 grammes or 6 fluid ounces

The solution was distinctly 'acid' in character; the carbonate of lead would leave a relatively harmless deposit on the skin, giving it the desired whitish colour that ladies liked. It was a common ingredient in face washes such as Goulard's Water – a popular lead-based solution used to relieve itching and inflammation – but it was not usual or safe to add hydrochloric acid to the mixture. Indeed its presence could generate lead chloride, which *could* penetrate the skin and cause eruptions. Such washes would do nothing to allay inflammation of the skin, as Rachel had claimed, and if used continuously might be 'deleterious' to it. Dr Thomas Bond, FRCS, of Westminster Hospital and a lecturer on forensic medicine concurred with Senior that the hydrochloric acid would produce a roughness of the skin and 'bring out an eruption' if applied sufficiently often. The 'toilette vinegars' generally on sale in London contained acetic acid which was soothing, but Rachel's formula would be the opposite. It was fundamentally an irritant, caused by the hydrochloric acid combining with the starch. At best the constituent parts of Rachel's nostrums were worth sixpence a bottle; but in Bond's opinion it was safer to stick to soap and water.

In response, the defence produced their own pet scientist, Professor Theophilus Redwood from the Institute of Pharmacy. The addition of chloride of lead to the washes would act as an astringent; he did not consider its presence harmful nor that of the starch and fuller's earth. Its effect in his opinion, was merely that of acetic acid; the whole solution combined would have whitened the skin as it dried. Hydrochloric acid was not normally used as an application to the skin, so having no experience of its effect in this way he could not pass comment but on some skins, he hastened to point out, even ordinary soap acted as much as an irritant as hydrochloric acid. Indeed, Madame's lotion might be effective in dealing with skin disease, 'where an abnormal state of the skin exists'.

The jury were not out for long when the evidence was concluded at the end of the second day. At the urging of Baron Huddlestone they agreed to reach their verdict that evening, in so doing sparing everyone from a third day. They retired at 6 p.m. Seven minutes later they were back with the expected verdict of guilty, in time for Baron Huddlestone to pass sentence before going home for his supper. Before he did so, Madame Rachel begged leave to address the court, which she did in a 'long and somewhat incoherent speech', in the course of which she claimed that Mary Tucker Borradaile had come to see her at Millbank, when she had admitted to her that she, Rachel, had been the victim of a 'malicious prosecution'. She had visited her again after she was released and even wrote 'an affidavit' to this effect, sending her a ten pound note and saying 'how very sorry she had been'; since then Rachel had taken her case to the Treasury and had waited 'in the hope that a good Providence might think it proper to bring it out'. She went on to complain of how her previous conviction had been 'a most monstrous charge got up by Mr George Lewis and his father'. As a result, since her release from prison, she had 'fitted up' her rooms at Great Portland Street 'more like a solicitor's office than a perfumer's shop', for she had been assembling facts about the conspiracy against her for many years past and had 'gone many weary miles to collect them' in the hopes of clearing her name. Much like the claimants in Jarndyce & Jarndyce, Madame Rachel lived in hope that the machinery of the law would one day grind slowly but surely in her direction.

Her appeal from the dock then took on a much more lachrymose tone. She admitted that, to her sorrow, she was not educated but that she had made up for it by educating her children. 'The greatest misfortune I had,' she now told the court, 'was when I introduced Mrs Turner to Mrs Pearse and her poor father, whom I am sure I respected, my lord, as much as you do.' In an extraordinary turn, Rachel now launched into a diatribe against what she perceived as Cecilia Pearse's neglect of her aging father Mario:

The lady who would allow her father to sell his last chair from under him, and go to a poor friend to beg bread while she herself acknowledges that she laid out £20 for her cosmetics, tells you, my lord, that the things she sold were for a charitable purpose, and her father meantime dying for bread! ... My children [have] raised heaven and earth for the benefit of her father, and I am not ashamed that I did the same.

In conclusion, the sick and now cowed Rachel did the one thing any cornered female animal would do: protect her young. She could do nothing more than reiterate that her children had had 'nothing to do with this affair whatever'. In a final plea, full of biblical overtones, she left Mrs Pearse to 'her own conscience and the Judge of Judges' and – clearly alluding to Hélène's promising career – begged: 'Do not try to crush any young rising creature because she has the misfortune to be my child. I beg and implore you as Englishmen not to visit the sins and sorrows of the mother upon the children.'

Baron Huddlestone was unmoved by Rachel's plea for her children. Her calling was, he said, 'as detestable a one as any I know of' and it would have been better if she had thought of her children before she determined to follow it. His only regret was that it was not in his power to pass a heavier sentence than that which the law allowed – of five years imprisonment.

In a state of collapse, Madame Rachel was taken down to the cells and from there to Millbank. Her sentence brought to a close this 'curious tale of simplicity on the one hand and of practiced craft and roguery on the other' which one journalist thought read like a chapter from the pages of Dumas *père*. The society ladies who had crowded out the courtroom for two days had sat there with bated breath, hoping for the revelation of 'extraordinary mysteries in connection with Madame Rachel's business' – mysteries from which 'even a mouse would fly in terror' – only to be disappointed. The trial had been something of an anticlimax, the only revelation being the true ingredients of Madame's face washes and Arabian baths. As for the rest, the evidence had been 'dull and uninteresting to the last degree'. Nevertheless, the trial had provided the aimless, moneyed socialites who populated the Central Criminal Court with 'a show for idle women'.

But how could any intelligent woman, people continued to ask, place herself 'in the hands of a convicted impostor like Madame Rachel in the childish hope that by washes and baths she could retain the beauty of her youth to the grave?' There was little public sympathy for Cecilia Pearse; indeed, some papers such as the *Evening Telegraph* pointed out that Baron Huddlestone, in condemning Rachel had failed to take to task the women who patronized her – married women who should know better. Perhaps there should be some punishment for ladies who, without consulting their husbands, 'enter into compacts to pay large sums of money ... for "enamelling",' suggested the *Derby Mercury*.

A golden opportunity had been lost by Huddlestone for striking home the moral message of the case, for 'There are more Rachels in London than are dreamed of in our philosophy, who no doubt justly declare this one to be justly punished for being found out.' But women would go on seeking the holy grail of eternal beauty, even though in the wake of the trial the medical press reiterated that 'no cosmetic wash, enamel, powder, paste or lotion can ever subvert the natural process of waste and repair which is ever taking place in our bodies.'

Ten years on from Rachel's much talked about first trial, the British press did not have the stomach for a long post mortem on her crimes. It had all been said before, ad nauseam, in 1868. Newspaper comment on the case died down very rapidly, aside from the syndication across the British press of an announcement that Madame's effigy had been dusted off and put back on display at Tussauds, where the curious could view her for a shilling a time. The collective lack of will to rake over the coals probably helped Cecilia Pearse in living down the ignominy of her exploitation by Rachel fairly quickly. She conducted herself with an excess of virtue and dignity throughout the trial and thanks to her good social connections she did not, like Mary Tucker Borradaile, find the door to polite society slammed in her face. The benefit concert for her father Signor Mario went ahead shortly afterwards and raised £1,150 for his twilight years. Thereafter, Cecilia and her husband continued to be regular guests at royal drawing rooms and garden parties as she went on to redeem herself with charitable work for the Westminster Working Women's Home and the Irish Distressed Ladies' Fund. She even gave the occasional amateur performances for charity events, such as singing at a benefit concert for Count Leo Tolstoi's Soup Kitchens for the Russian Starving during the famine of 1892. Her major work however was organizing fund-raising events for the home set up by the Church of England Waifs and Strays Society. In 1911 she published a biography of her father, *The Romance of a Great Singer*, and increasingly spent much of her time in Italy. She died in May 1926 at Bordighera, Italy, the year her memoirs – *The Enchanted Past* – were published. But they contain not a word about her run-in with Madame Rachel.

***

By the summer of 1878 Rachel was a chronically sick woman. Her health deteriorated further within the unhealthy confines of Millbank and on 15 July she was transferred to Woking Invalid Convict Prison, in a state of 'indifferent health'. Four days after her arrival, she was admitted to the infirmary suffering from catarrh and remained a patient there for most of the time. She might be ill but she still had the energy to entertain fellow inmates and matrons alike with anecdotes of her career, dropping 'many significant hints' of how, when she was released, she would make use of her 'considerable wealth' in helping out those who had been 'kind to her in her present misfortune'. Her stories failed to impress anyone, any more than did her offers of passing on her secrets for improving the complexion. Everyone thought her an ugly old woman, who had clearly made no attempt to beautify herself. But Rachel persisted in trying to ingratiate herself in every possible way by barefaced flattery. Upon receiving the answer from a matron 'Pretty well, thank you,' to an inquiry as to how she was that morning, she had unctuously replied: '*Pretty*, I know you are; *well*, I am glad to hear.' In similar fashion she had launched into a discourse on her enamelling arts to another member of staff: 'But there,' she concluded, your splendid complexion, Miss—, will never require enamelling. Gold cannot purchase anything like that.'

At the end of December that year, Rachel's sixty-three year old common law husband Phillip Levison died in Finsbury Park, north London, of cancer of the kidney and bowels. He appears to have cut himself off totally by then and had reverted to calling himself Levy. When his death was announced in the *Jewish Chronicle* he was described as the 'father of David Levy ... and Mlle Hélène Crosmond', but there was no mention of his other surviving children – Léontine, Arthur and Harry – suggesting that they were either estranged from him or perhaps still living in France.

In prison at Woking, Rachel was suffering badly from

heart disease, leaving her fatigued and breathless. She never complained about her treatment and continued to express herself grateful for the attention she received from the prison authorities, full of flattery to the last. A prison visitor recorded seeing her one day, sitting up in bed, 'making little dolls for the favourite child of some official.' She never showed any remorse for her supposed crimes – rather the reverse, she was proud of her name and the noise she had made in the world; it was *she* who was the injured party. As her health declined rapidly she continued to receive visits from her now glamorous and successful daughter, Hélène, who was noted by the prison officials as being 'encumbered in much jewellery and gorgeous wearing apparel' and who showed a 'considerable degree of affection' for her mother to the last.

Madame Rachel died in Woking jail, at 5.30 am. on Tuesday 12 October 1880, having been seriously ill for several weeks. An inquest was held at the prison on Saturday 16 and a death certificate issued, recording that Sarah Rachel Leverson, aged 60 years, and 'formerly a perfumer' had died of 'Natural Dropsy'. Dropsy was the old way of describing water retention or oedema; in Rachel's case it was probably linked to congestive heart failure – the result of the rheumatic fever she had suffered in the 1850s. On 18 October, the Beth Din of the United Synagogue in London issued a burial certificate so that Rachel could be taken to a Jewish cemetery for interment. Her body was placed in a 'handsome coffin of polished oak', and wreaths of immortelles were laid on her breast. From there it was conveyed to Brookwood Necropolis railway terminus and loaded on a train for Victoria Station. A hearse was waiting to meet it, after which it processed the solemn six-mile journey north across London to Willesden Jewish Cemetery. Here, at her children's wish, Rachel was buried privately, and without fuss, in an unmarked grave.

The newspapers noted her death with little interest. As far as they were concerned the notorious old criminal had finally received her just deserts. Ding dong, the witch was dead. All good Victorians could now sleep more easily in their beds, for the evil Madame Rachel had at last died – most appropriately as the inquest jury had agreed – 'by the visitation of God'.

CHAPTER TWELVE

The Final Curtain

MADAME RACHEL HAD only been in her grave for six months when a terrible whisper caught the wind among 'theatrical coteries' and the demi monde in London and Paris. In May 1881 rumours began circulating that the much-despised enameller of ladies faces might yet have her revenge from the other side of the grave. Rumours were flying that the 'old sorceress' had left behind memoirs of some kind, as well as a 'good deal of correspondence with distinguished persons and private memoranda of all sorts'. Worse – there was talk of her 'natural heirs' publishing it all.

It was the regional press who picked up on the story, which probably originated from one of the Paris correspondents. From Manchester, to Exeter, to Dublin, to Yorkshire, the gossip spread. The rumours that Rachel might yet wreak further scandal on Victorian society were so dreadful that they did not bear thinking about. For her memoirs, if published, threatened to contain 'startling revelations concerning the personal relations between Rachel and many celebrated beauties whose charms were heightened by her arts'; the 'cunning and vindictive old woman' might yet cause 'inconceivable grief' in London society.

It is certainly clear that Rachel kept some kind of account book; even if she couldn't write, this was done for her by Leontie and Rachel junior, as well as other hired amanuenses. In them, she kept the names and addresses of her lady clients, the amounts they owed and the jewels they sometimes left in hock with her. When she gave evidence at the 1878 trial, Cecilia Pearse's maid Orsalina Palmieri had stated that on visits with her mistress to the Great Portland Street salon, Rachel had 'mentioned the names of princesses, countesses and all the principal ladies in London' as being her clients. The fashionable elite of London therefore had good reason to be very afraid.

The correspondent of the *Northern Echo*, in confirming the existence of this potentially scandalous material, remembered how, at the trial, he had noted that Baron Huddlestone had had Rachel's account and address books, even her cosmetics recipes in front of him and had sat there 'turning over the pages' as he passed sentence. Huddlestone had hinted 'very significantly' that he had no doubt from their perusal that 'the prisoner's trade was of the most disgraceful character'. Indeed, he had also had one of Rachel's cheque books that confirmed that her business was, even in its relatively reduced circumstances in the 1870s, 'considerable'.

Having said all this, the papers then reassured their anxious readers by quickly dismissing the 'Parisian rumour'. No such book would ever appear, for it would have been immediately slapped with 'a dozen injunctions' to prevent publication, not to mention possible libel actions. The rumour was not trustworthy; it was no doubt the invention of some 'boulevard lounger'. It was, most certainly, not the work of her eminently respectable daughter Hélène Crosmond.

***

Having allowed the talk to die down for a few months after her mother's trial, Hélène had resumed her career in July 1878; she worked hard to mitigate against any damage it might have caused her, relieved at least that Cecilia Pearse had been only too anxious to assert in court that she had 'nothing at all to say against the daughter of the defendant' (Mrs Crosmond Turner) and that she had always found her 'a perfect lady.' With her husband travelling back and forth between London and Paris on business, and having no children, Hélène returned to the London stage, earning good reviews as Susanna in *Le Nozze di Figaro*, the critics concurring that she 'justified the hopes entertained of her from the first'. Various concert performances for Mapleson's Company followed that summer at Her Majesty's Theatre and the Crystal Palace, as well as the offer of a tour to Dublin with Mapleson's in September. Whilst clearly above average to make it to Covent Garden as a singer and be hired by Mapleson's, nevertheless as an aspiring opera singer, even with her adopted, French-sounding name, the English-born Hélène was at a distinct disadvantage. During the late 1870s it was the more exotic, foreign singers such as the impeccably Italian Adelina Patti, who were highly fashionable and commanding huge fees.

Late that summer, just as Hélène was preparing to leave for Ireland, a new and glamorous rival had arrived on the scene in Covent Garden. On 30 July, 1878, announcing their eight-week season of promenade concerts at the Theatre Royal, impresarios Agostino and Stefano Gatti declared that among the 'eminent artists' to appear on the opening night of 3 August would be 'Mdlle Alma Verdini, making her first appearance in London'. She was, the advertisements claimed, 'an American soprano of Italian parentage', but no one knew anything about her. La Verdini quickly ensured that no one would forget. Her Covent Garden debut was, if not vocally a complete success, then physically very much a talking point. She certainly 'gave one plenty to look at for the money' thought the downmarket *Sporting Gazette*, by attracting enormous attention for her highly 'prepossessing' appearance and her risqué décolleté costume. Verdini's dress was so elaborately decorated with roses, thought the critic of the *Era*, that she looked like 'a perambulating bouquet'. But everyone agreed that she had ample natural beauty and talent and a pure soprano voice; in fact, she possessed 'one of the finest voices we'Verdini-where', leered *Funny Folks*. However Mlle Verdini's was a raw talent and she lacked vocal training. If she made an effort and studied under someone like the great French tenor and teacher, Signor Barbot, she might reach 'the top of the ladder'.

The story of Verdini's London debut reached New York. There was scarcely such a voice to be heard anywhere, even from the great Patti, wrote the *New York Times* critic excitedly: 'volume, strength, compass, flexibility, sweetness' – Verdini's voice possessed 'every quality joined to a most attractive exterior. And once she had perfected her technique 'she might command any price she chose to ask, as she would be unrivalled on the lyric stage.'

But who was Alma Verdini? The tale she told of her tragic beginnings was an extraordinary one: she was born in America; her Italian engineer father had been killed in a railway accident when she was a child; her mother had died not long after. Abducted by gypsies, the orphaned Verdini had been rescued and placed in a convent near Paris, where her marvellous singing voice had attracted the attention of the nuns. One of the convent's patrons, the Princess de Metternich, had taken up her cause and thanks to her,

Alma was able to study her art, making her debut in the winter of 1879 at Jacques Offenbach's Théâtre de la Gaîeté to great acclaim.

A fortnight or so after Verdini's sensational London debut, a small news item appeared in the *Era*. Mademoiselle Verdini, it appeared was 'not of American origin as had been stated'. She was in fact 'the daughter of a *parfumeuse* of great notoriety in London and Paris, and was herself engaged in that occupation before adopting the vocal profession.'

Léontine Rachel, formerly of the rue de la Paix, had reinvented herself.

Whether or not she had come to London in a deliberate attempt to upstage her sister Hélène is not known. But the newly incarnated Alma Verdini's aspirations to stardom were considerable and her claims were grand to say the least. Despite what the critics said to the contrary, 'for the last four or five years' she had, she claimed, been under the tutelage of none other than Maestro Verdi himself. But why the sudden career change? It would seem, from the scanty evidence available, that the business in Paris had come to as disastrous an end as that of her mother in London. French sources suggest that Léontine Rachel had been taken to court by a lady client whose face had become swollen after using her cosmetics. The woman had lost her case but it had been enough to force Léontine to shut up shop. The rue de la Paix salon appears to have

ceased advertising some time around 1874, although the
Léontine Rachel cosmetics franchise in the form of her
L'Eau d'Albâtre lotion for removing wrinkles and Extrait
de Rose face powder continued to be available, through
agents, for many years afterwards. Indeed, 'Poudre Rachel'
was still on sale in the 1900s.

It was December 1881 before the public was finally
disabused about Alma Verdini's exotic background. The
legend she had put about was 'quite a romance' wrote
the music correspondent of the *New York Times*, and one
where the scenario changed with every telling. Yet another
version ran thus: Verdini had been 'stolen by gypsies near
New York', after which she had been forced to 'wander
with mountebanks all over both continents, dancing and
tightroping and tumbling at provincial fairs', before at
last being reclaimed by her disconsolate parents 'from the
booth of a suburban juggler'. It was a pretty story but a lie.

Thanks to her mother's insistence on an education in all
the social graces for her daughters, Alma had like Hélène
enjoyed the benefit of singing lessons as a young girl.
Whilst still at the Bond Street shop, her talents had been
spotted by one of Rachel's clients, Lady Cardigan who had,
so a contemporary source claims, encouraged them. Later,
in Paris, she had taken singing lessons with a certain Signor
Muzio, who, 'failing to make a rival to Patti, as he might
have done if she had minded to study, which she would
not', had finally given up on Alma and 'left her to her own

devices.' Muzio as it turned out was a friend and business manager of Verdi and had taught singing in New York and Paris – one of many very loose connections put to clever use by the inventive Alma.

Having inherited her mother's talent for con-artisty, with a fair amount of talent and a hefty dose of Levison *chutzpah*, an inexperienced Alma had managed to wangle the Gatti season at Covent Garden, probably recruited by them in Paris. Unlike her conventional and middle ranking sister Hélène, who within a couple of years was stuck in a groove as a good, workaday *comprimaria* – a vocalist who could take small parts and always perform them with credit but who would never be a leading prima donna – Alma had no interest in applying herself to years of study. The easier and quicker route to stardom was not via the rarefied world of high opera which her sister aspired to with dogged determination, but to go down-market, where the money and popular fame was. And so she sang for entrepreneurs like the Gattis (Swiss ice cream-makers turned impresarios), following the promenade concerts with an appearance at the end of August 1878 at Hengler's Grand Cirque on Argyll Street – a venue that today is the London Palladium. After a season on tour for another pseudo-Italian Signor Campobello (a Scottish impresario who's real name was Campbell) in Belfast, Dublin, Denbigh and Bath, Alma was last seen on the London stage in February 1882 before returning to the Continent.

Four years later she was back – in August 1886 – and in apparent triumph, now billed as 'Prima Donna, Grand Opera Paris'. In fact, in the intervening time, she had made her name not at the legendary Opéra but a few doors down the road, singing for wealthy guests in the concert room of the posh Grand Hotel, as well as in a Parisian recital room, the Salle Erard. However, although Alma might claim to be a diva, the venue at which she now demonstrated her talents was Mr Robert Bignell's New Autumn Holiday Company at the Trocadero Palace of Varieties, on the corner of Great Windmill Street. Better known as the 'Troc' by the prostitutes who worked it, this glorified music hall was the home of the *poses plastiques*; a far cry indeed from the Royal Opera House in Covent Garden.

While Alma had been out conquering the musical stage in London and Paris, her sister Hélène had decamped to Italy in pursuit of her own more purist operatic dream. Her London reviews had never stretched beyond the lukewarm of 'clever', 'admirable', 'generally satisfactory'. Hélène Crosmond was 'pleasingly mediochre' – although in the best possible sense of the word. Nevertheless, she continued her vocal training in Italy and 'won high fame as a dramatic soprano', so the obituaries later claimed, in Milan, Bergamo, Ferrara and elsewhere. It was in Italy that she achieved her goal of singing *Aida*, at the operatic mecca of La Scala in Milan. But by now she was increasingly prone to emotional breakdown; one night at La Scala, one of her fellow female artistes was alarmed when Hélène claimed to have recognized among the audience, one of her younger brothers (either Aaron or Abraham) 'whose loss she had mourned for many years'. So convinced had Hélène been of his presence in one of the stalls that she had sent a message enquiring the name of the gentleman who sat there, and when told that the seat was empty had fainted, and 'remained senseless for a considerable time'.

Whilst Hélène was away in Italy, her husband back in England had been plagued by business problems, as well as being troubled by the ongoing social stigma of being a son-in-law of Madame Rachel. On 8 March 1881 he left their home on the Finchley Road, North London and took a room at a hotel near London Bridge. It was 8 p.m. the following day before a chambermaid using a pass key finally got into his room. She found him lying on the floor in a pool of blood. Edward Turner, having chosen a poignantly appropriate venue – the Terminus Hotel – had shot himself in the mouth with a Colt revolver.

His brother-in-law testified at the inquest that Edward had been out of business for some time; suffering from depression and irritability, he had feared that 'he would be affected with paralysis'. A verdict of suicide while temporarily insane was returned; Turner's will, written in July 1879, was brief and to the point. He bequeathed what little he had to Hélène, with the proviso that she arrange for his sister Eliza to live with her and that 'she on no account whatever receives at home any member of her family'; Eliza would only live with her on this condition.

Edward's death shattered Hélène's Italian career. She returned to London to bury him and, rejecting the demand of his will, immediately retreated, as 'Hannah Turner', to the protection of her brother David and his wife in Camberwell, Surrey. Quite how long she put her career on hold is not clear; it was almost four years before she was seen again on the London stage. In the interim she had almost been forgotten, referred to in reviews as a 'newcomer'. She was now in her late thirties and somewhat *passée* as a singer, struggling to maintain her position in a profession constantly being repopulated by rising young sopranos. She knocked four years off her age, which might have helped her achieve a coveted chance to sing *Aida* at theatrical impresario Augustus Harris's Royal Italian Opera in Covent Garden on 26 July 1884 – but for one night only. A return to Italy seemed the only salvation for her declining career. Concert engagements in Europe and in England followed; Hélène earned plenty of money, but her friends would later observe that she had found it difficult to 'save or economise'.

***

It was the *Glasgow Herald* on 28 April 1888 that identified the lady who had so sensationally shot herself in a cab in

London as the 'well-known operatic prima donna Hélène Crosmond'. The final crisis in Hélène's long mental decline had been the cancellation of a contract with Harris for another Italian Opera season. Hélène had stipulated that she sing *Aida*, as she had done the previous year. He had offered her the same terms as the previous year, but 'not as a leading attraction'; this time she would be a member of the company 'in reserve in case of necessity'. It was a bitter blow for Hélène, even though Harris had advanced her £20 on account. She signed the contract but returned it with the written proviso: 'It is clearly understood that I make my *re-entrée* in *Aida. E basta.* [And that's that].'

Harris had not been planning to stage *Aida* again and refused to budge. Hélène went to see him, tore up the contract in front of him when she could not get her way and stormed out. Soon after Harris hired someone else; as far as he was concerned the contract was at an end. Hélène quickly realized she had been rash in throwing away a generous salary of £40 per week for four weeks, which would undoubtedly help to salvage her financial situation and relaunch her career in England. Her solicitor Mr Young tried to persuade Harris to reinstate the contract, but he refused. Hélène seemed to Young quite 'broken down' by the news; in addition, her hopes of getting a musical professorship had, she told him, been 'blighted'. Burdened by debt and close to bankruptcy, two days before her death she wrote to a friend on the *Glasgow Herald*:

I have been at death's door. Sleepless nights, through intense neuralgia in my head, obliged me to take an overdose of a mixture which has been prescribed me by my doctor to relieve pain. After some considerable hours I was brought to life by the vigilant care of two medical men. I feel still queer, especially about the eyes. I am thinking of going away for a little while.

The loss of her contract, Hélène added would be 'pretty well the death of me through worry'. She told her solicitor she was going to head north, to Manchester, to pursue a concert tour in the area and she would telegraph him in a day or so.

But instead, on the afternoon of Thursday 27 April, Hélène Crosmond had carefully packed up her things at her lodgings at Bedford Place, changed into a red and brown striped dress with a brown and black checked ulster trimmed with imitation beaver – not one of her best outfits, as her landlady Mrs Godbold later observed – and left at 4 p.m., saying she was going out for dinner. She would return for her luggage later, she told her, as she would be leaving the following morning to go on tour. Mrs Godbold thought she had seemed rather anxious; she knew that several people had recently been pursuing her for the settlement of bills though she did not know for how much. And then she noticed that Madame Crosmond had left her door keys behind on her dressing table; so she thought she had better wait up to let her in. The following day she saw the suicide story in the newspaper and knew it was her.

In her private life, the papers subsequently observed, Hélène Crosmond had been 'distinguished by her brilliant conversational powers, her command of languages, and her wit'; she was much liked and had been regarded as 'one of the most open minded and sensible of women'. Had she not succumbed to mental strain she would 'probably have been considered the last person in the world likely to take away her life by violence'. More to the point, she had had many friends in London and Milan who would have come to her rescue had her pride not prevented her from appealing to them: shortly after her death it was revealed that another theatrical manager had been preparing to offer her a decent contract.

***

To the north of the narrow waters of the legendary Golden Horn that divides the city of Constantinople lies the suburb of Pera – the city's European quarter. In the late nineteenth century, after leaving the steamer at the quayside, you reached its main tourist thoroughfare – the Grande Rue – by toiling uphill in the heat of the day through a succession of picturesque, winding alleyways. The Grande Rue teemed with life in a city at the axis of European *fin de siècle* culture and the exotic mysteries of the Orient, its shops, and cafes carrying French names but redolent with all the smells and sounds of the Turkish bazaar and standing alongside grandly built foreign consulates, hotels and restaurants in *bell époque* style.

If you were looking for nightlife and entertainment in Pera you headed for the Grande Rue and either the Palais de Crystal or the Théâtre Français 'Concordia', two of the most cosmopolitan theatres-cum-music halls in the world, where you could rub shoulders with Greeks, Jews, Germans, Austrians, Italians, Russians, Armenians and the English. At the Concordia you had two choices: a game of roulette at the gambling tables in the saloon upstairs, where the gold coins rolled thick and fast across the green baize; or you could lounge downstairs amidst the thick fug of Turkish cigarettes, with the pretty whores circulating around you in droves, as you enjoyed a night's musical entertainment in the style of the French *cafés-chantants*. High opera it wasn't, more a second-rate mixture of popular music and variety acts, but they occasionally had good singers from Europe.

It was here, some time in the late 1880s–1890s, that Alma Verdini landed up. After her 1886 appearance in London she had continued a somewhat lurid career in Paris, during which she had titillated theatregoers by appearing in outrageous costumes, if not 'semi-nude'. Many men had pursued her; the Parisian 'king of the valse' Jules Klein had dedicated his melody 'Rayons Perdus' to her, but she had finally been forced out of Paris by a jealous lover, who had shot at her from the stalls one night. Alma had refused to prosecute; she had simply disappeared.

Years later, visiting the Concordia Theatre in Pera, one of her former admirers recognized her up on the stage. All Alma's exotically Jewish *beauté du diable* had vanished; the caste in her eye was still there, but it was no longer seductive. Nature had worked its way through the cosmetics which she had peddled and with which she had caked her skin for years and she had now become 'a living example of how "Time turns the old days to derision".'

With her looks gone and her once beautiful soprano voice cracking and fading, let us here ring down the curtain on Madame Rachel's last surviving daughter, Alma Verdini, aka Léontine Rachel, or rather just plain Leah Levy of Drury Lane. No longer beautiful for ever as her mother had promised, she ended her professional days sharing the bill with the likes of Mademoiselle Lucelle's Comic Pantomime Troupe, Miss Nellie Frazelli the Champion Lady Rifle Shot, and other 'grotesque artistes', 'eccentric comics' and contortionists whose second rate careers flickered and died at the Concordia Theatre in Pera and are now forever lost to history.

Who Was Madame Rachel?

LET ME TELL you a story.

In County Galway in the wild and woolly west of Ireland there is a little town called Aughrim, where, some time in the 1830s a Dr Fuller arrived and set himself up in medical practice. Business was thin in such an impoverished and rural spot, so the good doctor turned his hand to distilling lotions and concoctions 'to preserve and improve the delicacy of the female complexion'. He sent his young servant girl out to scout for herbs and leaves and flowers to be used in his preparations and bit by bit taught her his skills. Her name was Rachael Booker. A barefoot wench of fourteen or so, she was the daughter of Jewish gypsies who had settled in the area and spent much of their time stealing cordwood from the local landowner's park. Before too long economic decline – probably the Irish potato famine – drove the doctor and his family from Ireland to the less romantic location of Manchester, where the young Rachael 'won the heart and hand of an assistant in a chemist's shop' and from him put the finishing touches to her new found skills.

That untamed, half-literate young girl from the bogs of Ireland was the woman who became Madame Rachel. That, at least, was what Victorian readers were told by the weekly magazine *Truth* one week after Madame Rachel's death, in a piece of triumphant reporting that claimed, finally, to have tracked down her true identity. After twenty-five years of confused and contradictory reporting, at last the enameller of ladies' faces was revealed in all her dubious past history.

But there is something worryingly familiar in this tale as it was then told – a tale of poverty, abandonment, gypsies, romantic adventures. It all smacks of another similar story – that told by Alma Verdini – of her own mysterious beginnings. In 1880 it seems likely that Alma, who clearly had a fertile imagination and a talent for telling tall stories, had had the last laugh on the Victorian public by reinventing her own mother and setting up this false trail. Perhaps too she had been the source of the rumours about the proposed publication of Madame Rachel's memoirs. But why did Alma fabricate this absurd Irish story? Was it an altruistic act to protect her siblings, or, at their insistence, Rachel's relatives? Or had she simply wished to distance herself from her mother's notoriety, as she furthered her own stage career? We shall never know; but it seems highly unlikely that her siblings would have colluded in such a fiction.

Throughout the many years of press reporting on Madame Rachel, from 1852 to her death in 1880 and even beyond, she and her two eldest daughters were referred to by a variety of names, most commonly corruptions of her 'married name' – as Levison, Leverson, Levyson, Levenson and Lewison. Even the indictments for the two trials varied between Levison in 1868 and Leverson in 1878 – with the press querying the change of spelling and seeing it all as very suspicious. There was further confusion with the name Levy – the original surname, so it seemed of Phillip Levison and the one under which his and Rachel's children's births were registered. Yet perplexingly, in court in 1854, he denied ever having gone by that name.

Yet more names came and went as the rumours about Madame Rachel circulated: her real name was Moses; no, it was Jacobs, or possibly Levi or – as had originally been alleged by those who knew her around the theatres of Drury Lane – Russell. At one point in February 1878, during the remand hearings for the Pearse case, the speculation had become so intense that the *Sporting Times* had ill-advisedly published an article claiming that one of the proprietors of the *Daily Telegraph*, Joseph Moses Levy, was Madame Rachel's brother – a claim perhaps born of a confusion with the name of her errant husband, Joseph Moses. An enraged Levy had hired George Lewis and taken the editor and printer of the *Sporting Times* to court, where they were forced into a grovelling public apology.

One thing at least was certain about Madame Rachel: she had indeed been Mrs Sarah Moses, legal wife of Joseph Moses, although his name too was misreported as 'Jacob Moss' leading probably to the confusion with Jacobs as another possible surname. When Rachel junior had been cross-examined during her bankruptcy hearing in 1861, she had denied that her mother had ever gone by the name of Moses, but admitted it was the name of her mother's husband; but she made no mention that Moses was her own natural father. The reason Madame Rachel had never become Mrs Sarah Levy or Levison legitimately is, of course, that she never obtained a divorce. Many years after he had deserted her, Joseph Moses did finally reappear in her life – but as a corpse. He had been returning to England from Melbourne as a steerage passenger on the iron-clad steamship the *Royal Charter* when, after a two-month journey, the ship hit a force 12 gale at Red Wharf Bay, off Anglesey. The storm drove it onto rocks where it broke up. All but about 39 out of 498 passengers and crew went down with the ship, as well as a cargo of half a million in gold bullion, not to mention the gold brought back by individual travellers, some of whom like Moses had been out in Australia prospecting. His mutilated body was eventually found and claimed for burial by his first wife's father, Moise Marks. There is no record of Rachel's response to this disaster; she would have been free at last to marry Phillip Levison but there is no sign that she did, even though she used his name. Indeed, shortly after Moses' death, in April of 1860, she took out an insurance policy on the contents of her home at 480 New Bond Street as 'Mrs Rachel Levison'.

Then there was the question of exactly how old Madame Rachel was. Her age varies on census returns, giving a date of birth between 1814 and 1820. Her death certificate issued at Woking Prison described her as 60 years old in 1880, but in 1877 she had told her maid Sabina Pinney that she was sixty-three. She had further muddied the waters by saying that she had been born in the United States – a claim also made on the 1871 census in prison. Phillip Leverson similarly claimed in statements in court that he had been born in New York and that he had known Sarah since she was 'a little girl'. But there is no way of knowing whether the two of them had actually ever spent time there.

The one name above all others that Madame Rachel consistently denied as being her true one was Russell, which in any event, seemed a decidedly un-Jewish name. In 1861 Rachel junior had confirmed in court that Russell was her mama's maiden name but vehemently denied that she had ever been known around Drury Lane as 'Sally Russell'. Madame Rachel's own typically inflated assertion in her promotional material in 1865 was that the enamelling art she practiced had 'descended from generation to generation of her family'. But no, Madame Rachel's ancestors were not Jewish perfumers and cosmeticians of yore. Far from it.

The truth had been out there waiting to be found all along – if only some diligent journalist had done some digging. The pamphlet Rachel had brought out after the first Borradaile trial – the 'History and Trial of Mdm Rachel or, Beautiful For Ever' – had claimed in passing that she was 'first cousin to one of our most popular singers and music composers'. At the time it had probably been dismissed as yet another of her many lies but this much, in fact, was true.

***

Sarah bat David was born in Long Acre, Covent Garden in around 1814, the daughter of David Russell (David ben Michael) and his wife Rachel HaCohen (Rachel bat Jacob), who had married at the New Synagogue in Leadenhall Street in the City of London in 1805. She had two siblings: Lewis born in 1810 and Rosa born 1819. David Russell, who later lived at Cobb's Yard near Petticoat Lane – an area then densely populated by Jews – was described on his death in 1839 as a 'broker', probably a euphemism for a money lender or pawnbroker. He had been born in around 1774 in the East End, one of seven children of Michael Russell. But Michael Russell was an immigrant to London: he had moved there from the tiny Jewish enclave at Sheerness, on the Isle of Sheppey in north Kent, where he had been born c.1735. The Russells of Sheerness were

Ashkenazi Jews who had, so the story went, been settled there since they first immigrated some time in the 1600s – who knows from where; family legend has it that they had changed their name to Russell from Levy on arrival in this country. Up to and during the Napoleonic Wars the Russells had prospered in the area known as 'Blue Town', with much trade coming and going in the local naval dockyard, but economic decline in north Kent at the end of the wars drove most of them out.

Madam Rachel's illustrious Russell family connection came from her father David's nephew and her first cousin – Henry Russell – son of Moses Russell, a naval agent in Sheerness. Henry, who had been born there in around 1812, went on to become a celebrated pianist and composer, and, with his fine baritone voice, one of the leading popular singers of his day both in England as well as America and Canada (where he spent his early years till 1845). As a song writer, he was celebrated as the author of the songs 'Woodman, Spare that Tree', 'Cheer Boys, Cheer' and 'A Life on the Ocean Wave' among over two hundred songs in his repertoire. Singing was clearly in the Russell family's blood. Three of Henry's nieces – Ann, Charlotte and Maria – formed an ensemble as 'The Russell Family' and made a decorous debut giving musical entertainments in London in 1853 under the patronage of the influential Rothschild family of Jewish bankers. Charlotte went on to enjoy a singing career, becoming the leading soprano at the

Oxford Music Hall in London in the 1860s.

Henry Russell's side of the family had very distinguished Jewish connections – through his mother Sarah Levin's Russian line – to a succession of eminent rabbis, including Solomon Herschel, British Chief Rabbi from 1802 to 1842. All of this was reason enough for the wider Russell family not to want their names dragged through the mire of Madame Rachel's notorious criminal career. Whether she herself drew a smokescreen over her Russell name voluntarily or under duress from the family (she made no mention of her Russell connections at the 1878 trial) we shall never know.

The Jewish community at Sheerness did not survive the century: its small wooden synagogue built in 1811 had only five Jewish families in its congregation by 1841, many having moved to Glasgow ten years previously. Those remaining worked in the main as pawnbrokers, haberdashers and furniture-brokers. By 1853 only fifteen seat holders remained at the synagogue and by 1887 the community was too small to keep it going. It was closed soon after but the synagogue was not finally dismantled until 1935. Today a handful of forlorn headstones survive in the Hope Street Jewish Cemetery in Sheerness, their Hebrew inscriptions almost obliterated by the salt and sea air.

After 1868 it is clear that Madame Rachel's children tried to loosen their ties with the name Levison: when Hélène committed suicide in 1888, an unnamed journalist on *Truth* revealed that 'After their mother's disgrace all the children took different names,' and portentously announced that 'I for one, do not intend to lift the veil, to the disparagement of those who are still seeking to gain an honest livelihood.' Hélène had long since divested herself of her Levison association; Rachel junior retreated into respectability as Mrs Llewellyn Pritchard before her death and Madame Rachel's two other sons – Abraham and Aaron both appear to have dropped their Jewish given names and to have been later known as Harry and Arthur – though one of them, apparently suffering from 'melancholia', had died young. David, however, having given up his medical training to become a financial journalist in the city, retained his Levison surname until his death in 1909, leaving one son Harry, Madame Rachel's only known grandchild.

***

If you walk down New Bond Street today you will still find a shop at no. 47, but it isn't the original building Madame Rachel had in the 1860s. The whole of the façade was extensively revamped in the early 1900s, since when it has been the premises of François Pinet, a French couture shoe maker. The house at 50 Maddox Street is still there, just round the corner, but the terrace of houses of which it forms part has recently been extensively refurbished. We shall never know the truth of Madame Rachel's supposed grand properties at Blackheath and St Cloud in Paris, nor answer the one remaining question: what happened to all the money she made? The answer may well lie in Paris. But at least now, her story can, after many false trails and blind alleys, at last be laid to rest.

There remains one final tantalizing puzzle: what happened to those account books and the details of Madame Rachel's many and celebrated clients? The key to the truth about her dubious business concerns and criminal activities, from her early days in Drury Lane till her 1878 trial, almost certainly went to the grave with Sir George Lewis, knighted in 1902 and for fifty years London's leading criminal lawyer. Whilst Léontine/Alma may, in the end, have had pressure brought upon her not to publish or had even been bought off, the ultimate scandalous memoirs of the century would undoubtedly have been those of the highly-connected Lewis. But he gave up keeping a diary in the 1870s, when representing clients in some very high profile court cases including the Tranby Croft gambling scandal involving the Prince of Wales. Interviewed in 1893, he remarked in typically sphinxlike manner that 'No novel was ever written, no play ever produced, that has or could contain such incidents and situations as at the present moment are securely locked up in the archives of memory which no man will ever discover.' He later destroyed all his professional papers, long held in the strong room at 10 Ely

Place, swearing that when he died 'all the confidences of London society' would die with him.

It is therefore highly appropriate that the imposing granite chest tomb of Sir George Lewis, where he was laid to rest in 1911, is to be found at the Jewish Cemetery at Willesden. A hundred yards or so away, in a barren and forgotten corner amidst a row of children's graves, lies the unmarked resting place of Sarah Rachel Levison or Leverson or Levy – but who, as we now know, was born Sarah Russell – and who, unlike the illustrious Sir George, at last rests in eternal anonymity.

Notes on Sources

PROLOGUE

Hélène Crosmond's suicide: 'Attempted Suicide', *Times* 27 April 1888; 'The Piccadilly Tragedy', *Daily Telegraph*, 28 April; 'Tragedy at the West-End', *Daily News*, 28 April; 'The Tragedy at the West-End: Sad Story of a Prima Donna', *Pall Mall Gazette*, 28 April; 'Suicide of a Lady in a Cab', *Lloyds Weekly Newspaper*, 29 April; 'The Suicide in Piccadilly, *Leeds Mercury,* 1 May; 'Inquests', *Times,* 1 May; 'Sad Suicide of an Opera Singer', *Pall Mall Gazette*, 1 May; 'Fearful Death of Poor Hélène Crosmond', *Birmingham Daily Post,* 4 May; 'Suicide of an Opera Singer', *Reynolds's Newspaper*, 6 May. See also notes to Chapter 12.

CHAPTER 1:
SALLY RUSSELL OF DRURY LANE

St Clement Danes in the 1840s–1850s: Dickens, *Dickens Dictionary of London*; Diprose, *Some Account of the Parish of Saint Clement Danes,*

1868, vol. I, pp. 76-7; 160-8; vol. 2, 1876, pp. 55, 60, 217–18; Heckethorn, *Lincoln's Inn Fields*; Hibbert, *London Encyclopedia;* Kilch, 'A Corner of London'; Thornbury, Walter, *Old and New London* vol. 3; 'Sketches of life by A Radical' (Alton Locke), *Harpers New Monthly Magazine* vol. 1, 1850, p. 806. Henry Mayhew's 'Labour and the Poor', has a fascinating description of the baked potato and fried fish trade. The *Brighton Observer* 2 October 1868 names Sarah's business in Clare Court. For the brothels of London, notably Kate Hamilton's, see Pearl, *Girl with the Swansdown Seat,* esp. pp. 177-80. Insulting proposal to an actress: Ballantine, *Some Experiences* vol. 2, p. 77. Phillip Levison bankrupt: *Jurist,* 1855 p. 335. Joanna Mack: *Morning Chronicle* 25 August 1857; assault on David Levison *Times* 16 July 1859. Rachel's loss of hair and early cosmetics career: H&T p. 2: Arabian recipes: Madame Rachael *Spatula* p. XX. Spurious claim re Mademoiselle Rachel: *Morning Chronicle* 8 July 1859. Mary Ann Christian: *Morning Chronicle* 13 November 1875, *Lloyds Weekly Newspaper* 15 November.

Biographical information on Sarah prior to 1868 is drawn from 'The Life of Madame Rachel', which forms the preface to *The Extraordinary Life and Trial of Madame Rachel* (hereafter ELTMR) pp. iii–iv. Boase, Frederic, 'Sarah Rachel Russell' and Boase, George, 'Madame Rachel', were the first to offer biographical information, drawing heavily – with some inevitable inaccuracy – on the pamphlets produced at the time of Madame Rachel's 1868 trials. Other information – often contradictory – about Sarah and Phillip Levison is scattered in nuggets across their many court appearances prior to 1868, especially the David Belasco trial – see e.g. *Lloyds Weekly* 9 May 1852, though Rachel's evidence is only to be found at

David Belasco, 10 May 1852 at Old Bailey Online. See also evidence in Levison v. Broadhurst, *Times,* 5 June 1854 and sources in ch. 2 for Levison v Atloff 1857, Rachel junior's bankruptcy 1861 and the Carnegie case 1862.

CHAPTER 2:
MADAME RACHEL'S COSTLY ARABIAN PREPARATIONS

See Cosmetics bibliography for general overviews by esp. Ellis, Cooley, McLaughlin, Montez, Williams. Raven recipe: 'Face Enamelling', p. 23; 1770; William Arthur Poucher, *Perfumes, Cosmetics and Soaps*, vol. 2, London: Chapman & Hall, 1993, pp. 12–13. Buch'hoz's recipes: *Toilet of Flora* pp. 35-8; *Beeton's* prognostications on female beauty are at pp. 88–9, 148; see also Walker *Female Beauty*. Adulteration: 'Cosmetic Poisons', *Journal of the Society of Arts* 5 August 1864 pp. 614-15. Rimmel: *Book of Perfumes* and his entry in DNB; for his advertisements see e.g. *Era,* 20 January 1839. *Figaro in London* on Queen Victoria: 16 September 1837. See also Rowland biography in DNB and his *Toilette of Health, Beauty and Fashion*. For advertising puffery including Rowland, see Roughead *Bad Companions* p. 40, Strachan *Advertising and the Satirical Culture*, pp. 208–10.

Levison v Atloff: *Daily News* 8 November 1857; *Times* 9 November; *Bristol Mercury* 13 November; *Trewman's Exeter Flying Post* 18 November. Exchange between Rachel junior and Mr Temple: *Freeman's Journal,* 9 November. Further commentary: 'The Cause of the Cosmetics and 'Stucco for the Softer Sex' *Punch* 20 November 1858 and 26 March 1859; 'Face Enamelling' and Montez, *Arts of Beauty*, p. 37.

Rachel's 1859 advertisements: e.g. *Morning Chronicle* July–August; *Era* 5 and 12 May. Rachel's junior's bankruptcy: *Times* and *Morning Chronicle* 13 November, 1861; *Era* 17 November; *Daily News* 18 January and 1 February 1862. Renewed advertising campaign 1862 : *Era* 2, 9, 16 March, 27 July, 3 and 10 August, 14 September, 12 and 19 October. Milton case: *Daily News* 3 and 10 May 1862, *Lloyds Weekly* 4 May, *Standard* 3 and 10 May, *Reynolds's Newspaper* 11 May; Rachel's letter to *The Times* 5 May.

CHAPTER 3:
THE INNER LIFE OF FASHIONABLE PEOPLE

History of Bond Street: Desebrock *The Book of Bond Street*; Brereton, *A Walk Down Bond Street*, Tallis *London Street Views*, Margetson, *Leisure and Pleasure*, Adburgham. *Shops and Shopping*. Beauty doctor at Mr Trout's: Thompson, *Quacks of Old London* pp.201–3. Madame Rachel's Bond Street premises: A. O. Tibbits *Cassell's Saturday Journal* 1898, 'Madame Rachael', *Spatula* p. 328; Rachel junior's testimony EH&T pp.67–9; Jenkins *Six Criminal Women*, p. 5; Wyndham *Blotted Scutcheons* p. 243; Anon *London in the Sixties*, pp. 279–80; Kelly's *Post Office, Trade and Court Directory* 1862, pp. 284-5.

Carnegie trial: see especially *Times* 19 June 1862, *Daily News* 20 June, *Examiner* 21 June, *Belfast News-Letter* 24 June. For wider press comments on the issues raised see: *Morning Advertiser* quoted in BFE

p. 16; *Glasgow Herald* 24 June; *Birmingham Post* 21 June; *Caledonian Mercury* 21 and 30 June.

For Wilkie Collins see Ellis *Wilkie Collins* and Peters *The King of Inventors*; and for a very useful site on his work *www.wilkie-collins.info/index.htm*

CHAPTER 4:
BEAUTIFUL FOR EVER

Quotations are all from Madame Rachel's privately printed pamphlet, 'Beautiful For Ever' – copies in the British Library and Bodleian Library Oxford, among others. Madame Rachel's price list is listed on pp. vi–viii of ELTMR. Average earnings are from Geoffrey Best *Mid-Victorian Britain*, London: Weidenfeld & Nicolson, 1971 p. 124. Exotic names of Rachel's products: 'Beautiful For Ever' *Chambers's Journal.* Typical Rachel advertisements: November 1863 to December 1864 in the classified ads of *Times* and *Era* among others. Madame Rachel's male customers: Anon., *London in the Sixties*, p. 280.

Rachel junior's run-in with the cab driver: *Era* 22 March and *Times*, 23 March 1863. Madame Rachel paying the cabbie's fine, H&T p. 2; 'Take care of the putty'

Pall Mall Gazette, 22 February 1865. The Frederick Beaver case was most extensively reported in the *Belfast News-Letter* 12 April 1865; see also: *Observer* 9 April; *Times* 10 April; *Liverpool Mercury* 11 April. The Cardigan story was published by *Belfast News-Letter* 27 October 1863. Aurora Knight's claim: *Times* 13 December 1865,

Glasgow Herald and *Liverpool Mercury* 16 December, *Trewman's Flying Post* 20 December, *Birmingham Daily Post* 22 December, *Hampshire Telegraph* 23 December.

Rachel's debts for advertising: *Birmingham Daily Post* 25 August 1864; 'Bull and Middleton v Levi [sic]': *Caledonian Mercury* 27 September 1866.

Collins's *Armadale* re Mother Oldershaw is from p. 160. Wilkie Collins's appendix can be read at *www.wilkie-collins.info/index.htm* / Advertisements for abortifacients: Miller *Framed* pp. 75–6; see also John Sutherland's introduction to the Penguin edition, pp. ix–x. Rachel junior's statement about her mother's activities in Paris: ELT pp. 68-9. Rachel's carriage accident in Paris: *Daily Telegraph* 10 August 1867 – the award of damages was later mentioned in Levison v Stack , *Lloyds Weekly,* 20 June 1868.

CHAPTER 5:
LEWIS & LEWIS

George Lewis: see entry in DNB; profile in *New York Times* 29 Sept 1907; obituaries, 8 December 1911 in *Times* and *New York Times*; 'Sir George Lewis', in *Strand* and Juxon, *Lewis & Lewis* ch. 5, where the Esdaile case is discussed on pp. 64–6, though it is possible that the name is bogus to protect the subjects' true identities, as too that of Alice Maynard, whose story is told on pp. 69–70 of Kingston *Remarkable Rogues.* See also Williams *Leaves of a Life* p. 140. Rumours about Rachel's premises at Bond Street are in Parry *Vagabonds All*, p. 112 and Boase 'Madame Rachel', p. 323. Kingston *Remarkable Rogues* pp. 67–70 contains veiled allusions but with no substantiating cross references. Haymarket and houses of assignation: Pearl *Swansdown Seat* pp. 22–3, 169–80, Chesney, *Victorian Underworld* p. 241.

Ranelagh: Harré *Heavenly Sinner*, p. 15; Anon *London in the Sixties* p.2. Numerous Montes biographies recount the Ranelagh incident, e.g. Harré *Heavenly Sinner* pp. 179–82, Wyndham *Magnificent Montez* pp. 51–6. For his affair with Annie Miller see *My Grandfather* pp. 165–6. For Mrs Borradaile's early visits to Rachel see trial reports for chapter 6, especially *Daily Telegraph* 21 August. Press run up to trial: *Era* 14 June 1868, *Lloyds Weekly* 14 and 28 June, *Liverpool Mercury* 10 June. Lady Palmerston: Theo Aronson *Victoria and Disraeli* London: Macmillan, 1977 p. 104; 'Widow of the Period' *Lloyds Weekly* 14 June. Crabbe and Houston assault: *Reynolds's Newspaper* 21 June; Rachel ill: Van Winkle *Sixty Famous Cases* pp. 13–14, *Daily News* 23 June, Wyndham *Blotted Scutcheons* p. 253. Judge & Jury mock trials: *Bell's Life in London* 13 June; *Tomahawk* parody 27 June; street ballad: *Curiosities of Street Literature* Reeves & Turner 1871 p. 142; Byron parody Walter Hamilton: *Parodies of the Works of English and American Authors*, vol. III, London: Reeves and Turner, 1886 p. 194; Rachel's royal warrant *Pall Mall Gazette* 19 June. Trial postponed and Rachel's bail: *Daily News* 8 July, *Times* 10 July. Ranelagh and 'flunkeyism': *Reynolds's Newspaper* 21 June, *Glasgow Herald* 25 June. Louisa Gould: *Pall Mall Gazette* and *Daily News* 25 June, *Birmingham Daily Post* 25, 26, 27 June. Gould was back in jail in October 1868, see: *Illustrated Police News* 24 October.

CHAPTER 6:
A CHARLATAN AND HER WILLING DUPE

Victorian women criminals: Knelman *Twisting in the Wind*, ch. 2. Barrett's execution: *Times* and *Daily News* 27 May 1868. Old Bailey, Rachel's legal team and the run up to the trial: Jackson *Old Bailey* p. 68; Anon, *London in the Sixties* p. 131; Wyndham *Blotted Escutcheons* p. 253; *Times* 17 August.

Madame Rachel's trial was extensively reported in the national press 21–23 August 1868. See especially *Daily Telegraph* and *Times* for the fullest accounts, as well as newspapers digitized in 19th Century British Library Newspapers. See also: H&T and NMM and Hogg, 'The Piccadilly Papers'; *Pall Mall Gazette* 21 and 22 August; *Reynolds's Newspaper* 23 August. The following accounts cover both the August and September trials, often merging the two and quoting extensively from the William letters: Williams *Leaves from a Life* pp. 126–39; Van Winkle, *Sixty Famous Cases* pp. 3–65. Roughead *Bad Companions,* pp.50–65; See also Kingston *Dramatic Days* pp. 21–2; Wyndham, *Blotted Scutcheons* pp. 249–59; Ballantine, *Some Experiences of a Barrister's Life,* pp. Rachel in the dock: Kingston *Remarkable Rogues* p. 76 and Hogg, 'Piccadilly Papers' p. 380; Borradaile described: Roughead *Bad Companions,* p. 51, Williams *Leaves of a Life* pp. 127–8. 'I'll beautify them': Kingston *Dramatic Days* p. 21; 'charlatan and dupe': *Pall Mall Gazette,* 22 August.

CHAPTER 7:
MRS PLUCKER SPARROWTAIL

Post mortem on Rachel's first trial: *Daily News*, 22 August 1868, *Times* 27 August; *Glasgow Herald*, 25 August; *Scotsman* quoted in NMM p. 6; 'Madame Rachel', *Saturday Review*, *Penny Illustrated Times*, 29 August; Kingston *Dramatic Days*, p. 22. 'Old lawyer' *Trewman's Exeter Flying Post*, 30 September; juryman *Daily News* 1 September; Toryism *Reynolds's Newspaper* 13 September; Mat Robson *Era*, 11 October; Arthur Lloyd *Era* 6 September and Newton, *Crime and the Drama*, p. 137. 'Extraordinary disclosures' *Reynolds's Newspaper* 23 August; 'The Persecuted Jewess' *Tomahawk*; Roberts's appeal to have the trial moved *Manchester Times* 19 September; business booming at Bond Street, *Hull Packet* 18 September.

CHAPTER 8:
THE BOND STREET MYSTERY

The national press covered the 21–5 September 1868 trial exhaustively, in particular the *Daily Telegraph* and *The Times* which quote Borradaile's 'Dear William' letters at length – see sources for chapter 6, ELTMR; Van Winkle *Sixty Famous Cases* pp. 194-252; *Reynolds's Newspaper* 27 September; Roughhead, *Bad Companions* pp. 52–65; *Illustrated Police News* 26 September. Rachel in the dock: *Liverpool Mercury* 23 September; 'self-confessed idiot': *Pall Mall Gazette* 22 September; shirtless Lord Ranelagh: ELTMR p. 32, *Reynolds's Newspaper* 27 September. Leontie called to give evidence:

Manchester Times 26 September, *Pall Mall Gazette* 23 September. Mrs Borradaile and Rachel's children: *Glasgow Herald* 23 September, ELTMR p. 36; Rachel and Leontie as witnesses: Roughead, *Bad Companions* p. 62–4; Rachel junior's cross-examination *Daily News* 25 September, ELTMR p.67–71; Leontie's: ELTMR pp. 73–5. Digby Seymour 'affliction of Providence' and 'hang a cat', ELTMR p. 90. Ballantine's summing up: ELTMR pp. 93-100 and *Times, Telegraph and Pall Mall Gazette* 26 September. Lyon v. Home: Van Winkle, p. 241; Watermark evidence: *Times* 28 September. Madame Rachel's final words from the dock: *Reynolds's Newspaper* 27 September, *Glasgow Herald* 26 September, *Jackson's Oxford Journal* 3 October, Wyndham *Blotted Scutcheons* p. 359. Anti-Semitic comments: ELTMR p. 105, 122,; *Reynolds's Newspaper* 27 September; 'Last of Madame Rachel', *Saturday Review* p. 119; *Trewman's flying Gazette* 20 September See also Miller *Framed* p. 78. Opinions on Kerr: *Trewman's Flying Post* 30 September, *times* 26 September, *Preston Guardian* 26 September; *Pall Mall Gazette* 26 September and 3 October, *Specatator* 3 October. Speculation on the 'real' William: Parry *Vagabonds All* p. 121, NMM pp. 4–5. 'Moral pest': Ballantine *Some Experiences* p. 80; Borradaile's money: ELTMR p. 23; 'senescent Sappho': L&T p. 72; Ranelagh: peeping Tom, Anon, *London in the Sixties* p. 241; 'Madame Rachel's man' *Hampshire Telegraph* 23 July; letter to *Daily News* 8 October. 'Deep cunning': ELTMR p. 117; Rachel's appeal: *Lloyds Weekly Newspaper* 27 September. See also front cover cartoons *Illustrated Police News* 24 October 1868.

CHAPTER 9:
CLOSED DURING ALTERATIONS

The Writ of Error was discussed extensively in the legal press but for more lucid summaries see O'Donnell *Old Bailey* pp. 160-1 and *Times* 3 May 1869. Tussauds effigy: *Freeman's Journal* 9 November; 'Beautiful For Ever' waltzes: *Daily Telegraph* 21 October; Herr Schutze: *Era* 8 November; Bonfire night: *Aberdeen Journal* 11 November; *Girl of the Period Miscellany* no. 1 March 1860 p. 138.

Millbank: Mayhew and Binny 'Female Convict Prison', pp. 269–73; *Murray's Modern London* pp. 149-50; Byrne, *Prisons and Punishments of London,* pp. 93–7; Hibbert *London Encyclopaedia.,* pp. 518–19; *Penny Illustrated Paper* 14 October 1865. 'Melancholy waste', *David Copperfield,*ch. 47; Kate Summerscale *The Suspicions of Mr Whicher*, London: Bloomsbury, 2007, pp. 161–2; 'Two Hours in Millbank'. Millbank was closed in 1890 and demolished in 1903.

For the case against Haynes see: *Daily News* 25 and 26 January 1869, *Liverpool Mercury* 27 January, *Illustrated Police News* 30 January, *Reynolds's Newspaper,* 31 January. Philip Leverson: *Belfast News-Letter* 19 February. 'Motives of delicacy': *Glasgow Herald* 18 February; 'children live after': *Liverpool Mercury* 19 February; charge dismissed: *Pall Mall Gazette* 6 May; 'Beware of the paint': *Every Saturday* 20 February. Maddox Street contents sale: *Times* 26 February and 10 March; *Glasgow Herald* 18 March; 'Madame Rachel Under the Hammer', *Illustrated Police News* 20 March. Rachel back in Newgate: *Reynolds's Newspaper* 21 March; date for appeal: *Examiner* 10 April, *Pall Mall Gazette* 22 April. *Punch* 10 April; *Judy* satire 24 March.

Sutton v Borradaile: *Times* 31 March and 1 April; *Pall Mall Gazette*

31 March; *Daily News* 31 March, 1–4 April; *Reynolds's Newspaper* and *Lloyds Weekly* 4 April; *Examiner* 10 April). Rachel junior v Stack *Lloyds Weekly* 20 and 27 June; refusal of McNeil writ: *Belfast News-Letter* 3 August and 11 September.

Léontine Rachel in Paris: *Times* classified ads 26 April, 5 May, 11 June 1869. 1871 Census 27 Burghley Road, RG10 217 fo. 42–3. Rachel at Millbank: Griffiths, *Memorials of Millbank* p. 381, *Secrets of the Prison- House* p. 11; at Woking: info from Corinne Garstang's blog *www.wokingprison.blogspot.com/*. Back in business: *Era,* 1 December 1872.

CHAPTER 10:
GONE TO GROUND

Rachel's return to business: *Belfast News-Letter* 20 November 1873, *Newcastle Courant* 7 August 1874; prize heifer *Times* 12 December 1877. Hannah's career: Register of Auditions and Committee Minutes, Royal Academy of Music, GRO marriage and death certificates. For Paris see: Bottin de Commerce; *Paris Mode* 16 April 1872. Paris Morgue: Archives de la Préfecture de Paris. See also Schwartz *Spectacular Realities*, pp. 4–88 and Emile Zola's *Therese Raquin*, Oxford: Oxford University Press, 2008, ch XIII pp. 73–8 for a chilling description written in 1867. Elise's death announced: Berger, *Jewish Victorian* p. 323.

Hélène's debut: *Graphic* 29 December 1877, *Daily News* 4 February 1878, *Times* 6 February, *Pall Mall Gazette* 8 February; *Hull Packet* 22 March. Rachel on a charge again *Era* 17 February.

CHAPTER 11:
A SHOW FOR IDLE WOMEN

Cecilia Pearse: see her *The Enchanted Past* and *The Romance of a Great Singer*; Jopling, *Twenty Years of My Life* pp. 227–8; biographical notes on her in The Correspondence of James McNeill Whistler at Glasgow University, *www.whistler.arts.gla.ac.uk/jmw*

For Pearse's patronage of Rachel see remand hearings: *Daily News* 15 February, *Reynolds's Newspaper* 17 February 1878, *Times* 18 and 25 February – which has Rachel's comments on Lewis, *Hampshire Telegraph* 23 February, *Cardiff Western Mail* 22 February *Illustrated Police News* 16 March. Theft of Lady Dudley's jewels: *Pall Mall Gazette* 14 December, *Birmingham Daily Post* 16 December and *Times* 15 and 16 December 1874. The Dudleys deny patronage of Rachel: *Liverpool Mercury* and *Times* 25 February 1878, *Newcastle Courant* 1 March. Postponement of trial: *Times* 13 and 14 March.

The online Old Bailey version of the trial whilst giving Cecilia Pearse's statement in full is heavily truncated on the remaining evidence, therefore see national press, especially *Daily News* 6 April, which included Rachel's statement from the dock; *The Times*, *Daily Telegraph*, *Birmingham Post* 11 and 12 April; *Belfast News-Letter* 11 and 23 April. The *Penny Illustrated Paper* for 20 April contains an illustration of Rachel in the Central Criminal Court as well as a profile of Judge Huddlestone. Women wanting tickets for trial: *Newcastle Courant* 15 March and 5 April, *Western Mail* 2 April, *Illustrated Police News* 16 March. Madame Restell: Allan Keller *Scandalous Lady: The Life and Times of Madame Restell*, New York: Atheneum, 1981,

Cynthia Watkins Richardson, 'In the Eye of Power: The Notorious Madame Restell', an online e-journal article.

The description of Rachel in the dock is from Horler *Black Souls* p. 34; Pearse's jewellery described in Indictment PRO; Sabina Pinney's evidence: Old Bailey online and *Belfast News-Letter* and *Leeds Mercury* 11 April; Orsalina Palmiera and forensic evidence of Senior, Bond and Redwood all repeated as per the remand hearings – see *Times* 18 February; *Daily News* 15 and 25 February. Rachel's speech: *Daily News* and *Birmingham Daily Post* 12 April; *Jackson's Oxford Journal* 13 April; clearing her name *Daily News* and *Times* 18 February; Huddlestone's sentence *Penny Illustrated Paper* 20 April. Dumas pere *Times* 12 April; idle women *Belfast News-Letter* 17 April; lack of sympathy for Pearse: *Leeds Mercury* 12 April, *Freeman's Journal* 15 April, *Derby Mercury* 17 April. Medical press quoted in *Bristol Mercury* 22 April.

Rachel at Woking: Robinson, 'Female Convict Life p. 257; making dolls *Pall Mall Gazette* 28 September 1895; Phillip Leverson death Berger, *Jewish Victorian,* p. 340; Rachel's death and inquest *Times* and *Birmingham Daily Post* 18 October, *Penny Illustrated Paper* and *Illustrated Police News* 24 October; information from the Jewish Burial Society and GRO death certificates.

For front page cartoons see: *Illustrated Police News* 2 and 9 March, 20 April, 1878.

CHAPTER 12:
THE FINAL CURTAIN

Rumours about Rachel's account books and memoirs: *Manchester Times* 28 May 1881, *Trewman's Flying Post* 15 June, *Freeman's Journal* 9 August, *Northern Echo* 18 August. Palmieri *Birmingham Daily Post* 25 February 1878; Huddlestone at trial *Northern Echo* 13 June 1881, *Belfast News-Letter* 12 April 1878.

Pearse on Hélène *Reynolds's Newspaper* 17 February 1878; review of debut *Graphic* 2 July 1878. Verdini's debut: *Graphic* 10 August 1878, *Era* 11 August, *funny Folks* 17 August. See also: Anon., *London in the Sixties* pp. 280–1. Duaghter of *parfumeuse*: *Ear* 18 August; fanciful stories by Verdini: *New York Times*: 'Broken Marriage Vows', 6 May 1880, 'French Life and Affairs', 10 July 1881, 'Events in Paris Life', 22 December 1881; Verdi's tutelage *Newcastle Courant* 18 March 1881. The Paris salon: Sabin *Le Beauté* pp. 101-2, d'Almeras *La vie Parisienne*, pp. 67-8. Léontine Rachel's beauty products: *Myra's Journal of Dress and Fashion* 1 February 1882, *Myra's Threepenny Journal* 1 January 1886, *Le Figaro* 20 June 1891; Countess of Cardigan: Anon *London in the Sixties*, p. 280. 'Rayons Perdus', 1875, Biblioteca Nacional, Madrid.

For details of Hélène's aborted contract see *Pump Court*, vol. VIII NS no. 82, 12 May 1880, pp. 63-4. The run up to her suicide is discussed in obituaries such as: 'The Death of Madame Crosmond', *Musical World*, 5 May 1888; 'Music', *Truth,* vol. XXIII, 1888, 3 May, pp. 759–60 'Mme Héléne Crosmond', *Musical Standard*, 5 May. See also sources for chapter 1. Ghost of brother *Birmingham Daily Post* 28 April and 4 May, *Pall Mall Gazette* 12 Mar 1881; Edward Cooke

Turner 'Suicide in an Hotel', *Pall Mall Gazette* 12 March 1881, *Lloyds Weekly*, 13 March, *Times* 15 March 1881. His will is at London Probate Registry 10 May 1881. For the run-up to Helen's suicide see *Glasgow Herald*, 28 April, *Lloyds Weekly*, 29 April, *Pall Mall Gazette* and *Leeds Mercury* 1 May.

Context on Alma's last days in Pera, Istanbul can be gleaned from the many ads for the Concordia Theatre, in *Era* from 1878 onwards; see also: Albert Charles Wratislaw, *A Consul in the East*, Edinburgh: Blackwood, 1924, pp. 8–9; Richard Graf von Pfeil, *Experiences of a Prussian Officer in the Russian Service during the Turkish War of 1877–8,* London: Edward Stanford, 1893, p. 320; Demetrius Coufopoulus, *Guide to Constantinople*, London: Adam & Charles Black, 1910, p. 36.

POSTSCRIPT:
WHO WAS MADAME RACHEL?

For confusion over names and genealogy see sources for ch. 1. Levi libel case *Daily News* 7 March and 13 April 1878; Jacobs *Penny Illustrated Paper,* 20 April 1878. Death of Joseph Moses: *Archives Isréalites.*

Sally Russell: *Era* 17 November 1861, *Morning Chronicle* 13 November 1861; 'generation to generation', 'Beautiful For Ever', *Chambers's*, p. 451.

The Russell family genealogy is from Oliver *Meet the Family*, esp. pp. 55–69 and entry for Sarah Rachel Leverson at Dan Russell's Russell Family posting at Rootsweb. Further information from

Arna Samuels, Patricia Oliver, Dan Russell and Gordon Ashbury – the latter three are all descendants of the Sheerness Russell family – as well as GRO certificates in the author's possession. For Sheerness: W H Studt, ' A Jewish Community in Sheerness' pts 1 and 2, *Bygone Kent* vol. 12, nos 3 and 4, 1991; Roth, *Rise of Provincial Jewry,* pp. 96–7; 'lift the veil' *Truth* vol. XXIII, 1888 p. 759. Lewis 'all the confidences: 'Sir George Lewis', *Strand* p. 652.

Bibliography

ARCHIVES

Archives de la Préfecture de Paris: Morgue, Registre des disparus, hommes et femmes 1871-1878; Registre de la morgue, 1874.

Arna Samuels papers, author's collection

Attested List of the Convict Prison at Woking Surrey: Quarter ending 30 June 1871; Quarter ending 30 June 1872; HO 8/188 and 192, PRO, Kew.

Bottin de Commerce, Paris: rue de Choiseul, Carton 264, DP4, 1862; rue de la Paix, Carton 836, DP4, 1862; rue du Roi de Rome, Carton 971, DP 4, 1862

Old Bailey Sessions Papers, 1684–1913: Tenth Session 1867–8, Case 468 August 1868, Case 721m September 1868; Sixth Session, 1877–8, Case 883 April 1878.Guildhall Library, London.

Committee Minutes of the Royal Academy of Music, 1869–1877, microfilm MF 177 at RAM library.

Indictment, Sarah Rachel Leverson 1878, PRO CRIM 4/883

Register of Applicants for Ticket of Leave, 1872, PRO Kew, P.COM 6/17

Register of Auditions 1837–73, Royal Academy of Music

DIGITAL ARCHIVES AND SOURCES

19th Century UK Periodicals, British Library

19th Century British Library Newspapers

British Periodicals Index

England Census Returns at www.Ancestry.co.uk

Chicago Tribune Digital Archive 1852–1984

Google News Archive

Dictionary of National Biography (DNB)

Guardian and *Observer* Digital Archive, 1821–2000 and 1791–2000 respectively

Historic Australian Newspapers 1803-1954, National Library of Australia

Irish Times Digital Archive 1859 to the present

New York Times Article Archive 1851–1980

Newspaper Archive.com

Papers Past, New Zealand, 1839-1920

Scotsman Digital Archive 1817–1950

Times Digital Archive 1785–1985

Washington Post Digital Archive 1877–1986

Central Criminal Court: trial of David Belasco, 10 May 1852 (evidence of Sarah Levison). Online at www.oldbaileyonline.org (NB not full transcript)

Central Criminal Court: trials of Sarah Rachel Leverson: 17 August 1868, 21 September 1868, 8 April 1878. Online at *www.oldbaileyonline.org* (NB not full transcripts).

NEWSPAPERS AND JOURNALS NOT YET DIGITIZED

Brighton Observer
Daily Telegraph
Surrey Advertiser
Truth
Illustrated London News

PRIMARY SOURCES

'The Extraordinary Life and Trial of Madame Rachel, London: Diprose & Bateman, 1868 [ELTMR]

'History and Trial of Mdm Rachel or, Beautiful For Ever', London: William Swift, 1868 [H&T]

'No More Mystery! Sketch of "Dear William" the Gay Young Fellow …Account of Mrs Borradaile and the History of Madame Rachel; opinions of the press on this remarkable case', London: William Swift, 1868 [NMM]

'Life, Trial and Sentence of Madame Rachel' … 2nd edition, 1 penny with presentation plate gratis. London: Police News, 1868

Madame Rachel, 'Beautiful for Ever', London: privately printed, 1863.

Oliver, Patricia, *Meet the Family* [Russell Family History], privately printed, 2009, author's collection.

Sarah Rachel Russell entry, in Russell Family History at www.
rootsweb.ancestry.com

***

'The Affaire Rachel', *Saturday Review*, 26 September 1868, pp. 417-
18.

Anon [Captain Donald Shaw], *London in the Sixties, by One of the Old
Brigade*, London Everett 7 Co., 1908.

Ballantine, William, *Some Experiences of a Barrister's Life* vol. II,
London: R. Bentley, 1882.

'The Bond Street Mystery', *Christian World Magazine*, Nov 1868
pp. 801–16.

Kelly's London Post Office and Court Directory, 1858–77.

Berger, Doreen *The Jewish Victorian: Genealogical Information from
Jewish Newspapers 1871-80*, Witney: Robert Boyd, 1999.

Boase, Frederic, 'Sarah Rachel Russell aft. Moses, aft. Leverson',
Modern English Biography, vol III, reprint, London: Frank Cass,
1965 p. 3.

Boase, George C., 'Madame Rachel', *Notes and Queries*, series 8 vol.
6 1894 pp. 322–4.

'Celebrated Crimes and Criminals No. XXIII: An Account of
the "Bond Street" Mystery and the Subsequent Trials of the
Celebrated Madame Rachel', *Sporting Times*, 11 August 1888.

D'Heylli, Georges, *Dictionnaire des pseudonyms*, Paris: E. Dentu,
1869.

Diprose, John, *Some Account of the Parish of Saint Clement* Danes,
1868, vol. I, 1868, vol. II, 1876, London: Diprose & Bateman.

Robinson, F. W., 'Female Convict Life at Woking' part 1, *Graphic*, 31 August 1889, pp. 256–8.

Griffiths, Arthur, *Memorials of Millbank and Chapters in Prison History*, London: Chapman & Hall, 1884.

— , *Secrets of the Prison House* vol II, London: Chapman & Hall, 1894 .

Galignani's New Illustrated Paris Guide, Paris, 1872.

Heckethorn, Charles, *Lincoln's Inn Fields and the Localities Adjacent*, London: Elliot Stock, 1897.

Hogg, James, 'The Piccadilly Papers: A Day at the Old Bailey', *London Society*, vol. 14 1868, pp. 379-80.

Horler, Sidney, *Black Souls*, London: Jarrolds, 1931.

Juxon, John, *Lewis and Lewis: Life and Times of a Victorian Solicitor*, London: Collins, 1983.

'La Femme Passée' *Saturday Review*, 11 July 1868, pp. 49-50.

'The Last of Madame Rachel', *Saturday Review*, 3 October 1868, 455–6.

'Madame Rachel', *Saturday Review*, 28 August 1868, pp. 284–5.

Kingston, Charles, *Remarkable Rogues*, London: John Lane, 1921.

—, *Dramatic Days at the Old Bailey*, London: S. Paul & Co., 1923.

'The Law of the Rachel Case', *Irish Law Times and Solicitors' Journal*, vol. II, no. 84, 5 September 1868, pp. 483–4.

Lewis, George Pitt-, *Commissioner Kerr, An Individuality*, London: T. Fisher Unwin, 1903.

[Madame Rachel obituary], *Truth: A Weekly Journal*, vol. VIII, 21 October 1880, pp. 508-9.

Parry, Edward Abbott, *Vagabonds All*, London: Cassell & Co., 1926.

'The Persecuted Jewess', *Tomahawk*, 12 September 1868, vol. III, p. 107.

Roughead, William, '*Bad Companions*, Edinburgh: W. Green & sons, 1930.

Rowlands, Ernest Bowen, *Seventy-Two Years at the Bar*, London: Macmillan, 1924.

'Two Hours in Millbank Prison', *Illustrated Police News*, 19 December 1868.

Williams, Montagu, *Leaves of a Life: Being the Reminiscences of Montagu Williams QC*, London Macmillan, 1893.

Winkle, Marshall Van, 'The Bond Street Mystery', in Winkle *Sixty Famous Cases ... from 1778 to the Present*, vol. 1, Long Branch, NJ: Warren S. Ayres.

SECONDARY SOURCES

Adburgham, Alison, *Shops and Shopping 1800-1914*, London: Barrie & Jenkins, 1989.

Agate, James *Ego 5: Again More of the Autobiography of James Agate*, London: George G. Harrap, 1942.

Altick, Richard *Victorian Studies in Scarlet*, London: Dent, 1972.

—, *The English Common Reader: A Social History of the Mass Reading Public 1800–1900*, Ohio: Ohio State University Press, 1957.

Archives Israelites, vol. 21, 1860 p. 115.

Bailey, Catherine, *Black Diamonds: the Rise and Fall of an English Dynasty*, London: Penguin, 2008.

BIBLIOGRAPHY

Bennett, Alfred Rosling, *London and Londoners in the 1850s and 60s*, London: Fisher Unwin, 1924.

Benson, Theodora, *London Immortals*, London: A. Wingate, 1951.

Braddon, Mary Elizabeth *Lady Audley's Secret*, Oxford: Oxford University Press, 1998.

Brereton, Austin, *A Walk Down Bond Street*, London: Selwyn & Blount, 1920.

Byrne, Richard, *Prisons and Punishments of London,* London: Grafton, 1992.

Chancellor, Edwin, *Wanderings in Piccadilly, Mayfair and Pall Mall*, London: Ward, 1908.

Chesney, Kellow, *The Victorian Underworld*, London: Maurice Temple Smith, 1970.

Collins, Wilkie, *Armadale*, London: Penguin, 2004.

Crew, Albert, *The Criminal Prisons of Today and Yesterday*, London: Ivor Nicholson & Warson, 1933.

d'Almeras, Henri, *La vie Parisienne au second empire*, Paris: Albin Michel, 1952.

Desebrock, Jean, *The Book of Bond Street Old and New*, London: Tallis Press, 1978.

Dickens, Charles, Jr, *Dickens's Dictionary of London*, London, 1879.

Drinkwater, John, ed., *The Eighteen-Sixties, Essays by Fellows of the Royal Society of Literature*, Cambridge: Cambridge University Press, 1932.

Ellis, Stewart Marsh, *Wilkie Collins*, London: Constable, 1931.

Graves, Charles, *Mr Punch's History of Modern England* vol. 2., London: Cassell, 1921.

Hamilton, Walter, *Parodies of the Works of English and American Authors*, vol. 3. London: Reeves, 1886.

Hardman, Sir William, *A Mid-Victorian Pepys: Letters and Memoirs of Sir William Hardman* 1923.

Harré, Thomas Everett, *The Heavenly Sinner*, London: Jarrolds, 1936.

Hartmann, Mary S., *Victorian Murderesses*, London: Robson Books, 1977.

Hibbert, Christopher, *The London Encyclopedia*, Macmillan, 1983.

Hindley, C. *Curiosities of Street Literature*, London: Reeves & Turner, 1871.

Hunt, Diana Holman. *My Grandfather, His Wives and Loves*, London: Hamilton, 1969.

Jackson, Stanley, *The Old Bailey*, London: W. H. Allen, 1978.

Jenkins, Elizabeth *Six Criminal Women*, London: Sampson & Low, 1949.

Jopling, Louise, *Twenty Years of My Life* London: John Lane, 1925.

Kilch, George, 'A Corner of London, the Heart of the Campus', *LSE Magazine*, Summer 2006, pp. 15–17.

Knelman, Judith *Twisting in the Wind: The Murderess and the English Press*, Toronto: University of Toronto Press, 1998.

Lapinski, Pia-Pal, *The Exotic Woman in Nineteenth Century British Fiction and Culture*, Durham: University of New Hampshire Press, 2005.

Linton, Eliza Lynn, *The Girl of the Period and Other Social Essays*, vol. II, London: R. Bentley, 1883.

Loeb, Lori Anne, *Consuming Angels: Advertising and Victorian Women*, Oxford: Oxford University Press, 1994.

Mayhew, Henry, 'Labour and the Poor', Letter XIII, *Morning Chronicle* 30 Nov 1849.

Margetson, S. *Leisure and Pleasure in the 19th Century*, London: Cassell, 1969.

Lustgarten, Edgar, *The Judges and the Judged*, London: Odhams Press, 1961.

Mayhew, Henry and John Binny, 'The Female Convict Prison at Millbank', in *The Criminal Prisons of London*, London: Griffin, Bohn & Co., 1862.

McConville *English Local Prisons, 18601900*, London: Routledge, 1995.

Miller, Elizabeth Carolyn, *Framed: the New Woman Criminal in British Culture at the Fin de Siecle*, Ann Arbor: University of Michigan Press, 2008.

Murray's Modern London 1860: A Visitor's Guide, reprint, Moretonhampstead: Old House Books, 2003.

Newton, Henry Chance, *Crime and the Drama, or Dark Deeds Dramatized*, London: Stanley Paul, 1928.

O'Donnell, Bernard, *The Old Bailey and its Trials*, London: Clarke & Cockeran, 1950.

Palmer, Cecil, *A Mid-Victorian Pepys*, London: C. Palmer, 1923.

Pearl, Cyril, *The Girl with the Swansdown Seat*, London: Robin Clark, 1980.

Pearse, Mrs Godfrey, *The Romance of a Great Singer: A Memoir of Mario*, London: Smith Elder, 1910.

—, *The Enchanted Past,* London: Chapman & Hall, 1926.

Peters, Catherine, *The King of Inventors: A Life of Wilkie Collins*, London: Secker & Warburg, 1991.

Quennell *Mayhew's Characters*, London: Kimber, 1951.

Quennell, Peter ed. *Mayhew's London*, London: Spring Books, 1949.

Richards, Thomas, *The Commodity Culture of Victorian England: Advertising and Spectacle 1851-1914*, Stanford: Stanford University Press, 1990.

Robb, George, *White Collar Crime in Modern England: Financial Fraud and Business Morality 1845-1929*, Cambridge: Cambridge University Press, 1992.

Roth, Cecil, *The Rise of Provincial Jewry: the Early History of the Jewish Communities in the English Countryside, 1740–1840*, London: Jewish Monthly, 1950.

Sabine, Jeannin da Costa, *La Beauté: Les Coulisses de la seduction,* Paris:Editions de la Martinière, 1995.

Schwartz, Vanessa R.m *Spectacular Realities: Early Mass Culture in Fin-de-Siecle Paris,* Berkeley: University of California Press, 1998.

'Sketches of life by A Radical' (Alton Locke), *Harpers New Monthly Magazine* vol. 1, 1850, p. 806.

'Madame Rachel the Beauty Doctor', *Spatula A Magazine for Pharmacy*, 1908 p. 328–30.

Taylor, Afred Swaine, *A Manual of Medical Jurisprudence*, London: J & A Churchill, 1886.

Thornbury, *Old and New London: A Narrative of its History, its People and its Places* vol. 3, London: Cassell, Peter & Galpin, 1878.

Tibbetts, A. O., 'Romances of Our Own Times', *Cassell's Saturday Journal,* 1898.

Timbs, J., *Curiosites of London*, London: Green, Reader & Dyer, 1868.

Vielmas, Laurence Talairach, *Moulding the Female Body in Victorian*

Fairy Tales and Sensation Novels, Aldershot: Ashgate, 2007.

Vincent, Arthur ed. *Twelve Bad Women,* London: Unwin, 1911.

Willett, C. *Feminine Attitudes in the Nineteenth Century,* London: Heinemann, 1935.

Wyndham. *Blotted Scutcheons,* London: Hutchinson, 1926.

—, *The Magnificent Montez,* London: Hutchinson, 1935.

Zedner, Lucia, *Women, Crime and Custody in Victorian England,* Oxford: Clarendon Press, 1991.

COSMETICS

[Anon], *Toilette of Health, Beauty and Fashion,* London: Wittenoom and Cremer, 1832.

Beasley, Henry, *The Druggist's General Receipt Book,* London: John Churchill, 1857.

'Beautiful for Ever', *Chambers' Journal of Literature* v. 42, 1865, pp. 449–52.

'Beautiful for Ever', *Pall Mall Gazette,* 26 September 1868.

Beeton's Dictionary of Practical Recipes and Everyday Information London: Ward, Lock & Tyler, 1870.

Buc'hoz, Pierre-Joseph, *The Toilet of Flora* London, 1775.

Cooley, Arnold James, *The Toilet and Cosmetic Arts in Ancient and Modern Times,* London: Robert Hardwick, 1866.

Corson, Richard, *Fashions in Makeup: From Ancient to Modern* Times, London: Peter Owen, 1972.

Ellis, Aytoun, *The Essence of Beauty,* London: Secker & Warburg, 1960.

'Enamelled Ladies', *Vanity Fair*, 19 July 1862, vol. 6 no. 134, p. 30.

'Enamelling a Lady', *Saturday Evening Post*, 9 August 1862, p. 3.

'Face Enamelling', in *Every Saturday*, 24 October 1868 pp. 522-3.

Gunn, Fenja, *The Artificial Face, History of Cosmetics*, Newton Abbott: David & Charles,1973.

McLaughlin, Terence, *The Gilded Lily*, London: Cassell, 1972.

Montez, Lola, *The Arts of Beauty and Hints to Gentlemen on the Art of Fascination*, London: 1860.

'Paint and No Paint, *All the Year Round*, 9 August 1862, pp. 519-21.

Scoffern, J., MB, 'Cosmetics', in *Belgravia,* vol. 4, February 1868 pp. 208–16.

Strachan, John *Advertising and the Satirical Culture in the Romantic Period*, Cambridge: Cambridge University Press, 2007.

'Stucco for the Softer Sex', *Punch* 26 March 1859.

Tallis, John, *London Street Views, 1838–40*: London: Topographical Society, 1969.

Thompson, C. J. S. *Quacks of Old London*, reprint, New York: Barnes & Noble, 1993.

Walker, Mrs A. *Female Beauty as Preserved and Improved by Regimen, Cleanliness and Dress*, London: Thomas Hurst, 1837.

Williams, Neville *Powder and Paint: A History of the Englishwoman's Toilet* London: Longmans, 1957.

Index